W9-CTO-251

Long Ride on a Hobby-Horse

JIM COLEMAN

LONG RIDE ON A HOBBY-HORSE

MEMOIRS OF A SPORTING LIFE

KEY PORTER BOOKS

Canadian Cataloguing in Publication Data

Coleman, Jim.
Long ride on a hobby-horse

ISBN 1-55013-179-5

1. Coleman, Jim. 2. Sports journalism — Canada.
3. Sportswriters — Canada — Biography. I. Title.

GV742.42.C64A3 1990 070.4'49796'092 C90-093713-0

Typesetting: Southam Business Information and Communications Group Inc.
Printed and Bound in Canada by John Deyell Company

Key Porter Books Limited
70 The Esplanade
Toronto, Ontario
Canada M5E 1R2

90 91 92 93 5 4 3 2 1

For my wife Maggie, and my children, with love

CONTENTS

PART 1

LIFE ON THE RAILROAD

A RAILROADER'S SONS

I WISH I COULD SAY THAT THE FIRST SOUND I REMEMBER hearing was the haunting whistle of a railway steam-locomotive.

In my childhood, I heard that lonesome howl frequently as I lay in my berth with the bed-covers pulled tightly under my chin. In wintertime, as the train sped across the frozen prairies, the lingering wail of that whistle lulled me to sleep. I could hear the rhythmic click of steel wheels rolling over the joints in steel rails. The constant motion of the train, swaying slightly but always under control, was, to me, as reassuring as a giant hand gently rocking a cradle.

Of course, there must have been earlier sounds which penetrated my consciousness: the clip-clop of horses in the street, delivering the early-morning milk; the muffled voices of Hannah and Jenny in the kitchen as they prepared breakfast; in springtime, the chirping of robins as they foraged for worms on the lawn below my bedroom window on Donald Street.

Still, the sounds I remember best were those of railroading: the jerking clatter of steel couplings being extended to their limits as the locomotive engineer, making a standing start out of a depot, inched back his Johnson-bar and picked up the slack in the long line of heavy passenger coaches.

My brother and I were a railroader's sons. In our household the Canadian Pacific Railway was known as "The Company" and it dominated our lives. The Canadian Pacific nurtured us, raised us, educated us and today I am grateful still that it played such an important role in my life. Our good fortune was the result of our father's association with the Canadian Pacific. We spent our formative years travelling on Canadian Pacific trains, living in Canadian Pacific hotels and developing a warm lifelong attachment to a transportation enterprise which, for more than a century, has played a key role in Canada's history.

The 1920s was a great era of railroad transportation in North America. Airplane travel still was only a dream of the future. There were few major highways in Canada and automobile transportation between major cities was an adventure in pioneering.

To travel from Montreal to Vancouver by train took four nights and three days — approximately 89 hours. The time consumed by the transcontinental journey explains why Canada's two railways built their own hotels in cities such as Winnipeg, Calgary, Saskatoon and Edmonton. Looking back, it is apparent that the North American preoccupation with personal hygiene, including daily tub-baths or daily showers, wasn't quite as important 60 or 70 years ago as it is today.

Prior to the introduction of so-called luxury trains in the mid-1920s, there wasn't a full-scale bathroom on board.

Even then, the luxury facilities consisted only of one or two individual shower rooms on the observation car at the extreme rear of the train.

Accordingly, the vast majority of passengers who travelled from Montreal to Vancouver without a stopover in a major city arrived at their final destination in slightly grungy condition.

The more fastidious travellers on the Canadian Pacific transcontinental route usually broke their journey by stopping at the Royal Alexandra Hotel in Winnipeg or the Palliser Hotel in Calgary for a period of 24 hours, during which they could wallow happily in a tub of hot water.

Even less than 50 years ago, I can remember travelling from Vancouver to Toronto. Knowing that there was a 45-minute stop in Winnipeg, I rushed from the C.P.R. Station to the Royal Alexandra Hotel next door to rent a room where I could take a bath. Then, shining with cleanliness, I reboarded the train for the remaining 36-hour run to Toronto.

Actually, the staff of the Royal Alexandra didn't charge me for the use of their facilities. Aware of my Canadian Pacific antecedents, they gave me the use of the room with the compliments of the management.

For many years that same Royal Alexandra Hotel had been my permanent home. When I was eight years old, our mother had drowned at the Canadian Pacific bungalow-camp in Invermere, British Columbia, where we were spending our summer holidays.

I mention this only to explain, in some measure, why our father always overindulged his two sons and brought them up in circumstances which, in those days, certainly were unusual. My older brother had died, five years previously, at the age of six, and my mother's death compounded my father's family tragedy. He was intensely devoted to his two small boys and, although other parents felt that we were hopelessly spoiled, he was generously supportive of us until he left us at the age of 78.

For several years after we lost our mother, our upbringing was in the hands of our maternal aunt, Ella Grant. In 1920, my father decided to get us out of our house on Donald Street and he moved us into a six-room suite at the Royal Alexandra. Then, my father remarried in 1922 and we continued to live in the hotel until about a year after I took my first newspaper job on the Winnipeg *Tribune*.

Our father had risen very rapidly in the service of the Canadian Pacific. After being an exceptionally youthful editor of the Belleville *Intelligencer* and city editor of the Port Huron (Michigan) *Times*, he joined the railway as a clerk in the engineering department at Fort William before he was 21. When he was 39, he became vice-president of Western Lines. The Canadian Pacific's Western Lines encompassed the entire area between Fort William and the Pacific coast, including Vancouver Island.

In those days when railroading dominated continental transportation, company officials had their private business cars in which they travelled over their areas of jurisdiction. My father's first private car was Lillooet, named after a small town in B.C. I don't remember the Lillooet because it had been transferred to some other official before I was born. The first business car which I remember clearly was the Champlain which was assigned to my father when he became assistant general manager of Western Lines in Winnipeg in 1915.

Until the coming of the executive jet aircraft, the private railway car provided the ultimate in long-distance travelling comfort. The private cars were equipped with comfortable sleeping accommodation for as many as eight persons, including the car's crew of chef, steward and travelling-secretary. Each private car had its own galley in which the chef prepared full course meals.

It is quite probable that as a child I logged more train-mileage than 99 percent of the other children. After my father remarried in 1922, I was packed off to various boarding-schools which usually were situated about as far from my hometown of Winnipeg as you could go before falling off the edge of the continent. My younger brother and I became familiar with every conductor, dining-car waiter and sleeping-car porter on the mainline of the Canadian Pacific in those years when we travelled back and forth between Winnipeg and University School in Victoria on Vancouver Island, unaccompanied by any of our elders.

We managed to ride in the cab of the locomotives on quite a few of those trips. Obviously, we couldn't have enjoyed those rare privileges if our father didn't have at least a nodding acquaintance with almost every locomotive engineer on Western Lines. Any ride in a locomotive had to be approved by the railway's divisional superintendent. It was amazing how many of those superintendents we managed to know personally.

Our fellow-passengers were probably glad to be rid of us for an hour or so as we rode in the steam-powered locomotives at the head-end. We weren't particularly noisy children but, to while away the daylight hours on the long trip from Winnipeg to the Pacific coast, we sometimes amused ourselves by playing catch with an English rugby ball.

The engine-crews were invariably patient and protective. Usually, the engineer permitted one of us to share his small, hard seat on the right-hand side of the cab and allowed us to pull the whistle-cord as we hurtled across the prairies. It gave one a sense of power to pull the cord and then to hear the scream of the steam whistle directly overhead.

Our particular joy was riding the head-end through the five-mile Connaught Tunnel and the famous Spiral Tunnels in Rogers Pass. For the long ride up the steep mountain grade, passenger trains employed two engines, hooked together.

In the Connaught Tunnel, the smoke produced by these two labouring engines was heavy with soot that cascaded blindingly through the open windows into the cab. The engineer and fireman gave us gobs of a cotton material called "waste" to be held over our mouth and nose so that we wouldn't asphyxiate. By the time we pulled into the station at Field, B.C., we were dirty, sweaty and happy. Back in the sleeping-cars, our fellow-passengers nobly managed to restrain their enthusiasm as we rejoined them. If they envied our opportunity to ride the locomotives, they had no trouble in concealing it.

As was the case with most senior railway officials, my father spent a good deal of his time travelling on business trips over the large territory which was assigned to him — more than on-half the width of the continent. When I came home from boarding-school for the summer holidays, he took me with him on many of his business-trips on the Assiniboine, his railroad business car.

In 1922, my father and our stepmother married in St. Patrick's Cathedral in New York City. Although Ottawa-born, our stepmother was a New Yorker when she joined our family. She probably wasn't completely prepared for the task of presiding over our home in the Royal Alexandra Hotel. To ease her burden, my father took me with him on his business trips during the summer holidays. He felt that she would have enough on her hands with my comparatively docile younger brother.

My father conceivably reasoned that the other guests in the Royal Alexandra would be more comfortable if I was absent from that hostelry as much as possible. It is likely that most adults then regarded me as a juvenile pest. My father himself may have subscribed to that theory, but some very strong sense of paternal obligation compelled him to abide all my gauche indiscretions.

We had lived in the Royal Alexandra for two years before our father remarried and, in that period, several other families with children of our age had become permanent guests of the hotel.

The 450-room hotel proved to be a magnificent playground. Our principal playmates were two brothers of approximately our ages: T. Jeffares Porte, Jr., and his younger brother, Andy.

Within a few months, the four of us had explored every nook and cranny of that bulky six-storey building at the corner of Main Street and Higgins Avenue adjoining the western headquarters of the Canadian Pacific Railway.

The Royal Alexandra was a very lively place in our childhood. In those days of the Roaring Twenties, a dance-band, the Canary Cottage Orchestra, led by a highly talented, one-armed trumpeter named Wes Mortimer, played for supper-dances or dinner-dances every night except Sunday, and there was a tea-dance in the Grill Room every Wednesday and Saturday afternoon. Those were boom-days on the Winnipeg Grain Exchange. Winnipeggers flocked to the hotel to dance to the music of Mortimer's fine little band.

All of this gaiety should have been quite dazzling to a child's eyes, but we invented other activities which were considerably more interesting than standing in the doorway of the Grill Room, watching our elders waltzing, foxtrotting or doing the Charleston to the music of the Canary Cottage Orchestra.

We played hide-and-seek. Not surprisingly, there were hundreds of places to hide in a building of that size which had so many public rooms. We played floor-hockey with a tennis ball and real hockey sticks on the marble floors of the basement corridors which connected the Royal Alexandra with the Canadian Pacific Depot. We played football on the polished floors of the Crystal Ballroom although that pastime had to be discontinued when an assistant manager, attracted by unusual noises from the supposedly unoccupied ballroom, walked in just in time to see one of us drop-kicking a rugby ball dangerously close to the expensive, overhanging crystal chandeliers.

When our dear, unsuspecting stepmother first arrived in Winnipeg from New York, she brought two miniature bicycles as introductory gifts for my brother and me. She thought that we would ride those bicycles on visits to Assiniboine Park or in other pastoral and quiet areas of Winnipeg.

Certainly, she never anticipated that we would ride the bicycles along the broad corridors of the guest-room floors in the hotel. As soon as the two bicycles had been unpacked in our fifth-floor suite, we were bombing through the corridors of the Royal Alexandra, our shrill yelps warning any other guests of the impending danger. We rode with considerable skill and dexterity, never actually colliding with any guests, although I'm quite sure that we scared the pants off several old ladies who were waiting for the elevators.

After several near misses were reported to our father by the hotel management, the two bicycles were placed under lock and key. I don't recall that we sorrowed for long — we went back to playing football in the Crystal Ballroom with the Porte brothers. This time, the management didn't object. I presume the manager, Mr. Pierce, felt that the replacement of a few chandeliers was less expensive than paying hospital bills for guests who had been assaulted by hit-and-run cyclists.

During the long summer holidays, our father had devised other schemes for sparing the Royal Alexandra guests our quaint antics. His good friend Nelson Smith owned a 640-acre produce farm at Birds Hill, 12 miles northeast of Winnipeg. The Porte brothers and the Coleman brothers were driven to Mr. Smith's Agnoel Farm where, for as long as a week at a stretch, we were fed, watered and loosely supervised by Charlie, the Chinese cook.

Two ponies which had been given to me by Hon. Archie McLean, one of the four founders of the Calgary Stampede, already had become permanent residents of Mr. Smith's farm, and we put in long days, riding and skirmishing on those 640 acres. The farm foreman, Hugh Jones, permitted us to run on a rather long leash as long as we didn't terrorize the livestock.

Over several summers, we perpetrated only one major transgression. One night, we liberated a bottle of whiskey from our host's private stock, went to the hen-house and poured the whiskey into the mash which had been prepared for the birds' evening meal.

Early the next morning, the outraged screams of Charlie, the cook, warned us that the chicken-house was a mess. The hens, bedizened by the strong spirits which had been poured into their mash, had been laying eggs from their perching-rails instead of laying them in their nests.

Several of the frailer poultry had keeled over during the night and, when Charlie arrived to give them their feed in the morning, were found staggering around in bewilderment, obviously nursing monumental hang-overs. We cleaned up the hen-house in silence. The unsmiling face of Hugh Jones, as he stood in the doorway watching us, was a sufficiently chastening reproof. We didn't do quite such a stupid or cruel thing again.

My father still hadn't played his hole-card. Aware that my younger and more placid brother could be handled easily by our stepmother, whom he adored, my father began to take me away with him on the Assiniboine on many of his summer business trips through western Canada.

Those were trips to which I looked forward eagerly. I loved travelling; I loved the companionship of my father who, although he was a very busy man, always managed to find time to tell me interesting anecdotes about the land across which we rode or the towns which we visited.

My father had his little peculiarities. He retired rather early each night to his private stateroom and selected a book from his supply of reading-matter. Invariably, the chef and steward Harold Courtenay left an unpeeled orange and a small stack of soda-crackers on the bedside table. By morning my father had peeled and eaten the orange; he had eaten most of the crackers and had read his book, usually from cover to cover. He was a skip-reader and I never discovered how many hours he managed to devote to sleeping.

Before we pulled out of Winnipeg, his secretary would provide him with a slip of paper on which were typed the names of the train crew: the conductor, engineer, fireman, front-end trainman and rear-end trainman.

About five minutes before our scheduled departure, my father would walk up to the head-end of the train; he would shake hands with the engineer and chat briefly. Most of them were men he had known for many years. He repeated this friendly little ritual at every divisional-point where we had a change of train crews.

I was under instructions to keep out of sight as much as possible and I spent a good deal of my time in the galley with Harold Courtenay or in the little room occupied by the travelling-secretary. I must confess that, surreptitiously, I took an occasional squint into the voluminous files of correspondence which accompanied my father on those trips, but I came to the conclusion quite quickly that railway executives receive a great deal of damn dull mail.

As long as I kept my mouth shut, I was permitted to join my father, his travelling guests and the railway officials for meals at the dinner-table on the Assiniboine. Apparently, my presence didn't inhibit anyone since some of those old railroaders certainly enriched my vocabulary.

On one occasion, I hit the jackpot: I was permitted to travel from Winnipeg to the Pacific coast — and return — on the President's Special train. Once each year, the chairman and president, Sir Edward W. Beatty (he hadn't been knighted at the time of which I write), took the directors of the Canadian Pacific on a coast-to-coast tour of the company's properties.

At the time, it didn't occur to me that I was uniquely privileged. Not many other teen-aged boys had the opportunity of riding the President's Special from Manitoba to British Columbia and return. My father told me that this was "no ordinary trip." I was to confine myself to the Assiniboine. I was not to be seen or heard by the directors of the railway company.

The President's Special was quite a sight as it rolled across Canada. The locomotive and private cars positively gleamed. The official colour of the Canadian Pacific passenger equipment was described as Tuscan red or Honduras red. The words "Canadian Pacific" and the names of the individual private cars were painted in gold on that background of red.

At each stop along the line, the local officials of the Canadian Pacific, dressed in their Sunday-best dark suits, lined up on the platform to greet the president and the directors.

The annual tour of the President's Special was a triumphal progress. When we swished past little whistle-stop stations without reducing our speed measurably, I looked through the window and I could see bystanders on the platform staring curiously at the line of gleaming private cars trailing the locomotive.

On instructions, I stayed out of sight. Andy Manson was my father's travelling-secretary in that period and I spent most of the daylight hours in his little bedroom-office. Andy was a fascinating man, a jock with an encyclopedic knowledge of all sports. He played a part in my extracurricular education in the area of athletics and the entertainment world.

That trip on the President's Special was admittedly far out of the ordinary for me. But on other trips through the West, whenever we visited a city where a horse-racing meeting was in progress, my father sent Andy and me to the races while, probably a bit enviously, he went about the business of solidifying the interests of the Canadian Pacific.

My brother and I quickly became familiar with other major hotels in addition to the Royal Alexandra on the main line of the Canadian Pacific: the Palliser in Calgary, the Hotel Vancouver and the Empress. There were also two major hotels which were open only in the summer tourist season, the Banff Springs Hotel and Château Lake Louise. Also open only in the summer were Glacier House and numerous company-operated bungalow-camps, all of which we visited.

During the years of our incarceration in University School at Victoria, the Empress Hotel served as our surrogate home. The Empress was the bountiful oasis to which we scurried each Saturday when it was the school's practice to release the inmates for the afternoon, unescorted. Most of the boys would attend a motion picture, followed by a visit to the ice-cream parlour in Terry's Drugstore, at the corner of Fort and Douglas streets.

Our father had enrolled us in University School because Victoria was the westernmost city in the territory which he managed for the Canadian Pacific. It was sufficiently remote that we weren't likely to run away from school and attempt to ride the rods all the way back to Winnipeg. Also, our father's duties obliged him to make at least three or four trips to Victoria during the school year.

Always overly generous, our father had arranged with the manager of the Empress, Herbert G. Wilson, that we should be permitted to have a charge-account for meals at the hotel.

The provender which was provided by Chong and his assistant cooks at University School was quite adequate for growing boys, but certainly, it wasn't haute cuisine.

Accordingly, each Saturday morning after the obligatory 11:00 A.M. roll-call, my brother and I would take the Mount Tolmie number 10 tram and, after disembarking at the corner of Fort and Douglas, would run the remaining three blocks to the Empress as swiftly as our knobby little legs would carry us. Scarcely pausing to pay our respects to Mr. Wilson in his office, we would sprint to the main dining-room where we would dine in style.

Those Saturday-noon feasts more than compensated for the six days of boarding-school fare. At the end of the meal, as unofficial treasurer or manager of our joint enterprises, I signed our father's name to the bill and I added a 10 percent tip from my weekly pocket-money.

Not surprisingly, we acquired some new friends when news of our signing privileges at the Empress reached the ears of our classmates at University School. We never bothered to ask what happened to those luncheon-tabs after I signed them but, presumably, Mr. Wilson sent them to my father's office in Winnipeg at the end of each month. Typically, my father never mentioned them.

If we didn't go to a movie after lunch, we'd amuse ourselves around the Empress on Saturday afternoons. Mr. Wilson's secretary didn't work on weekends and the hotel manager permitted me to use her Underwood typewriter on which I banged out fairly lengthy letters to our parents, in the course of which I fabricated some glowing accounts of my upward progress in the halls of academe.

We prowled the corridors and public rooms of the Empress, acquainting ourselves with the waiters, the housemaids, the Japanese bell-boys and the members of the three-piece string orchestra who played in the lobby for the afternoon tea-hour. Before long, we knew most of the Empress employees quite as well as we knew the men and women who toiled back home in the Royal Alexandra.

One Empress employee who viewed us with barely concealed distaste was the gardener, Mr. Saunders. The flowers and lawns around the hotel were beautifully tended and Mr. Saunders understandably became a bit testy when he watched my brother and me punting an English rugby ball on a nice plot of grass which had been laid out for a golf putting-green.

I still can see Mr. Saunders, a tiny peaked cap on his head, his hands thrust deep into the pockets of his gardener's apron, staring at us playing on his carefully manicured lawn. He had a strangely resigned look on his gloomy face — the look of a man who realizes that, if he keeps his mouth shut, he won't be forced to wait long to cash his well-deserved pension cheques.

Occasionally, my brother and I had the good fortune to hitch a ride on a private car when we were going to boarding-school or when we were returning from the Pacific coast for our Christmas or summer holidays.

We made most of our back-to-school trips on the regular passenger trains and, in addition to our rides on locomotives, we investigated all the other facets of rail transportation.

Although private-car chefs such as Harold Courtenay performed miracles of culinary expedience, the real magicians were the crews of dining-cars on the regular passenger trains. The dining-car steward, the chef and his assistants not only worked long hours on their car but they slept on it, too. On the trip from Winnipeg to Vancouver, the crew was compelled to spend at least two nights on the train.

After the last of the dinner-crowd had gone back to their comfortable berths or compartments in the passenger coaches, the dining-car tables were folded and packed away. Then, the members of the crew made uncomfortable beds for themselves by putting four chairs against the wall and covering these makeshift beds with a thin pallet and blankets.

They hung specially cut curtains from the ceiling so that they were at least hidden from view while they attempted to sleep. They were disturbed intermittently by the sound of opening doors at both ends of the car as the conductor and brakemen performed their regular inspection duties on the train during the night.

The entire crew of the dining-car was up at 5:00 A.M., after only a few hours of fitful sleep. The fires were lit in the galley; the tables were re-erected and covered with fresh linen and table-silver. The waiters donned fresh, white jackets for the day's work.

The chefs were among the highest paid of railway employees. They made as much as a conductor or an engineer and they genuinely earned their money. The kitchen staff performed almost incredible feats of catering since, working in a space which was approximately the size of four telephone booths, they produced more than 300 individual meals in the course of a day.

After one group of diners had finished their meal, they were replaced immediately by four more hungry passengers. While the new passengers were seated, the waiters deftly removed the soiled table-cloth and replaced it with fresh napery.

During the Depression, you could buy a three-course meal for 35 cents in the Chinese restaurants of many Canadian prairie towns. In that era, dining on a passenger train was regarded as a high point in luxury but, considering the conditions under which the kitchen crew, the steward and the waiters laboured, the meal prices on trains were exceptionally reasonable.

Among my souvenirs, I have a 1937 dinner-menu from the Dominion, one of the Canadian Pacific's three daily transcontinental trains. The passenger could have a full dinner for one dollar. He could start with the soup du jour. Then, there was a choice of three main dishes: ham steak, fish or a chicken omelet. Those main dishes were served with vegetables and/or a fresh salad. To top it off, the passenger was offered a choice of four desserts, plus tea, coffee, milk or buttermilk.

For more discriminating diners, the dining-car offered a wider gastronomical choice. In addition to the soup, salad, desserts and post-dinner coffee, tea, milk or buttermilk, the passenger willing to spend $1.50 could have a cooked-to-order Red Brand sirloin steak or a broiled chicken with dressing.

That was in 1937. I don't remember the price of dining-car meals when my brother and I were frequent travellers on our way to school a decade earlier, but I doubt that they were any more expensive than they were in 1937. On those trips to school, I was the treasurer and I'm reasonably sure that my father gave me about $25 before we left home. That was plenty of money for feeding us along the way to the Pacific coast, as well leaving me with enough change to give the sleeping-car porter a tip of $2 or $3.

There were several extra private cars — known officially as "the spare cars" — on the western lines of the Canadian Pacific. On at least one occasion, one of these spare cars was about to be hauled from Winnipeg to Vancouver on the exact day when we were scheduled to return to boarding-school. So, we went back to school in style on the car Penticton, accompanied by our stepmother. That trip on the Penticton provided us with the opportunity to meet and chat with our first living, breathing, published author, the Baroness Orczy.

Between the ages of six and 17, I managed to read my way through more books than I have perused in the remainder of my lifetime. Unquestionably, whatever smattering of education I received in my formative years resulted partly from my addiction to books. In prairie cities such as Winnipeg there were not yet the distractions of television — or even radio — in the early 1920s. I went through books, such as those by the Baroness Orczy, in the manner of a boll weevil gnawing its way through a field of cotton.

Baroness Orczy and her great adventure stories of the French Revolution and the Scarlet Pimpernel were guaranteed gassers. Egad — Sir Percy Blakeny certainly stood those Frenchies on their pates with his clever ruses. The Scarlet Pimpernel had more narrow escapes than Harry Houdini.

My stepmother wrote a note to Baroness Orczy inviting her to join us in the Penticton for dinner. Baroness Orczy and her husband, a gentleman named Mr. Montizambert, duly appeared on the Penticton in time for a pre-dinner martini. On invitation, they appeared for lunch and dinner the following day and, when we reached Vancouver, accompanied us on the steamer, *Princess Kathleen*, to Victoria where a suite at the Empress was put at their disposal by the Canadian Pacific.

My brother and I initially were a bit surprised that this tubby little lady, heavily made-up, was the Hungarian-born genius who had written those world-wide best selling novels about the Scarlet Pimpernel. However, the Baroness was a fascinating raconteur. Mr. Montizambert, a stout man with a military moustache, left most of the talking to his celebrated spouse.

Some other private-car trips were, for my brother and me, equally memorable. There was our first visit to New York City, when I was 11. Two days after Christmas, my father bundled us aboard the Assiniboine and, with Harold Courtenay cooking up a storm, we travelled east to Toronto, Ottawa and Montreal where my brother and I were introduced to our stepmother's family. Whether or not we passed muster must be a moot point, but I do not recall that tears were shed publicly when, our familial visits completed, we left Canada for New York.

To our young eyes, New York City was incredible. Our stepmother introduced us to many of her New York friends, including George Arliss, the distinguished English actor and an occupant of the same Park Avenue apartment building where she had lived before marrying our father.

We rode on the open upper deck of the Fifth Avenue and Madison Avenue buses. We went to the Aquarium and the Bronx Zoo. We saw the famous vaudeville show at the Hippodrome Theatre where 100 chorus-girls appeared to walk right into a water-filled lake on the stage. We went to the top of the Woolworth Building which, in 1923, was the tallest in the world.

All the colourful excitement of this New York trip was the build-up for a terrible let-down. Knowing what was in store for me, I couldn't enjoy myself fully. I went to bed each night with a knot of fear in my stomach and my meals turned to dust in my mouth. From New York City, I was being taken directly to Lennoxville, Quebec, to be enrolled in boarding-school for the first time. True, I was travelling to school by private car but it was much as if I was being served first-class meals in the tumbrel on the way to the guillotine.

There were to be other private-car trips to the United States which, happily, didn't conclude with my being dropped off at a boarding-school in the Eastern Townships of Quebec in the middle of winter.

During the Prohibition Era in the United States, my father's arrival in New York, Detroit, Chicago or Minneapolis was welcomed warmly by his American friends. My father had stocked quite a large private cellar back in Winnipeg and, before he left on a US trip, he arranged for bottles of excellent old Scotch whiskey and other alcoholic goodies to be brought aboard the Assiniboine to be given as gifts to friends.

Our father was keenly interested in all sports, most particularly hockey and horse-racing. Since I had become an incorrigible jock by the age of nine or ten, he encouraged my interest in the sporting scene and, whenever possible, took me to major sporting events.

In the summer of 1927, he decided that the time had come for my brother and me to be exposed to Major League Baseball. Before we left Winnipeg, he must have been provided with a copy of the American League schedule by his travelling-secretary, Andy Manson, who among other things, had played semi-professional baseball.

We attended American League games in Detroit, St. Louis and Chicago. In Chicago, Tom Wall, the Canadian Pacific's district passenger-agent, was waiting for us with four tickets to that afternoon's game between the White Sox and the Washington Senators. The tickets were a gift from Charles Comiskey, the "Old Roman" who owned the White Sox. He had given us seats in his private box, directly behind home-plate.

Before Tom Wall left the Assiniboine, my father nodded to Harold Courtenay, who retired to his secret recesses of the car. Within five minutes, Harold returned with a bottle of Johnny Walker Black Label. Tom Wall knew what was expected of him: he would deliver the precious elixir to Mr. Comiskey with my father's compliments.

Mr. Comiskey must have been profoundly touched by that gift. Before we left Chicago, Tom Wall appeared with an envelope from the Old Roman. The envelope contained a lifetime pass to Comiskey Park, with my father's name embossed in gold letters.

When my school days ended, I wasn't to have many more long trips in the Assiniboine. In 1934, Grant Hall, the senior vice-president of the C.P.R., died and my father moved to the head office at Montreal to succeed him. The Assiniboine and

Harold Courtenay stayed in Winnipeg. In Montreal, my father inherited Mr. Hall's private car, the Mount Royal.

After I moved to newspaper work in Toronto, I was to have many trips in the Mount Royal but none of those two-week journeys of inspection which I had enjoyed as a child with my father. My father took my wife and me and our two children on Christmas-holiday visits to Quebec City and the Seignory Club at Montebello. And once, he took me alone on a nostalgic return to Winnipeg and the Royal Alexandra Hotel where so many happy days of my childhood had been spent.

Best of all were the trips in August to the thoroughbred summer-racing meetings at beautiful Saratoga Springs in upstate New York. My father, my stepmother and I were always in perfect harmony at the horse-races. And Saratoga Springs, with its magnificent elms and its old-fashioned racecourse, spins its own special spell over visitors.

My last journey in the Mount Royal was the most poignant. My father had been in retirement for seven years when he died in 1956. He had expressed a desire to be buried in the little cemetery at Arnprior, Ontario, where he had been a schoolboy.

After a funeral service at Montreal, the Canadian Pacific provided a special train to take my father to Arnprior. In the most thoughtful of all possible gestures, the Canadian Pacific put the old Mount Royal at our family's disposal.

Surrounded by Canadian Pacific officials, we buried him in the cemetery on the banks of the Mississippi River. The adjoining plot was the burial place of H.J. "Gus" Main, a longtime colleague and friend of our father.

As the casket was being lowered into the grave, Alex Lyle, who had been associated with our father for more than 25 years, whispered in my ear: "Gus is sitting down there with an open bottle of whiskey. And he'll be saying: 'D.C., I've just been sitting here, waiting to pour you a drink.'"

After the graveside service, we rode back to Montreal in the Mount Royal. My last trip in the private car provided the opportunity for bittersweet reflection. I missed him terribly but I recognized that I had been singularly fortunate to know such a man. Now, a quarter-century after he died, I miss him, still.

PART 2

LIFE IN THE NEWS MEDIA

INK IN THEIR BLOOD

"Those oldtime newspapermen had ink in their blood."
– Britt Jessup

IN VIEW OF MY FAMILY BACKGROUND, SOME OF MY acquaintances have wondered why I didn't seek a career in the railroad business. The answer is simple: my father didn't believe in nepotism where his sons were concerned.

When I asked him about the possibility of getting a job with the Canadian Pacific, he explained the facts of life to me. Gently, he told me that my fellow-employees would have difficulty in overlooking the fact that I was his son. Even if I received a deserved promotion in the railway, some of these employees would feel that I was being favoured because I was his son.

Although he became an eminently successful railway executive, my father always remained fascinated by newspapers and the newspaper business, which had been his first vocation. *The Times of London* was delivered to him by mail throughout his lifetime and he read every edition thoroughly. His closest personal friends were newspaper publishers and editors and some of them were travelling guests on his private railway car when he went on business trips.

One of his frequent travelling guests was M.E. Nichols, publisher of the Winnipeg *Tribune*. And when the time came for me to think about doing something productive with my own life, I had no hesitation in presuming on the longtime family friendship with Mr. Nichols, who found me a job as a summer-replacement reporter on the *Tribune*.

At the time, it didn't occur to me that I was embarking on a writing career which, with some fairly lengthy side-trips, would continue for 60 years.

In those days the word "reporter" had a certain panache. A reporter, even if he was paid only a very modest salary, imagined that somehow he was slightly superior to the average working man, who was harnessed to a nine-to-five job.

The general public probably regarded reporters with mixed emotions. The average working man may have envied the largely fictitious "bohemian" life which newspapermen were reputed to live, but most of them hoped that their daughters wouldn't choose to marry a reporter.

Reporters, for the most part, took a truculent pride in their profession, but many of them hid that pride behind a facade of public cynicism. Among themselves, they made a pretence of being a bit derisive about "the newspaper game." This derision was strictly "inside stuff." They were quick to take offence when any outsider questioned the integrity of journalism.

A joke which was circulated among newspapermen when I was a cub reporter concerned two young men who had been close childhood friends in Winnipeg. However, when they grew up they didn't meet again for 20 years.

One of them, who had stayed in Winnipeg, went to Vancouver on a trip. Walking down Granville Street, he bumped into the old friend he hadn't seen for 20 years.

They exchanged back-thumping greetings, after which the Winnipegger said: "I still see your mother about once a week. When I get home, I'll tell her that you're looking great. By the way, what are you doing for a living?"

Lowering his voice, the Vancouverite replied: "Well, to tell the truth, I have a job as a newspaper reporter. But, please don't tell my mother what I'm doing. The dear old girl believes that I'm still playing the piano in a whore house."

When I made my first assault on an Underwood upright-standard in the editorial department of the Winnipeg *Tribune*, you could say that alcoholism was still the occupational disease of the newspaper business.

It was the tail-end of an era which had been glorified by Ben Hecht and Charles MacArthur in their successful play, The Front Page. Newspapering, at that time, was regarded as a somewhat bohemian business. It would be inaccurate to say that the major requirement for admission was semi-literacy, but admittedly there were very few university graduates working as reporters in Canadian newsrooms. The oldtimers on Canadian papers were disposed to be mildly contemptuous of journalism school products. Indeed, it was only a brash or naive job-applicant who would reveal that he was carrying a graduation diploma from a school of journalism.

When, timidly, I entered the newsroom of the Winnipeg *Tribune*, Mark Edgar Nichols, one of Canada's best-known journalists, was publisher of the *Tribune*, which was owned by the Southam family. The editor of the paper was W.L. "Biff" MacTavish and the senior editorial writer was John J. Moncrieff, a very tall, elderly gentleman who invariably wore his hat in the office and who seldom was seen without a smoking cigar between his lips.

John Moncrieff had been associated with M.E. Nichols in other journalistic enterprises and he could do as he wished. He refused to use a typewriter. He wrote his editorials with a fountain-pen on pads of copy-paper which had been reclaimed from the newsprint on which the paper was published. The ink from Mr. Moncrieff's pen soaked the copy-paper, leaving some very large smudges. There was only one veteran printer in the composing-room who, through years of practice, had mastered the art of deciphering the editor's inky handwriting and it was that one printer who was given the task of converting Mr. Moncrieff's vigorous prose into hot-type on the Mergenthaler linotype machine.

Another longtime newspaper colleague for whom M.E. Nichols provided office space in the *Tribune* was Colonel Garnet Clay Porter. Although he had no official status on the *Tribune*, Colonel Porter had been managing editor for Mr. Nichols on the defunct Winnipeg *Telegram*. For the remainder of his life Porter was given, without charge, an office on the editorial floor of the *Tribune* in which he made a fairly comfortable living, writing freelance pieces for American magazines.

Porter had come to Winnipeg from the United States via Calgary and always retained a strong trace of his hominy-and-grits Southern accent. His "Colonelcy" probably had been bestowed upon him by the governor of Kentucky, but he bore the title with pride.

Colonel Porter was a wonderfully friendly man, short and roly-poly. He wore a wig. On hot summer days, the editorial floor of the *Tribune* resembled a sauna. The Colonel would be composing stories in his little office and he would ruffle his headpiece in moments of frustration. The reporters used to delight in popping in on him — and finding his wig skewed sideways on his head, instead of pointing fore and aft. The Colonel concentrated on writing stories of violent crime and in some of those American magazines he created an impression that the natives of western Canada still hadn't been quelled completely by the Royal Northwest Mounted Police.

The *Tribune* just was recovering from the departure of a group of particularly gaudy reporters when I arrived. The departing scribes included such local legends as Chief Buffalo Child Long Lance, Jerry Hogan, Wales Thomas, Pete Galbraith, Lee Wilson and my own effervescent cousin, H. Travers Coleman. Chief Buffalo Child Long Lance and Trav Coleman both left the *Tribune* to go directly to the publicity staff of the Canadian Pacific Railway.

Long Lance was a tall, strapping, handsome man who made a distinct impression on wealthy American ladies who stayed at the Banff Springs Hotel or Château Lake Louise. Wealthy ladies and strong drink brought an end to his career as a Canadian Pacific publicist. He was permitted to "resign" after an incident in which he bent a poker over the skull of the chauffeur of an American lady who was occupying a suite at the Banff Springs. Apparently, the chauffeur resented the Chief's amorous interest in his employer.

After that, Long Lance found his spiritual home in Hollywood. He wrote for the studios and he starred in one picture, "The Silent Enemy." On March 20, 1932, he committed suicide in California. He was only 42 but he had done a lot of living.

Canadian newspapermen had been hearing rumours that Long Lance had fabricated some of his early history. It was only after he shot himself that the details began to come to light.

He had been born Sylvester Long in Winston Salem, North Carolina, in 1890. Under the name of Sylvester Long Lance, he volunteered for the Canadian Army in 1916. He went overseas and was wounded twice. After the war he went to Calgary where, while he was working as a reporter on the Calgary *Herald*, he was officially adopted by the Blood

Indian tribe and given the name of Buffalo Child. The Chief's reportorial career on the Calgary *Herald* terminated under spectacular circumstances.

On March 29, 1922, Mayor Sam Adams called an emergency meeting of his five closest advisors in his office at the Calgary City Hall. There was much unemployment in the city. There were rumours of an impending terrorist plot; only the previous day someone had hurled a brick through the glass door of the mayor's office.

The mayor and his advisors were meeting in this very tense atmosphere when suddenly they saw that the door to the office was opening. Crouching at the doorway was a masked man who, very slowly and carefully, shoved a small black satchel into the office. From the satchel protruded a burning fuse.

The mayor and his advisors immediately dove for cover. One of the councillors was cut quite badly when he went head-first through a glass partition. But there was no explosion! When the fuse burned down, it was discovered that the black satchel was quite empty.

The perpetrator of the "bomb-plot" was Big Chief Buffalo Child Long Lance. Despite the intercession of Mayor Sam Adams and City Solicitor L.W. Brockington, who sportingly were inclined to dismiss the incident as a well-executed practical joke, the *Herald* insisted on firing Long Lance. He was hired almost immediately by the Winnipeg *Tribune* which felt that any reporter with his imaginative enterprise would be a productive addition to their staff.

Stories about Wales Thomas still were circulating in the *Tribune* newsroom when I booked in. He had an artificial leg, and during one particularly alcoholic office party which was held in his apartment someone threw the leg through an open window. The limb fell into the street below; before it could be retrieved, it had been crushed by a passing automobile. The accident occurred in the middle of the night and his fellow-reporters had one hell of a time persuading a local medical-supply retailer to open his shop early so that Thomas could get a replacement limb on which he could report for duty at 8:00 A.M.

Jerry Hogan was one of those characters right out of The Front Page. He wasn't liked particularly, and when he was fired from the *Tribune*, the only tears shed were Hogan's. He had been a regular loser in the *Tribune*'s office poker-game, but one night he was a big winner, having cleaned out most of his competitors after a run of spectacular luck.

Jerry didn't give his colleagues an opportunity to recoup their losses. He pulled out a .38-calibre police service pistol, placed the gun in front of him as he swept the money off the table, and proclaimed flatly: "The game is over." The *Tribune* staffers thought that Hogan's method of ending their game was singularly unsporting.

After being fired, Jerry Hogan travelled immediately to Toronto where, with his gift of the gab, he talked himself into a reporting job on the Toronto *Telegram*. His term of employment at the *Telegram* was brief but memorable.

There was a shipwreck in a storm on Lake Ontario and Hogan hired a tugboat to take him to the scene of the wreck. When his assignment was completed, he turned in an expense account in which he charged the newspaper $300 for renting the tugboat. When a cheque was issued for the amount of his expense, he cashed it with alacrity.

A week later the owner of the tugboat arrived at the *Telegram* office on Bay Street to complain that, when paying him for the rental of the boat, Jerry Hogan had given him an N.S.F. cheque in the amount of $50. Hogan, who happened to see the tugboat owner standing at the cashier's cage in the *Telegram*'s ground floor lobby, went right through the doorway onto Bay Street and never returned.

* * * * *

In larger Canadian cities, the Winnipeg *Tribune* had a well-deserved reputation as an excellent training-school for young newspapermen. The standards of excellence were established by such deskmen as Bill Walling, Allan Bill, Ross Cameron, Bill Osler and the two editors on the city desk: Fred O'Malley and Fred Johnson.

O'Malley and Johnson were sticklers for taut, accurate writing and despised unnecessary adjectives. Their orders to rookie reporters were invariably: "Keep it short! The story of the Earth's creation can be written in half a column." They were patient and supportive but seldom did they go out of their way to inflate a young writer's ego.

Many years later when I was writing a syndicated column out of Toronto, I returned to Winnipeg for a Press Club bash, and Fred Johnson, then nearing retirement, took me aside. "I want to tell you that I'm proud of you, Jimmy," the veteran editor growled. "I've never seen anyone go so far with so little talent."

We had one holdover from the times when, as the late Jimmy Richardson wrote, "newspapermen drank themselves to sleep each night and went to bed, still wearing their socks." "Nick" Nicolls had been born for better things. Back in England, he had been educated at a proper public-school and he had attended Royal Military College in Sandhurst. Somewhere along the line he had disgraced himself and had been shipped off to Canada as a remittance-man.

When sober, he retained traces of his public-school good manners, but when in his cups he was a mess. He lived in a series of rented rooms; when he drank up his *Tribune* pay and his remittance-cheque was late in arriving from England, he was evicted frequently for non-payment of rent. Officially, his job was covering the city hall and police-beat activities in St. Boniface. And when he had been kicked out of his boarding-house room, he bedded down overnight in one of the now-unused horse stalls in the St. Boniface Fire Hall. Nick was a person to be avoided in the non-air-conditioned newsroom after he had spent a night of drinking, followed by a nap in a horse stall.

Guy White had been fired from the *Tribune* just before I arrived but his departure was still a topic of conversation in the newsroom. Guy had preceded "Nick" on the police-beat in St. Boniface. He had more than a small bit of larceny in his soul and that flaw was his undoing.

There were two undertakers in St. Boniface. Guy White had worked out a deal with undertaker "A." Whenever a drowning victim or accident victim remained unidentified after being brought to the St. Boniface morgue, White would put in a telephone call to undertaker "A." The importunate mortician would pick up the "stiff" and prepare it for burial. Burials of unidentified derelicts were financed by the Civic Health Department. Presumably, the mortician was giving Guy White a "cut" from those civic burial funds.

All went well until, after undertaker "A" had gone to the morgue to pick up the body of one of these unidentified accident victims, the deceased's family suddenly materialized. The family long had been devoted customers of undertaker "B" and objected strenuously to having their loved one buried by undertaker "A." There was a public hassle over the final disposition of the *corpus delicti*. Guy White's part in the merry little caper was brought to the attention of the *Tribune* and he was dismissed summarily. His newspaper playmates staged a farewell drinking party in Guy White's honour and he left town, announcing that he was going to the south of France to write the great Canadian novel.

Either the south of France proved to be climatically unsuitable — or the muse deserted him — but I met Guy White face to face less than two years after his dismissal. He had resurfaced in Winnipeg as a partner in a small bootlegging joint.

The star of the Winnipeg *Tribune*'s editorial staff was Victor Vereker Murray. A youthful veteran of the First World War, Murray had worked on the Winnipeg Grain Exchange before he persuaded M.E. Nichols to give him a newspaper job.

The amount of copy which Murray produced was mind-boggling. He was the senior reporter on the police-beat, in addition to writing a daily column of whimsies entitled "Tribune Trumps" for the editorial page. In the morning he would write all the major police and fire stories as well as covering the police court cases which were heard by Magistrate R.B. Graham.

Then shortly before noon, Murray would repair to the *Tribune* newsroom where he would shift gears mentally and hammer out his column. He played this dual role five days weekly; there were no police court hearings on Saturday. At that stage, Murray was turning out reams of delightful copy for less than $45 per week and it wasn't until some years later that the *Tribune* relieved him of his police-beat duties and assigned him to writing a new column, "Moss I Gather," six days a week.

Sports departments operated with a small staff in those days and the *Tribune* workhorse was Johnny Buss, a stout, good-natured beer-drinker who led long hours, six days weekly. However, there was a budding genius in the department, Ralph Allen, who had come directly from high school in Oxbow, Saskatchewan, and began writing the *Tribune*'s sports column at the age of eighteen. Even then, it was evident that Allen was going to be a writer of first magnitude and no one in Winnipeg was the slightest bit surprised when Ralph went on to be the editor of *Maclean's* magazine and the managing editor of the Toronto *Star*, Canada's largest newspaper.

* * * * *

When I joined the *Tribune* as a summer replacement during my holidays from McGill in May 1931, I was the last junior reporter of the Depression era to be hired at the longtime standard starting salary of $20 per week. One year later, when McGill University advised me to stop wasting their teaching staff's time, I went back to the *Tribune* and discovered that, in my absence, a salary reduction of 5 percent had been decreed for all employees. Accordingly, my new pay was $19 weekly.

All rookie reporters were given the task of writing obituaries. However, my father had bought me a Ford touring car for $300 and, since I was one of the few members of the staff with transportation, I was given the additional job of filling in for Vic Murray on the police-beat in the afternoons, evenings and weekends. After noon, I sat in the small press room at the Ruppert Street police headquarters and made hourly checks with the duty sergeant on the front desk to ascertain if any major accidents or fires had occurred. If there had been a fatal accident, it was my duty to drive to the victim's residence and ask the grieving survivors to provide me with a photograph of the deceased. Both the *Tribune* and the *Free Press* had a morbid fixation about printing pictures of accident victims.

These combined chores provided me with very little opportunity to write any journalistic masterpieces. In the mornings I telephoned all the funeral chapels and copied down brief biographical details of the newly-dead. I wrote these necrological tidbits on an Underwood Upright and turned in my finished products to Messrs. O'Malley and Johnson on the city desk.

However, if any person of genuine importance expired, I was under orders to turn over my notes to some senior reporter, such as N.B. Zimmerman, who could be expected to do justice to the dearly-departed.

The term "role model" hadn't been coined in those days but from the very beginning I admired Vic Murray intensely. He was certainly the most widely liked Winnipeg newspaperman of that era. The public liked him because humour columns were a comparative rarity in prairie journals. His colleagues and his competitors on the *Free Press* liked him because he was a man who appeared to be devoid of envy or malice.

It was merely coincidental that Murray, who was about 35 when I met him, had acquired a taste for alcohol while serving overseas and he had stepped into a profession where, at the time, almost everyone drank. Vic Murray and his lovely wife, Jean, managed to endure my adolescent antics and I spent many long evenings in their little apartment on Whitehall Avenue, directly across the street from Osborne Stadium.

It was Murray who introduced me to Ontario Concord wine, which was becoming a basic drink in Winnipeg newspaper circles at the time. Murray referred to it as Purple Peril and had a habit of starting his day with a modest libation of Concord wine to get his "blood circulating again." Thereafter, exuding good humour from every pore, he would betake himself to the *Tribune* and then saunter on to the police station.

One block west of police headquarters, on the southeast corner of Main Street and Ruppert Street, was the Cornwall Hotel with a beer parlour which attracted hangers-on from the police station. Murray presided over noon-hour gatherings in the Cornwall beer parlour. The daily assemblage included several criminal lawyers who, during the Depression, had been reduced to earning a few dollars by representing defendants in police court.

The proprietor of the Cornwall Hotel was a fat Irishman named Mahoney who, when he was in his cups, insisted upon giving palm-readings to his beer-parlour customers. Among the local fauna were Jackie, a waiter who was only four feet, ten inches tall, and Mr. Jones, a cultured but improvident Englishman who had become a permanent resident of the nearby Salvation Army Hostel. Mr. Jones suffered from the chronic shakes and, among the Cornwall regulars, was referred to as J. Jittering Jones.

When Cyril Evelyn Louth, the notably eccentric police reporter for the *Free Press*, took up permanent residence at the Cornwall, his hotel room became the unofficial headquarters for an oddly assorted group of lawyers, reporters, police constables and sundry other citizens whose daily ingestions of Ontario Concord wine inspired Murray to christen them the Purple Peril Pioneers.

About this time, there was an overnight break-in at a St. Boniface brewery, and some local brigands heisted thousands of gallons of pure grain alcohol. The brewery never publicly acknowledged the true extent of their loss, but immediately thereafter there was enough grain alcohol in illegal circulation to keep thirsty Winnipeggers satisfied for many months to come.

Suddenly it became possible for in-the-know newspapermen to acquire five-gallon jugs of grain alcohol at bargain prices. This led to the production of bathtub gin. The amateur distillers would take an empty 40-ounce whiskey bottle and, after cleaning it briskly, would pour 20 ounces of grain alcohol into it. Then they would add approximately 20 ounces of cold tap water, leaving only enough room for 12 drops of juniper juice and a teaspoon of glycerine. After vigorous shaking, the resultant mixture was an acceptable gin.

For big parties, the amateur distillers didn't bother to bottle the stuff; they just mixed it in the five-gallon jugs, thus saving a lot of time and energy.

A new form of bootlegging briefly became a cottage industry in Winnipeg. If you ran short of booze late at night, you could drive into the garage of the Blue Line Taxi, behind the Canada Block on Donald Street. Therein, a local racetrack character known as Gyp the Blood would retail a bottle of ersatz gin for only $2. The cottage distillers were whimsical chaps and they went to the extent of printing "brand name" labels which they affixed to their bottled products.

Vic Murray had a younger brother, Bruce, an accountant and amateur actor with a restless mind who invented a new drink by mixing equal quantities of bootleg gin and Purple Peril Concord wine. The resultant concoction, which Murray named "Kiss the Trolley Wire," became quite popular in Winnipeg newspaper and theatrical circles. The name of the new product was particularly appropriate; after a couple of glasses of the concoction, many of the drinkers reacted as if they had touched their tongues to the main generators at the local Manitoba hydroelectric plant.

Of all the *Free Press* staff, it was Cyril Evelyn Louth to whom I was exposed most frequently. Cy worked the full day-shift at the Ruppert Street police station. When Vic Murray left the police station after noon to return to the *Tribune* to write his humour column, I replaced him at Ruppert Street where Louth and I shared the press room until 3:00 P.M. when I usually drove him back to the *Free Press*.

Louth was a classic screwball beyond compare. He could write jaunty, staccato prose and was an exceptionally competent news-gatherer, but obviously he suffered from some tragic emotional imbalance. It was extremely unnerving to work with Cy in the police station because occasionally he would leap from his typewriter, throw open a window and startle passersby by barking ferociously.

In addition to barking, Louth could give a piercingly accurate imitation of a police siren. If we were blocked by heavy traffic when I was driving him back to the *Free Press* in my $300 Ford touring car, Louth would lean out of the Ford and give his imitation of a police siren. He would cackle happily as startled motorists made frantic efforts to turn their cars out of our path.

Winnipeg was a city of individualists, but among local newspapermen there were few, if any, who could match Arthur Carlyon "Tony" Allan.

Tony was the second of three sons — and the fourth of five children — in the remarkable family of Mr. and Mrs. George W. Allan. The senior Mr. Allan was a founder of the law firm of Allan Laird Haffner Hobkirk and MacInnis; he was Chairman of the Canadian Committee of the Hudson's Bay Company and he was a director of several major Canadian companies, including the National Trust.

Until the day he died, Mr. Allan presided over the family domain at 4 Roslyn Place. He was a wonderful gentleman: tall, erect and utterly imposing. For all his stately exterior, Mr. Allan was a very jolly man and his eastern friends and business associates regarded him as western Canada's foremost raconteur.

My exposure to the remarkable Allan family began with the youngest child, Ted, who had been my playmate at McGill. All the Allans inherited the intellectual brilliance and curiosity of their parents but Tony always was — well, *different*!

Tony spent a year at Royal Military College in Kingston and attended McGill briefly. Obviously, the confinements of academic life weren't for him and he disappeared from McGill before Christmas of his first year — never to return.

After the Christmas holidays, Tony left Winnipeg on an eastbound train and his family assumed that he had returned to McGill. When they didn't hear from him for several months, they weren't concerned unduly because, even in his prep school days at Appleby College in Oakville, Ontario, Tony's correspondence had been rather hit-and-miss — with more miss than hit.

Although Mr. George Allan wasn't a sports fan, Mrs. Allan and her adult children were enthusiastic supporters of all Winnipeg sports leagues — particularly hockey. So, when the Kenora Thistles and the Regina Pats met at the Winnipeg Amphitheatre to settle the junior hockey championship of western Canada, Mrs. Allan, her two daughters and two of her sons were in interested attendance.

Quickly, the Allan family espied a familiar figure on the ice. Tony Allan, whom they believed to be studying diligently at McGill, was playing defence for the Kenora Thistles, partnering Johnny Gallagher, who afterwards played in the NHL for the Montreal Maroons and the New York Americans.

Although he was only 20, Allan was already semi-bald. He had lost his front teeth in hockey scrimmages at RMC and McGill. He wore a bridge which he left in the dressing room whenever he went onto the ice to play for the Kenora Thistles. His semi-nude dome and his toothlessness inspired opposing players to refer to him as "Grandpa." And a sports columnist who knew him well described him as "the world's oldest-*looking* junior hockey player."

Tony simply hadn't bothered to tell his family that he wasn't returning to McGill. He had jumped off the train at Kenora where the Allans had a capacious summer home; he had taken a job in a local wholesale grocery establishment. Most of the players on the Thistles team were youngsters he knew from his years of spending his summer holidays in the Kenora area.

The Allans weren't particularly upset to discover that Tony had dropped out of university. They recognized that he was a free-thinker. They were pleased to see that he was alive and healthy.

Before the end of the hockey season, Tony had completed a journalism course offered by a correspondence school in the US. With that equipment he betook himself to Calgary to observe the infant Alberta oil industry. To sustain himself financially, he became the Calgary correspondent for a Tulsa trade paper devoted to the petroleum industry. When the oil boom began to peter out, he landed a job on the reporting staff of the Winnipeg *Tribune*.

Tony was a jazz buff. He introduced me to such international publications as the *Melody Maker* and *Down-Beat*. He was addicted particularly to the recordings of black musicians such as Duke Ellington, Louis Armstrong, McKinney's Cotton-Pickers, Earl Hines, Jelly Roll Morton, Bessie Smith, Sarah Vaughan and Billie Holiday. However, he had a fondness too for the recordings of Benny Goodman, the Dorsey Brothers, the Teagarden Brothers, Red Nichols and other white bands. He had an affection for those pioneering boogie-woogie pianists, Pine Top Smith and Albert Ammons, and he collected the works of such instrumentalists as Fats Waller, Eddie Lang and Joe Venuti.

By the time he married, left the parental home at 4 Roslyn Place and moved to his own house in suburban Fort Garry, Tony must have assembled Winnipeg's most complete collection of jazz recordings on those old 78-rpm discs.

Originally, Allan bought most of his recordings from the Dominion News around the corner on Main Street and only three blocks from the *Tribune*. However, he divided his trade after a close family friend, Charlie Counsell, opened The Music Box on Osborne Street. The Music Box was a lending library in addition to being a retail outlet for 78-rpm recordings.

Charlie Counsell was a particular pal of Tony's older brother, Bill Allan. All three were passionate admirers of Bing Crosby. By the same token, all three despised another crooner, Russ Colombo who, in their opinion, was an indifferent singer who had the consummate gall to attempt to imitate Crosby's succcessful style.

One Sunday evening, Charlie Counsell and Bill Allan returned from a day of duck shooting and, still carrying their armaments, repaired to the back office of The Music Box and opened a fresh bottle of whiskey. It wasn't the first bottle they had opened that day.

When they had attained a mood of considerable jollity, Counsell switched on the radio in his back office. Their mood was destroyed completely when, to their horror, the radio emitted the sounds of Russ Colombo shamelessly singing Bing Crosby's theme song: "When the Blue of the Night Meets the Gold of the Day." Calmly, Counsell and Allan loaded their shotguns; they took point-blank range and they blasted the radio all to hell.

The Allans and their friends were slightly unusual.

Tony Allan seldom joined in the general roistering of the local newspaper fraternity. He enjoyed a drink but he preferred the company of small groups of special friends. With his wide-roving interest in the trivia of the world, he didn't require the stimulus of alcohol to get his kicks.

On sheer journalistic merit, he became city editor of the *Tribune*. Then, in a moment of whimsical inspiration, he arranged to exchange jobs with Herb Manning, the sports editor.

Allan brought genuine distinction to his new job. He had a photographic memory for Canadian sports history. He was at heart a traditionalist. He felt that history was more important than the children's games of the immediate present — which were played by athletes who were, in his opinion, overpaid in the context of the entertainment they were providing in North America. He made one exception: as far as he was concerned, Canadian football was one game which was improving annually and he wrote of that game enthusiastically until, finally, he pulled the hood over his typewriter.

That he did suddenly and unexpectedly. At the age of only 47, he retired from the newspaper business. His father had died during the Second World War, leaving a rather substantial inheritance. Among the newspapermen of my acquaintance, he was the first to walk away from his typewriter when he still was at the very top of his game. And once retired, he never went back to writing. He died in 1979 at the age of 72.

Some other Winnipeg newspapermen didn't live to reach the age of retirement. Cy Louth, the flamboyant police reporter, always fought a losing battle against alcoholism. Sporadic sessions of sobriety brought him some surcease and, in a final, gallant effort to emerge from his private hell, he wrote a sad autobiography entitled *But for the Grace of God.*

Dick Malone, who at that time was general manager of the *Free Press*, always had encouraged Louth to write a book but he despaired of Cy ever completing such a project. Then one afternoon, Louth marched into Malone's office and dropped a copy of the completed manuscript on the general manager's desk.

But that final effort had been too much for him. With the job completed, it wasn't long before Cyril Evelyn Louth returned to the bottle. He was dead within the year.

On the other hand, Victor Vereker Murray, the jovial founder of the Purple Peril Pioneers, lived until he was over 90. And he didn't take a drink in the final 30 years of his life. His abstinence disproved the old newspaper theory that alcohol is necessary in stimulating the creative processes. After he abandoned Purple Peril, Murray's columns continued to sparkle with wit and good humour.

If I ever return to Winnipeg, there are some graves on which I must place a few floral tokens of grateful remembrance.

LOTUS LAND DURING THE DEPRESSION

DURING THE DEVASTATING ECONOMIC DEPRESSION OF the Threadbare Thirties, thousands of the unemployed pulled up their stakes in prairie cities and small towns and somehow managed to make their way to the Pacific coast. Many rode the rods.

Some of the migrants nourished the false dream that they would find jobs in Vancouver or Victoria.

Alas, the lotus land of the Pacific coast proved to be, in some respects, only a mirage. Vancouver was having its own depression. There were few opportunities for work; the city soon was overwhelmed by the influx of the jobless from the prairies. The situation worsened steadily until, in desperation, the federal government relieved some of the pressure on Vancouver by setting up work camps for the unemployed in the interior of British Columbia.

In those singularly inauspicious circumstances, I made my first career change: I quit the Winnipeg *Tribune* in the early summer of 1933. Although I was only 21, I was fast becoming a drunk. I persuaded myself that, if I got away from my Winnipeg friends, I could moderate my drinking. Regrettably, another 25 years would pass before I quit.

The old legends had it that when a reporter decided to quit his job he would put in a telephone call to the city editor and tell that gentleman exactly what he could do with the entire newspaper building, brick by brick.

I did nothing of the kind. From the press room at the police station, I made a telephone call to city editor, Fred O'Malley. I informed him, very politely, that I was resigning and I intended to leave for Vancouver the following day. Mr. O'Malley did absolutely nothing to dissuade me. My departure created no void in Winnipeg journalism. Without me, the *Tribune* managed to stagger along for another 47 years.

And there was no welcoming party awaiting me on the railway-depot platform at Vancouver. The publishers of Vancouver's three daily newspapers were blissfully unaware that I was open to offers. In fact, the Vancouver papers had imposed a staff freeze — they didn't plan to hire anyone in the foreseeable future.

Overly confident that I would secure employment when I arrived from Winnipeg, I registered at the Hotel Vancouver, the city's largest hotel. Tom Chester, who had been assistant manager of the Royal Alexandra when I was in short pants, had become manager of the Hotel Vancouver. For the incredible bargain price of only $25 per month, he provided me with a room and bath. I couldn't have improved on that rate even if I had canvassed the worst flea-bags in town.

I lived in the Hotel Vancouver, but I couldn't afford to eat there. Each morning I sauntered down Granville Street to a tiny restaurant which was situated in the back-end of a cigar store. For a total outlay of 25-cents, I breakfasted on orange juice, two boiled eggs, toast and coffee. For dinner,

I could eat for 50-cents in some of the smaller restaurants within walking distance of the hotel.

It was my cousin, Travers Coleman, who rescued me from the Hotel Vancouver before I became a basket-case. My room in the hotel at Granville and Georgia had become much too convenient a stopping place for my friends who had decided to stay downtown in the evenings for a bit of partying.

Trav Coleman had become press representative for the Canadian Pacific in Vancouver after leaving the Winnipeg *Tribune*.

When he was still with the *Tribune*, Trav was regarded not only with respect, but also with genuine affection by most working newspapermen. He wrote competently and with wit. His comedic talents as a dialectician-raconteur were known in every Canadian newsroom from coast to coast, and he was always what reporters described as "very good company."

He made light of the fact that my father — and his uncle — was vice-president of the company for which he worked. Actually, Trav had been selected personally by Hugh Campbell, a close colleague of Torchy Anderson on the Calgary *Herald*. Campbell had left the *Herald* to become the chief of public relations for Canadian Pacific in western Canada. He had been intrigued by Trav's ebullient personality when Trav was a reporter.

When my father became president of Canadian Pacific, Trav sent telegrams to many of his media friends across Canada. The telegrams read: "I am accepting congratulations on my promotion from nephew-to-the-vice-president to nephew-to-the-president."

Always to me, Trav had acted as an older brother, rather than as a cousin. Now, he and his wife generously scooped me out of the Hotel Vancouver and took me home to live with them in their bungalow on Third Avenue in Kitsilano. I used to say that they had me to dinner one Sunday night and I stayed for seven months. They provided me with a room in their basement and I paid them nominal room and board. I might have remained there forever, but, after seven months, I married and moved out.

Living with my popular cousin gave me the opportunity to become familiar with almost everyone in the editorial departments of the Vancouver newspapers. Trav entertained his many newspaper friends in his home. Eventually, it was Bob Elson, the sports editor of the *Province*, who permitted me to get a foot in the door. I had known Elson when he was promotion manager of the Winnipeg *Tribune*. However, he was a Vancouverite and he quit the *Tribune* when he had the opportunity to return to Vancouver to be a sports editor.

Because the staff freeze was in effect, there was no chance of my getting on the regular payroll of the paper. Elson worked out a scheme with Aubrey Roberts, the city editor. I would be a "stringer" at $25 a week, and $15 of that amount would be charged to the sports department while the other $10 was charged to the city news department. Each Friday I received a blue voucher slip which I took to the cashier on the main floor. In return for the voucher, the cashier would give me $25.

Bob Elson was a large, very dynamic man. I believe that he was one of the two or three best newspapermen with whom I had the privilege of working in the past 55 years. As a sports editor, Bob Elson was super-charged and imaginative but he had some very strange nervous habits. When he was contemplating a new enterprise with which to galvanize his willing staff, he would pick several pages of copy-paper from his desk and would chew on them thoughtfully. Often, reporters had written stories on those particular sheets of copy-paper and had submitted them for editing. In the *Province* sports department, we used to joke, half in truth, that Elson "ate some of the best stories we'd ever written."

In 1934, Vancouver had three dailies. The *News-Herald* was the morning newspaper, while the *Province* and the Vancouver *Sun* shared the afternoon field. The *Province* was considerably larger than the *Sun*, which was a very lively paper with a distinctly home-town bias.

As far as news content was concerned, the Vancouver *Province* was probably one of the three best newspapers in Canada in 1935–45 the period. It had access to all the leading news services in the world. In addition to the wires of the Canadian Press, Associated Press, United Press and International News Service, it subscribed to the special reports of the Chicago *Daily News* foreign service, the North American Newspaper Alliance and the Newspaper Enterprises of America. The *Province* made good use of all this material and it provided its readers with a wealth of informed international commentary which few other Canadian papers bothered to print.

Even the newsroom of the *Province* had a slightly international atmosphere. Two of the genuine characters on the staff were Bert Greenwood, from England, and M.A. Earle Kelly, from New Zealand.

Bert Greenwood, an irascible old gentleman who had served on *The Times of London*, was the night editor of the *Province* when I arrived. He lived alone in a room at the nearby Avalon Hotel. Although his best days were behind him, he still aspired to write a blockbusting historical motion-picture script which he could sell to Hollywood. Before coming to work at the *Province* for the night-shift, he would sit in his hotel room, pounding away on his Underwood. Regrettably, Hollywood never recognized Greenwood's potential as a playwright.

Bert Greenwood loved flowers and he hated whistling. On the window ledge, directly behind the chair in which he sat as night editor, he cultivated a garden of blooms in flowerpots. The messenger boys of the Canadian Pacific

Telegraphs, who each night made regular deliveries of the wire copy from the Canadian Press office, were well aware that Greenwood hated whistling; but being kids, there were occasions when they deliberately dared to irritate the old editor.

One summer night, Greenwood was sitting in his chair at the news desk. Because of the warmth of the evening, he had opened his second-floor window which looked onto Pender Street. His potted flowers were in full bloom.

A Canadian Pacific messenger boy, making one of his deliveries to the *Province* newsroom, parked his bicycle on the sidewalk directly beneath Bert's window. As the boy began to stroll from his bike around the corner to the Cambie Street door of the newspaper, he whistled with all the power in his lungs.

Greenwood rose in fury. He picked up two of his most precious flowerpots and hurled them through the window at the disappearing messenger boy. The boy didn't dare to come into the *Province* to face the raging Greenwood. He went back to the C.P. Telegraph office and resigned his job.

M.A. Earle Kelly came to work about 4:00 each afternoon and he shared the huge newsdesk with Bert Greenwood, although he was careful to sit as far as possible from Bert's flowerpots. At that time, Earle Kelly probably was Vancouver's most widely known media personality. He was heard each evening on radio station CKCD, reading the Vancouver *Province* newscast.

Earle Kelly, who had come to Vancouver from New Zealand, was a tall, erect, distinguished-looking man, who always dressed beautifully. When first he came to Vancouver, he lived in the Patricia Hotel on raffish Hastings Street East, but he contrived to employ the services of a "gentleman's gentleman" to look after his extensive wardrobe.

He was a very handsome man with a flowing white moustache. In good weather, he was a familiar figure on the tennis courts in Stanley Park, clad impeccably in white flannel trousers, a white shirt and a V-necked sweater bordered in the colours of his "old school" in Dunedin, New Zealand.

Mr. Kelly had a twinkle in his eyes and he would have been the last to deny that he was a bit of a rogue. He had a long list of "secretaries" who accompanied him to the *Province* where they typed the broadcast scripts which he dictated to them. Invariably, these "secretaries" were tall young ladies of commendable pulchritude. Mr. Kelly quickly discouraged any reporters from chatting with the "secretaries."

Through the 1920s and the first few years of the 1930s, Vancouver was a boisterous, wide-open city. In the words of one contemporary historian, "In Vancouver, you could do anything you were big enough to do." Gambling clubs operated until the small hours of the morning and you could buy a drink at almost any hour.

Bookmaking was big business in Vancouver, even when I was working for the *Province*. The city's most reliable bookmakers banded together under the name of the Big Nine and they rented the top floor of the Vancouver Block, one of the tallest buildings in town. There were three racetracks in the Vancouver area and two more tracks at Victoria. The Big Nine operated on a year-round basis and subscribed to the wire-service of the General News Bureau which the Annenberg Brothers operated out of Chicago. The General News Bureau provided entries and results from every track in North America. Each afternoon, patrons who wished to bet on the races visited the offices of the Big Nine. Free alcoholic drinks were provided for big betters. A fairly regular visitor was a police chief. He didn't bet but he availed himself of an occasional glass of refreshing spirits.

The atmosphere changed in 1934 when Gerry McGeer, a flamboyant lawyer, ran for the mayoralty on a reform platform. When McGeer defeated the longtime incumbent, Louis D.Taylor, he fulfilled his election promise to clean up the city. He ordered his police to crack down on prostitution and he warned the bookmakers that, thenceforth, they must adopt a lower profile.

Nevertheless, bootlegging still flourished in licensed "clubs" where the only qualification for membership was an outlay of 35-cents to buy a drink. One of these estaminets was the Irish-Canadian Social & Athletic Club, on the second floor of a building immediately next door to the *Province* on Hastings Street. You could step out of the side door of the *Province*, walk about 50 feet through an alley, and climb a flight of stairs to the Irish-Canadian Club. A cheerful waiter named Jerry would "book" your bet on a horse-race in addition to serving your drink.

In the early years of Gerry McGeer's mayoralty, the provincial government took a swipe at the bootlegging industry by opening an all-night liquor store on Howe Street. Now there was no excuse for running out of booze at an all-night drinking party.

In the 1930s the alcoholic staple in Vancouver newspaper circles was rum — 30-overproof Demerara rum which the B.C. Liquor Board imported. For all but the most corroded palates, the overproof rum was much too strong to be taken straight. It was customary to dilute it in a glass, one part of rum to two parts of tap water. The bootleggers sold Hot Rums at 35-cents per glass adding hot water and lemon juice. Even when diluted, it packed a ferocious clout and any overindulgence was almost certain to produce a monumental hang-over.

The star of the *Province*'s reportorial staff was H.H.C. "Torchy" Anderson. He was in his mid-forties by this time and the red hair which had inspired his nickname when he was a copy-boy on the Calgary *Herald* had turned dark brown, sprinkled with grey. His Christian name was Harold but only old friends in very good standing dared to address him as Harold.

Torchy founded the Rum Tum Tum Club, an informal group which met irregularly in the photographer's office at the *Province*. The meetings were convened after the day's final edition had gone to bed.

The club was inaugurated with a gift of several bottles of 30-overproof rum, donated by Gordon Wismer, the attorney-general of British Columbia. Payola was frowned upon at the *Province* but Anderson, whose authority always was unquestioned, ruled that occasional gifts of rum for on-the-premises consumption by members of the staff were acceptable if given by publicists of companies or institutions which were held in particularly high regard by the reporters.

Torchy Anderson and his pal, Hugh Campbell, shared a growling distaste for any type of pomposity. Torchy was consistent in his deflation of overripe egos. At an early session of the Rum Tum Tum Club, Anderson declared that the membership would accept nominations for a non-active group to be known as the Son of a Bitch Club.

Candidates for membership in the Son of a Bitch Club would be local business, professional or academic personalities who generally were a pain-in-the-ass to reporters. The candidates would be elected in absentia, but considerable care was taken to apprise new members that they were, indeed, certified *Sons of Bitches*.

Anderson decreed an important limitation. No politician who lived more than 50 miles from mid-town Vancouver was eligible for the Son of a Bitch Club. Anderson pointed out that if the 50-mile zone wasn't observed, the club very quickly would be overstocked with politicians.

The first president of the Son of a Bitch Club, who naturally was elected without his knowledge, was a prominent Vancouver businessman. After considerable alcoholic debate in the photographer's office at the *Province*, the first president was awarded the title of Grand Ultimate Supreme Son of a Bitch.

Regrettably, the poor gentleman suffered an emotional breakdown soon after his election and he was packed away in a mental hospital. It was necessary to select a new Grand Ultimate Supreme Son of a Bitch. However, the members of the Rum Tum Tum Club didn't forget the old president whose mental breakdown had compelled him to be removed from office. With a courteous nod in the direction of the former president's padded room, he was unanimously awarded a new title: Poor, Lonely Son of a Bitch.

The two editorial page columnists on the *Province* were James Butterfield and Phillip W. Luce. Mr. Luce was a quiet man and a stylish writer who seldom appeared in the building apart from those occasions when he delivered his columns which he had written at home.

Butterfield was a well-educated Englishman who somehow had drifted to British Columbia in his younger days and turned to writing for small papers in the interior of the province. He delighted in playing the role of the bohemian journalist. At times he was given to wearing flowing bow ties in the manner of turn-of-the-century Parisian artists; on occasion he would carry a cane.

His writings in the *Province* attracted a large following. Whenever he felt that his fans' interest was wavering, he would write a column attacking pet dogs or maligning the heroine of the era's favourite newspaper comic strip, "Little Orphan Annie." An attack on pet dogs or Little Orphan Annie invariably elicited a deluge of indignant letters or outraged telephone calls. The mail and the phone calls would provide him with column material for weeks to come.

Butterfield insisted upon having a ready supply of whiskey in his desk. The management of the *Province* therefore provided him with a small, private office on the fourth floor of the building where it was hoped his activities would be shielded from the eyes of younger, more impressionable members of the staff. However, it was impossible for anyone in the building to be unaware for long of Mr. Butterfield's flamboyant conduct.

In his latter years, he formed an attachment with a lady named Rosalee, a freelance writer. Rosalee used to join the columnist in his office for drinking sessions. One afternoon, Rosalee's husband arrived at the *Province*, fresh out of Oakalla jail where he had been serving some time for writing rubber cheques. The husband, finding Rosalee comfortably ensconced in Butterfield's office, joined the couple in a prolonged session of drinking.

At some stage in the afternoon, the discussion between the three of them took an acrimonious turn and Butterfield, picking up a whiskey bottle, broke it over the head of Rosalee's husband.

A few minutes later the husband, with blood spurting from a rent in his pate, stormed into the office of the publisher of the *Province* to protest this assault. The publisher put in an emergency call for staff assistance; an ambulance was called and Rosalee's husband was taken to hospital for surgical repairs.

Apparently the little sanguinary altercation didn't seriously impair a beautiful friendship. The very next afternoon, Rosalee, her bandaged husband and Jim Butterfield were seen staggering down Hastings Street, arm-in-arm.

For many years, Bob Bouchette's editorial-page column in the *Sun* vied with Butterfield's column in the *Province* for local popularity. The pair of them managed to promote a profitable rivalry by occasionally insulting one another in print.

One December, someone talked them into carrying their feud beyond the limits of public credulity by engaging in a phony boxing bout. The bout was designed to raise money for the Christmas funds which the *Province* and the *Sun* operated to provide yuletide dinners and toys for Vancouver's needy families. Naturally Butterfield and Bouchette loved the limelight and prepared themselves enthusiastically for the charity bout. However, the preparations didn't include any physical conditioning. They trained at bar-room tables.

On the evening of the bout, both men were close to the peak of alcoholic condition. They waddled into the ring wearing boxing shorts and stripped to the waist. Butterfield set the tone for what was to follow when he removed his upper plate and placed the gleaming dentures atop the ring post in his corner.

The bout was brief and no blood was spilled. In fact, it was doubtful that either man was sober enough to land even one solid punch. After clowning around the ring for slightly more than two minutes, both men swooned on the canvas in what was described as "a double knock-out." However, the spectators loved it. The Christmas funds of the two evening newspapers were suitably enriched — and no one was hurt.

For a brief period, Bouchette and Butterfield both were working for the Vancouver *Province*. Bouchette's drinking had been out of control for several years and finally he did something which ended the patience of his superiors at the *Sun*. Whether he was fired or whether he quit was a moot point, but one day Bouchette arrived at the *Province* looking for employment.

There was no room on the paper for another editorial-page columnist, as long as Butterfield was producing with regularity, so Bouchette was hired as a feature writer on the reportorial staff.

The new arrangement didn't last long. Bouchette, deprived of his regular *Sun* readers to bolster his ego, was never genuinely happy at the *Province*. One night, deep in his cups, he borrowed taxi fare from another reporter and said that he was going down to English Bay with the intention of swimming all the way to Point Atkinson, which was approximately five miles across open water. The reporter from whom he borrowed the taxi fare shrugged off Bob's talk about a midnight swim. But before dawn, Bouchette's clothing was found in a heap at English Bay. And his body was washed ashore several days later.

The editor of the *Province* was Roy W. Brown, a solemn gentleman who sat in his glass-enclosed office at the northwest corner of the newsroom. He wore tremendously thick spectacles and, behind those lenses, his blue eyes had a bovine calm. Although he was a non-drinker, Roy Brown was extraordinarily tolerant of human frailty. And he was paternalistic and protective where some *Province* employees were concerned.

After Bert Greenwood finally had been retired from his night editor's job, it was understood that he had Mr. Brown's approval to come into the office every night and occupy his favourite seat on the newsdesk, next to the Pender Street windows, while he typed away at his motion-picture scripts which never were produced as films.

Another employee who had Roy Brown's protection was Johnny Park who wrote horse-racing for the paper under the nom de plume, the Little Colonel. This relationship was an attraction of opposites. Roy Brown was abstemious; his gambling was confined to the cattle market and he was quite strait-laced. On the other hand, Johnny Park was a drinker, a gambler and, all in all, a rather delightful little rascal. He was a short, tubby man who, in his youth, had been a very successful poolroom hustler.

More than once, middle-management executives had succeeded in bouncing the Little Colonel from the paper. But invariably, after Johnny had spent a brief exile working for the *Daily Racing Form* of the local bookmaking syndicate, Roy Brown found some excuse for rehiring him.

The thoroughbred horse-racing season lasted for only five months of each year in British Columbia. However, it was a major spectator sport in Vancouver and both evening papers published "Racing Extras" which were rushed off the presses about 15 minutes after the running of each day's last race. These extra editions carried the complete form charts of the day's seven races, plus a full front page of entries and graded selections for the next day's program.

The comparative brevity of the racing season resulted in the racing writer being assigned to other duties in the remaining seven months of the year. When I arrived on the *Province*, Johnny Park had the somewhat nebulous job of night sports editor, once he returned from the racing-beat.

No one was ever entirely successful in firing Johnny Park. Even after Roy Brown retired and went over to the *Sun* as a highly paid consultant, the Little Colonel continued to defy the fates. Successive sports editors at the *Province* always found themselves mysteriously in need of his services.

Charles Ramsbottom Foster also adhered tenaciously to the sports staff of the Vancouver *Province*. Strangely enough, he never became a full-time employee although he was hanging around until he was an old man. He was always a space-writer and received weekly vouchers for his stories on rugger and soccer.

Charlie, who smoked a foul-smelling pipe and who was equipped with a remarkably foul vocabulary, was a widowed cockney who lived alone in a hotel room, across the street from the C.P.R. depot. Early each morning he left his hotel with several loaves of stale bread which had been given to him by the grocer in Spencer's Department Store, a few doors from his seedy hotel. Charlie would walk all the way to Stanley Park, rain or shine, to feed the stale bread to the swans and ducks which congregated in the pool just within the entrance to the park.

As with Johnny Park, Charlie Foster appeared to live a charmed life around the *Province*. He wrote voluminously and went into fearful rages when the editors cut his stories to comply with the limitations of space. He feuded noisily with every sports editor, beginning with the autocratic Bob Elson who, uncharacteristically, abided Foster's fulminations.

Charlie's tender feet became too much for him; one day, he just didn't turn up at the *Province*. It wasn't until then that anyone realized that he never had been a payroll employee; he didn't qualify for the paper's new pensions. Merv Moore, who had been a reporter with me in 1933, had become managing editor of the *Province*. He managed to wangle a $200 per month pension for the old man. Charlie never had been a gracious receiver; probably he cursed the *Province* all the way to the bank.

The closing of the *Morning Star* in 1932 had created quite a void in Vancouver. Some survivors of the *Star* had gone on to create the ill-fated Vancouver *News* and its successor, the *News-Herald*. After the *Star* collapsed, however, some reporters felt that the time had come to get out of the newspaper business.

One reporter who decided that the newspaper business was doomed was Bill Rose. After the *Star* went belly-up, Bill kept himself for several years by becoming an oyster fisherman. At that time, Palmolive Soap was one of North America's major advertisers and popularized the well-known slogan, "Use Palmolive Soap — And Keep That Schoolgirl Complexion."

Bill Rose displayed not the slightest compunction in stealing the slogan. As he went from restaurant to restaurant, seeking customers for his personally collected molluscs, he always left his business cards on which were printed the words, "Eat Rose's Oysters — And Keep That Schoolboy Erection!"

The *News-Herald*'s early years should be remembered as an outstanding tribute to the indomitability of the human spirit — not to mention a tribute to slightly conniving human ingenuity. No one at either evening newspaper had anything but sympathy for those courageous souls who toiled on the *News-Herald*. The morning paper was struggling along as a staff-owned enterprise with little or no visible means of support.

The reportorial staff performed a good job of filling the little paper with "local" news, but the *News-Herald* couldn't afford a Canadian Press franchise and consequently carried only the sketchiest stories of the major international news of each day. When it came to "Canadian" news beyond the confines of the Lower Mainland, the *News-Herald* was forced to steal its stories from the evening newscasts of the Canadian Radio Broadcasting Corporation, as the CBC was known in those days. For a couple of years, the *News-Herald*'s entire international news budget consisted of a 30-minute pony service which it received by telephone from the Portland, Oregon, bureau of the United Press wire service.

Each evening, Al Williamson, a pipe-smoking New Zealander who well may have been the speediest typist in the history of Canadian journalism, wore a set of headphones and sat in front of a typewriter. For 30 minutes, an editor in the United Press office at Portland dictated the day's main stories to Williamson.

After Williamson typed furiously for the stipulated 30 minutes, he distributed his collection of news briefs to his fellow-editors on the newsdesk. These editors "fleshed out" the stories, adding details which they had heard on radio newscasts. In this manner, the *News-Herald* managed to provide rudimentary coverage of the main international news on its front page each morning. Bare-faced skullduggery enabled the *News-Herald* editors to plug any important gaps in their coverage of international or national news.

Himie Koshevoy, a university graduate with brief experience on the defunct *Star*, was the first sports editor of the *News-Herald* and he was paid the magnificent salary of $5 per week — when he could get it. But Koshevoy's slightly larcenous activities, which were instrumental in keeping the paper afloat, should have earned him immortality. Himie was very popular in the newspaper fraternity and one of his closest friends was J. Everett "Red" Graeme, the night editor of the Canadian Press.

Early every evening, Koshevoy would toddle over to the Canadian Press office, only a block from the *News-Herald*, ostensibly to have a drink with his good buddy, Red. While Graeme was in the bathroom getting some water for their drinks, Himie would help himself to the third copies of the Canadian Press's news report. The Canadian Press made three copies of every incoming news item. The third copies were superfluous and usually were filed away in a storage room.

Himie's real purpose in grabbing these third copies was to obtain the NHL hockey scores, or any other Canadian sports scores which weren't provided in the 30 minutes of telephone conversation which Al Williamson had each evening with the United Press bureau in Portland. However, Koshevoy felt that he might as well take along all the general news copies, in addition to the sports. Not surprisingly, the editors back at the *News-Herald* made good use of the news copy to "flesh out" their modest wire service. Of course, they carefully rewrote anything which had been purloined from the Canadian Press.

Himie Koshevoy went on to work at the Vancouver *Province* and the Vancouver *Sun*, and he served briefly as managing editor of the Toronto *Star*. He returned to Vancouver to write a column for the *Province* until he retired at the age of 65.

I am left wondering: whatever became of Tex? He was a deskman with whom Himie and I worked at the *Province* when Bob Elson was the autocratic news editor.

Under ordinary circumstances, Tex was a dignified gentleman. He was the son of a Protestant minister of the Gospel and he wore pince-nez spectacles which, when they weren't in use, dangled from a black ribbon which hung around his neck. For all his genteel background, Tex was an alcoholic floater and his nickname stemmed from the fact that he had spent some time on a daily newspaper in Houston.

A nice, mild man, Tex became a tiger when he got into the booze. His binges were extraordinarily memorable. Once, he disappeared from home and office for two days. Elson dispatched a posse of reporters to find him. Tex finally was located in a flea-bag hotel, a joint which, when Tex was sober, he would have avoided like the plague. The reason for this 48-hour bender? Tex's 12-year-old daughter had suggested that he was cheating when the two of them were playing a game of Chinese Checkers.

After that incident, Elson took Tex off the copy desk and made him night editor. Elson's reasoning for this move was obscure — possibly he felt that he could abide Tex if he didn't have to watch him in action. Tex never forgave Elson for this shift in jobs, which he regarded as a demotion.

One night, Tex left his desk long enough to go across the alley to the Irish-Canadian Social & Athletic Club where he got himself well loaded before returning to the *Province* newsroom. He picked up all the night wire stories and placed them atop Elson's desk. Then, very solemnly, he piddled on the pile of papers. This wasn't the first or the last time that a disgruntled newspaperman resorted to such unseemly tactics to express his distaste for one of his bosses.

Many years later, I had a friend who, against his will, had been retired by the Montreal *Star*. The *Star* continued to give him part-time employment writing a weekly piece which was printed in the Saturday editions.

However, the managing editor of the *Star* gave strict instructions that the night watchman was to collect my friend's "copy" from him when he came to the back door of the paper. Under no circumstances was the watchman to let my fellow-newspaperman make his way to the editorial department. My old friend had developed a regrettable habit of opening the desk drawers of editors and piddling into them.

One night, a new watchman was on duty. He was unaware of the restrictions which were to be enforced. So my friend, carrying his copy, made his way to the editorial department unimpeded.

The next morning, the managing editor discovered that one of his desk drawers had been left ajar. And the papers in the drawer were soaking wet.

On the managing editor's desk was the typewritten note: "The Phantom Pisser Strikes Again!"

EDMONTON: OASIS IN THE DUST BOWL

MY PRECARIOUS EMPLOYMENT AS A STRINGER WITH the Vancouver *Province* ended early in the summer of 1935 when sports editor Bob Elson suspended me for three days after an in-office argument which, stupidly, I had provoked in the presence of the regular members of his staff. I went home to brood and I didn't return.

To augment my voucher pay from the *Province*, I had been writing weekly feature stories which were bought by the Edmonton *Journal*, the Calgary *Herald* and the Winnipeg *Tribune* — the three Southam papers on the prairies.

My fairy godmother must have been keeping an eye on me because a few days after Elson suspended me, I received a telegram from C.S. Wallace, managing editor of the *Journal*, offering me permanent employment at $25 per week. The *Journal* was beefing up its editorial staff in the final month of the election campaign which eventually culminated in W.A. Aberhart's Social Credit Party becoming the government of the Province of Alberta.

My career on the Edmonton *Journal* was spectacularly brief. The election of Bible-Bill Aberhart's party became the hottest news story in Canada. Delighted to be back on a regular salary, I worked long hours, gratefully and happily. I must have been productive because at the end of two months I received a raise of $10 per week — which was highly unusual on a prairie newspaper in the depths of the Depression. But exactly one month later, I was fired for throwing a copy of the *Canada Year Book* at city editor Fraser Gerrie.

Within an hour of being fired from the *Journal*, I walked down Jasper Avenue and was immediately hired by the Edmonton *Bulletin*. It was a stroke of sheer good fortune. I was interviewed by W.A. de Graves, the managing editor of the *Bulletin*, who had been impressed by a couple of stories I had written for the *Journal* in the previous week. Besides, he had been on the lookout for some young man to understudy his paper's veteran news editor, the monumentally irascible D.C. Jenkins. De Graves appointed me city editor of the *Bulletin* shortly after my arrival.

The *Bulletin* had a stormy history. It had been founded and edited by Hon. Frank Oliver, one of the last of the Old School of western publishers. Mr. Oliver always believed in calling a spade a spade. Once, in a scathing editorial, he turned on a man who had been one of his colleagues in the Liberal cabinet of Alberta. Mr. Oliver wrote: "Mr. ——— has the face and manner of an honest man — , but he has the guts of a louse."

Mr. Oliver had gone broke even before the beginning of the Depression. After that, the *Bulletin* was operated briefly by a group of Edmonton businessmen who had strong affiliations with the Liberal party. By the time I arrived in Edmonton, the *Bulletin* was being published by Charles E.

Campbell, who was previously the proprietor of papers in Vancouver and Regina.

The *Bulletin* was a hand-to-mouth operation. Among "boomer" reporters and "boomer" printers who habitually moved from city to city on alcoholic whims, the *Bulletin* had become known as the "Last Stop." If you were fired from one newspaper job, usually you could find another elsewhere, but not if you were fired from the Edmonton *Bulletin* — that was the end of the line!

The *Bulletin* presented itself as the brisk, noisy alternative to the sober, businesslike *Journal*, and was the only northern Alberta mouthpiece for devout Liberals. It struggled along with a circulation of slightly more than 18,000, while the *Journal* had a circulation of 35,000.

The *Bulletin* had one source of income which was declined by the *Journal*. John M. Imrie, who published the *Journal* for the Southams, was a staunch prohibitionist and he didn't permit his paper to accept any liquor advertising. Accordingly, the *Bulletin* was the only daily advertising medium for distillers and brewers who wished to bring their wares to the attention of thirsty northern Albertans.

When I started working at the *Bulletin*, I was mildly mystified by the cavalier manner in which managing editor de Graves treated our publisher, Charlie Campbell. Sometimes when the publisher was sounding off in the newsroom, espousing one of his theories for producing attention-grabbing, front-page news stories, de Graves would ignore him and stare into space, his steely-blue eyes fixed on some far-distant landscape.

Bill de Graves long had been regarded as one of Alberta's most competent, all-round reporters, a man who had contacts in high and low places. And when we became friends, he told me why Charlie Campbell would be unlikely to fire him.

When Campbell became publisher of the *Bulletin*, it was necessary for him to obtain a franchise for the wire service of the Canadian Press — it would be almost impossible to produce a daily newspaper in Canada without it. Knowing that Charlie Campbell would be applying for a Canadian Press franchise, John Imrie of the *Journal* committed a slight indiscretion. He sent a telegram to certain other publishers suggesting that he would be happy if Campbell's application was denied.

An Edmonton employee of Canadian Pacific Telegraphs told Bill de Graves that a copy of the telegram was on file in an office on the second floor of the C.P.R. Building on Jasper Avenue. Late at night, de Graves had an accomplice boost him through the transom above the door of that second-storey office. Bill de Graves stole the telegram and gave it to Charlie Campbell. It was a clear case of breaking-and-entering and theft. Not surprisingly, there wasn't much opposition when the *Bulletin*'s application for a Canadian Press franchise came to a vote.

Charlie Campbell played the role of the whip-cracking publisher, but de Graves was his one employee who could get away with murder. A handsome, debonair man, Bill seldom bothered to arrive in the *Bulletin* office until just before the first edition rolled off the presses at 10:00 A.M. Before coming to the office, he dropped into the barbershop at the nearby Macdonald Hotel for a shave and a shoeshine. Occasionally, he tarried longer for a manicure.

De Graves's nonchalance frequently would enrage the publisher. Campbell would storm into the newsroom where D.C. Jenkins and I would be working busily at the two-man universal desk. He would glare at us and ask, "Has anyone seen de Graves?" Neither of us would answer.

Campbell would pick up one of the telephones on the desk and he would bellow into the mouthpiece at Flo Nelson, the voluptuous switchboard operator: "Florence, get hold of that son-of-a-bitch de Graves. I want to find out why the hell he hasn't come to the office."

After Florence had located the genial managing editor, she would ring the phone on the newsdesk. But Campbell would be all sweetness and light when de Graves came on the line. He would say gently, "Billy, are you planning to come into the office this morning?"

The publication of the Edmonton *Bulletin* six days weekly was one of the miracles of the Canadian newspaper business. The Goss rotary press which produced the paper was, at least, third-hand and before arriving in Alberta it had been operating in Salt Lake City. In the first half of the twentieth century, old newspaper presses were shipped from city to city and they were kept in use until they finally fell apart. In 1935, the *Bulletin*'s old press was very balky. Occasionally, the pressroom foreman felt compelled to kick it savagely before it began to roll.

There were only eight linotype machines in the composing room at the *Bulletin*. Amazingly, two shifts of printers working at top speed managed to produce enough hot type to fill a 24-page paper every day.

Marsh Hodgins, the composing room foreman, would stand behind the row of eight linotype machines, making sure that none of the printers wasted a minute of precious time. He begrudged even their trips to the bathroom. As Marsh strode up and down behind the printers he reminded me of the barge-master of a Roman galley, standing over the galley slaves as they pulled the oars to propel the ship through the seas. The only thing missing was a long snake whip with which Hodgins could lash his printers to greater efforts.

The reportorial staff of the paper was small. Necessity made its members versatile. Some of them went on to bigger and better things.

Our office-boy was Bruce "Man Mountain" MacDonald, who became a major-general in the Canadian Armed Forces.

Another young member of the staff was Harper Prowse who, after the Second World War, became the leader of the provincial Liberal party in Alberta. Later, he was appointed to the Senate of Canada.

A journalistic celebrity was D.C. Jenkins, who referred to himself as "Jenx." He was a tiny man of indeterminate age who, in the great tradition of old newspaper deskmen, wore a green eyeshade on the job. Jenx was probably in his sixties at that time because he had worked on the Vancouver *Province* in 1919 and he had been a deskman on the Denver *Post* during the First World War. In fact, Jenx vowed that he was the man who had written the infamous headline which appeared on the front page of the rowdy Denver daily when the British forces under Lord Allenby liberated Jerusalem. The Denver *Post*'s headline proclaimed: "British Capture Christ's Home Town."

Jenx was given to newsroom histrionics, shouting and snapping when things went amiss, but actually he was a very warm-hearted man who, once his bouts of irritability had subsided, went out of his way to encourage struggling young newspapermen.

He had emerged battle-scarred from a couple of unsuccessful marriages and, during his years at the *Bulletin*, was living with a middle-aged Irish seamstress in a Jasper Avenue apartment building, which had the hilariously inappropriate name of "Harmony Block." When Jenkins and his lady engaged in domestic debate, their voices could be heard on every level of the four-storey building. Their apartment resembled the Old Curiosity Shop. Jenx had acquired many souvenirs and gadgets in his newspaper travels and, apparently, he had brought most of them to Edmonton.

Jenx and his lady drank sparingly but they enjoyed having parties for the members of the *Bulletin* staff in their gaudy apartment. They weren't very elaborate parties — just a little booze which Jenkins poured carefully from a measuring glass. He warned his young newspaper guests to be sure to get out onto Jasper Avenue before they became actively ill.

Jenx owned a parrot with a disposition almost as irascible as that of the old news editor. The parrot spent its time perched atop the shower curtain in the apartment bathroom. Jenx had rigged up a loudspeaker system which was triggered by the flush-handle on the toilet. Whenever anyone flushed the toilet, the loudspeaker emitted the stirring strains of "The Stars and Stripes Forever," played by a military band. At the first sound of the music, the parrot would leave its perch and circle menacingly around the head of the unfortunate person who had flushed the toilet. It was very disconcerting to be dive-bombed by a parrot while standing with your trousers unzippered. The parrot never bit anyone but it scared the hell out of many first-time visitors to the apartment.

For all his personal eccentricities, Jenkins was a crackerjack editor. He was an unrivalled expert in the areas of typography and make-up. Patiently, he taught me the elements of editing stories and writing headings for those stories. He emphasized speed and accuracy and I worked diligently to earn his approval. After coaching me for a year, Jenx moved me into the news editor's slot and he took over the city desk. When I left the *Bulletin*, I had become a good, all-round newspaper deskman.

The paper's sports department consisted of three men: Jack Kelly, Jack Deakin and Joffre Miville Dechene. Kelly's family owned a farm at nearby Ponoka and Kelly never appeared to be short of food or tobacco for his pipe. Red Deakin's wife worked for the Great West Garment factory and they managed to scrape along on their combined incomes. But Joffre Miville Dechene was a candidate for the intensive-care list. Joffre's total unsupplemented income from the *Bulletin* was $50 a *month*! He managed to exist — but barely. He arrived on the staff as a healthy young man but became wasted and gaunt as we watched him. So one day, Joffre Dechene decided to bite the bullet. Summoning all his courage, he marched downstairs and strode right into the publisher's office. Charlie Campbell looked up from his chair but made no other move as the earnest young sportswriter confronted him.

"Mr. Campbell," Joffre blurted, "I must have a raise. I simply can't get enough to eat on $50 a month."

The publisher was unsmiling, so Dechene delivered his punch-line.

Glaring at Campbell, Joffre said firmly, "If you don't give me a raise, I'm going to quit."

Charlie Campbell rose slowly from his chair. When he stood erect, he reached out his right hand and said sorrowfully, "Well, then, this must be goodbye, Joffre!" However, Dechene didn't quit right then. He stayed on the job; even a meagre $50 a month was considerably better than nothing.

A couple of years on the Edmonton *Bulletin* prepared Joffre Miville Dechene to conquer the business world. He and I were associated again many years later when he was general manager of the Canada Wide Feature Service, owned by the Montreal *Star*. After that, he became the most successful of all *Bulletin* graduates when he was appointed vice-president of the Canadian International Paper Company.

The busiest and most enterprising of the *Bulletin* reporters was Dick Jackson, a young man who, unlike his newsroom colleagues, never appeared to be short of money. Early in 1937, he left to work for the Windsor *Star* (then known as the *Border Cities Star*); later he had a long and successful employment with the Ottawa *Journal*.

Dick Jackson had many sidelines for earning money but he was never too busy to dream up some new dodge. Once, he promoted a heavyweight boxing bout in Leduc, a small town just south of Edmonton. One of the participants in the planned bout was Harold McMasters, a fierce-looking Edmonton roustabout who was just a couple of bricks short of a full load. Harold kept himself in victuals by walking around town wearing a sandwich board which advertised a local beanery. Between periods of hockey games in the local arena, Harold would don skates to advertise the restaurant out on the ice. His prat-falls aroused much laughter among the unfeeling hockey fans, but Harold was no dummy — he stuffed a pillow in the seat of his pants before he took to the ice.

Jackson, who wrote all the publicity releases for the proposed bout, billed Harold as "Heartless Harold McMasters — The Alberta Assassin."

With the assistance of lawyer Jack McClung (a son of famous women's rights advocate, Nellie McClung) and Hal Laird, a Lacombe automobile dealer, Jackson induced a Lacombe blacksmith, named Fred Doberman, to be McMasters's opponent. Always one for hyperbole, Jackson billed the blacksmith as "Frisky Fred Doberman — The Lacombe Larruper."

A large crowd had paid to get into the little arena in Leduc on the appointed evening. Jackson, taking no chances that his gladiators might provide a dull show, brought a bottle of whiskey into McMasters's dressing cubicle and persuaded Harold to swallow about 50 percent of it, neat, before he lumbered towards the ring. If Harold loved anything more than a drink and a cigar, it would be two drinks and two cigars.

Harold was well loaded before he clambered onto the stool in his corner of the ring. Meanwhile, Doberman, whom Jackson had neglected to stimulate, made his appearance in the opposite corner of the ring. McClung and Laird had exhausted all their eloquence in persuading the blacksmith to accept the bout. They told him not to worry — Jackson's script called for McMasters to take a dive no later than the third round.

Unfortunately, Doberman had been reading Jackson's publicity stories in the Leduc weekly paper. That fearsome nickname, "Heartless Harold," was beginning to make him nervous.

So, just before the referee called the two fighters to the middle of the ring to give them their instructions, Heartless Harold went wacko in his corner. Enflamed by the ingestion of about 14 ounces of neat whiskey — consumed in the space of 15 minutes — he rose and began to beat his chest and make Tarzan yells.

Frisky Fred Doberman immediately lost what little remained of his advertised friskiness. As he watched the extraordinary performance in the opposite corner of the ring, Doberman decided that he wanted no part of this opponent who, obviously, was completely out of control. Muttering to himself, Doberman climbed out of the ring and fled for the safety of the dressing room.

Watching this craven but eminently sensible defection, the crowd reacted angrily. Soon, a small-scale riot was in progress. Picking up the folding chairs which had been assigned to them as seats, the outraged customers began to hurl them into the ring.

While two RCMP constables attempted to quell the mob, Jackson and McMasters escaped through a side door and spent the next two hours hiding in a potato field. Eventually, they managed to get back to Edmonton safely, but Heartless Harold had to be rushed into hospital because he was suffering from incipient pneumonia.

Friends kept me informed of the subsequent career of McMasters, long after I left Edmonton. About 1953, he died of a heart attack while sitting in a comfortable chair in an Edmonton bootlegging joint. Heartless Harold passed away with a gentle smile on his face — he had a big cigar between his lips and a glass of whiskey in his right hand. The other inmates of the bootlegging establishment didn't notice that

Harold had lost interest in all further earthly matters until his cigar and whiskey glass hit the floor almost simultaneously.

Dick Jackson wrote crisp, clean copy and his newspaper prose always was lively. He was one of the first western reporters to realize that some eastern publications could be gullible when they were offered highly coloured — and indeed fictionalized — stories of life on the traplines and in the remote outposts of Canada's northlands.

Outlets for space writers included the Central Press Canadian and the Toronto *Star Weekly* syndicate. By writing stories for those two agencies, Jackson earned more money, in all probability, than he was receiving in salary from the Edmonton *Bulletin*.

Jackson quickly realized that there was a vast treasure trove of material for fiction writers to be found in the legends of Nahanni Land and the Headless Valley. The discovery of some human skulls in those sparsely settled areas had given rise to the theory that some natives of the northlands had practiced cannibalism. It was, in all probability, a crass libel on the inhabitants of the bushland but, more than half a century ago, readers were willing to believe many outlandish tales.

By 1935, Dick Jackson was mining the Headless Valley lode very profitably. Approximately twice a month, he was sending "exclusive interviews" to Central Press Canadian and the news service of the *Star Weekly*. The subjects of the interviews purported to be trappers who had come "outside" after spending a year or more in isolation along their traplines. To add authenticity to his stories, Jackson enclosed photographs of his "interviewees," which he had taken with his own camera.

Unquestionably, Jackson did interview some legitimate trappers when they disembarked from the weekly Alberta & Great Waterways train. But it was a matter of common knowledge that occasionally he would pick up some compliant derelict in the city hall park, take him to Uncle Ben's Exchange on 101st Street, and outfit him in borrowed trapper's gear for photographic purposes.

Jackson wrote so engagingly that it was difficult to discern the line between truth and fantasy. When I was city editor, he would submit these stories for publication in the *Bulletin*. When I questioned the authenticity of some particularly hair-raising interview, he would vow that it was the real McCoy. At that point, we would submit the matter to W.A. de Graves and D.C. Jenkins for arbitration. Occasionally, those two worthies would rule that the interview in question was a bit too unbelievable for publication, even in the carefree columns of our little newspaper. Jackson accepted such decisions good-naturedly. He would mail the rejected piece to one of his eastern outlets, confident that he would receive a cheque in return.

I was more naive than I had imagined. It wasn't until 1950, when Dick Jackson and I were attending Bill de Graves's funeral in Ottawa, that he told me de Graves was the person who, originally, urged him to send those fables to eastern publications. Furthermore, when de Graves offered to rewrite Jackson's stories and add colourful embellishments, Jackson cut him in for a piece of the action.

Dick Jackson wasn't the first fiction writer to prosper while in the employ of the Edmonton *Bulletin*. When Albert Johnson, "The Mad Trapper," was the quarry of the Royal Canadian Mounted Police during a 52-day chase through the frozen wastes in 1932, the "eye-witness" stories in the Edmonton *Bulletin* were written by a reporter named Gilroy who certainly was the oddest of all journalistic odd-balls.

Gilroy was a recluse who lived in a hut which he built on the banks of the North Saskatchewan River. While mere mortals walked or used public transportation to go to their offices, Gilroy paddled to the Edmonton *Bulletin* in a birchbark canoe. In wintertime, when the North Sakatchewan River was frozen, Gilroy came to the office on snowshoes.

The Mad Trapper story broke in 1932. It quickly became a daily front-page saga in many North American papers. The Edmonton *Journal*, well aware that this was one of the most intriguing news stories which ever would come its way, chartered a bush plane equipped with skis to report the pursuit of Albert Johnson by the RCMP.

Gilroy was the *Bulletin*'s answer to the Edmonton *Journal*'s bush plane. The *Bulletin* couldn't afford to charter a plane, but Gilroy had a source of information which had been ignored by the *Journal*. Gilroy was friendly with Bill Newsom, the local superintendent of the Mounted Police. The RCMP had a two-way radio system by which headquarters in Edmonton kept in touch with the search party. Newsom permitted Gilroy to listen in on the daily conversations between the search party and headquarters in Edmonton.

The 52-day chase across the wilderness produced some colourful prose. Gilroy, who never left Edmonton, more than held his own with the *Journal* reporters in their chartered plane. Sometimes, the *Journal*'s communications failed and they couldn't get their stories back to the paper in Edmonton. Gilroy, in the meantime, was obtaining some great material from the RCMP radio in Edmonton and his stories frequently were picked up by the Canadian Press news service and relayed across the country as "eye-witness, on-the-spot" reports.

Gilroy, according to those who knew him, was a highly imaginative eccentric. He would take notes while listening to the RCMP radio and then get himself into the proper emotional frame of mind to write his stories overnight for the following day's editions. He would go to his cabin on the banks of the North Saskatchewan River, dress himself in parka and mukluks and don a pair of snowshoes. Then, imagining that he was one of the Mounties pursuing Albert Johnson, he'd clop-clop through the snow to the battered old *Bulletin* building on the northern bank of the river.

But here's the payoff — he would be carrying his .303 rifle, loaded!

Clambering up the backstairs to the second floor of the *Bulletin*, he would seat himself in front of his typewriter, removing only his toque and fur mitts. His loaded rifle lay on the desk in front of him while, carefully, he composed his deathless prose. Needless to say, no one dared to interrupt him.

The point is that those "eye-witness" stories which were carried in the *Bulletin* and reprinted in many other Canadian papers were written by a highly imaginative man who wasn't within 1,000 miles of the dramatic events which were transpiring out on the frozen wastes.

Gilroy had left the *Bulletin* and disappeared completely from the newspaper scene before I came to Edmonton. However, Bill de Graves vowed that the legend of Gilroy's Mad Trapper coverage was no mere legend but the truth.

I never met Gilroy but I am grateful that I wasn't city editor in his time. I wouldn't have dared to delete even a single comma from any story written by a reporter who typed his copy while a loaded, high-powered rifle lay on his desk next to the typewriter.

Dick Jackson, bless his ingenious soul, saw to it that Gilroy's stories were marketed to Central Press Canadian and the *Star Weekly* Syndicate. Probably, Dick cut himself in for a percentage of the profits.

Purists may look back on those years and, with justice, accuse us of being lamentably lacking in journalistic ethics. After all, we permitted the publication of stories which were suspected of being fabrications. We were aware that some of the stuff which sneaked into print was fiction — but it was harmless fiction. The fiction writers were careful not to submit anything which would cause unhappiness in the lives of any of our readers.

Most of us were privy to sensitive information about people and we kept that information to ourselves. For instance, it was common knowledge that the brother of one of Canada's leading politicians lived in a northern settlement where his continual drinking binges were ignored by the other residents. As long as he remained in that northern settlement, the drinker was kept handsomely in funds from his politician-brother. And he was cared for by a doctor who had been deprived of his practicing rights in a hospital in a major city.

For what crime had the doctor been exiled to this remote settlement? He had performed an abortion for a teenager whose wealthy and pious parents would have disowned her if she had borne an illegitimate child.

No one was practicing investigative journalism in western Canadian cities in those years. For the most part, a man's private affairs were his private affairs. Probably, as journalists we fell far short of the principles of our profession, but possibly the average person simply had more compassion for his fellow man, 55 years ago.

I am reminded of a story about the late Captain Stanley Harrison, a famous Canadian horse lover and writer who lived at Fort Qu'Appelle, Saskatchewan. Cap'n Harrison bred race-horses; he wrote graceful prose and poetry. He had come to Canada as a young man after attending one of Britain's leading public schools and he settled immediately near Fort Qu'Appelle where he lived until his death at the age of 93.

Well, one day Cap'n Harrison was in the town of Fort Qu'Appelle and he bumped into a man who, many years earlier, had been his schoolmate at Charterhouse. The former schoolmate was uncommunicative but Cap'n Harrison was persistent. He pried until he elucidated the fact that the schoolmate lived only 40 miles from Harrison's own farm. Furthermore, the old schoolmate had been living in that particular home for more than ten years.

Harrison was incredulous. He blurted, "For the past ten years you have been living less than 40 miles from me and I haven't even seen you. Good God, man — what have you been doing with yourself?" The old schoolmate wasn't forthcoming. He stared at Cap'n Harrison and he replied coldly, "I've been minding my own damn business."

Possibly that explains why, on western Canada's smaller dailies 55 years ago, we may have been slightly careless about the truth, but we weren't prying into the lives of our fellow citizens. We were minding our own damn business.

THE EAST

MY CURRICULUM VITAE REVEALS THAT ONLY ONCE WAS I fired from a newspaper job — in October 1935, when I lobbed that copy of the *Canada Year Book* at Fraser Gerrie, city editor of the Edmonton *Journal*. However, I sensed that I would be terminated again, this time from the Edmonton *Bulletin*. My salary of $160 (I had received a monthly raise of $10 in 1936) was becoming a burden to the paper. Publisher Charlie Campbell had developed a habit of staring at me and mumbling when he passed my desk. I wasn't entirely stupid — the time had come to seek other employment, and I left the *Bulletin* in July 1937.

Fortuitously for me, two changes had occurred on the Vancouver *Province*. M.E. Nichols, the publisher of the *Tribune* who had given me my first job in Winnipeg, had become publisher of the Vancouver paper. Bob Elson had moved up to be news editor of the *Province*. To all intents and purposes, he was the managing editor although, for some unexplained reason, he was never given that title.

Elson apparently was willing to forgive me for the tiff which upset him two years earlier. He was looking for a young, energetic deskman and he had heard reports from Edmonton that I had become a speedy and efficient copy editor, thanks to the tutelage of D.C. Jenkins on the *Bulletin*. Bob couldn't have been entirely displeased by my return because, for the next two years, he picked me up at my home and drove me to work every morning, but perhaps he wished only to assure himself that I would arrive at the office in time for my daily shift.

This second-time around, I spent four years at the *Province*. During that period, among other things, I wrote sports columns for the first time, survived a crippling automobile accident in which the driver of our car was killed, and was co-promoter of Vancouver's first Canadian professional football team.

However, I began to be troubled by the spectre of the future. There were no newspaper pensions at the time, so that my older colleagues had no guarantee of financial security when they reached retirement age. About that time, some of us who were comparative youngsters on the paper had attempted to form a branch of the American Newspaper Guild. We weren't entirely discreet and soon management knew the names of the organizers. Each of us was told we were jeopardizing any chances of future advancement. Possibly that automobile accident had made me morbidly introspective but all things added up to the fact that I was no longer happy in Vancouver.

Coincidentally, the Canadian Press was starting a special news service for radio stations. This service, named Press News, would have its editorial office in Toronto and the general manager of the operation would be Sam Ross. At the time, Sam Ross was superintendent of the Pacific Bureau of the Canadian Press in Vancouver. We were friends and Sam recommended me for a job with Press News in Toronto.

I was the object of specious pity among my Vancouver friends when it became known that I was moving to Toronto. My colleagues on the *Province* must have thought that I had taken leave of my senses. I was making $60 per week in Vancouver. The job in Toronto would pay only $50 per week. Who the hell would ever think of trading the "promised land" of Vancouver for austere Toronto, and compounding that idiocy by taking a pay cut of $10 per week? I left Vancouver, my head ringing with predictions that within six months I would be desperately eager to return to the Pacific coast.

I have a theory that a newspaperman can be happy in *any* city, as long as he is surrounded by compatible newspaper colleagues. In any event, I went to Toronto "temporarily" — and ended up living there for 42 years.

When I arrived in Toronto, there were three daily newspapers in the city, the *Globe and Mail*, the *Star* and the *Telegram*. George McCullagh, a stockbroker who was once a financial writer for the Toronto *Globe*, had bought two morning papers — the *Globe* and the *Mail & Empire*, which amalgamated as the *Globe and Mail*.

McCullagh's purchase of the two morning papers had been backed by his older friend, William R. Wright, a partner in the rich Wright-Hargreaves mine. To provide a proper setting for the *Globe and Mail* they built the magnificent W.H. Wright Building on the northeast corner of King and York streets. The new structure, which was occupied entirely by the newspaper and the newspaper staff, was modelled on Lord Beaverbrook's Daily Express Building in Fleet Street.

The afternoon field was occupied by the Toronto *Star* and the Toronto *Telegram*. They were bitter competitors, although the *Star* was dominant in circulation. The *Star*'s technique for important news stories was to overwhelm the opposition with manpower. When a story broke, the *Star* would send out every available reporter and photographer.

The *Star* had only a couple of staff photographers at that time, but at least half a dozen freelance photographers in the city were dependent on the *Star* for the major portion of their income. When there was a big story in the wind, those freelance photographers debouched from the front door of the *Star* like popcorn being propelled from an overheated oven.

The *Star* was published by the staunchly abstemious Joseph Atkinson and the editorial operation of the paper was handled by Atkinson's son-in-law, the autocratic H.J. Hindmarsh. Officially, the *Star* had a strict "no drinking" rule for employees, but, of course, the staff included some vigorous imbibers who flirted constantly with unemployment. The wise old veterans on the paper were careful to do their drinking in secrecy, preferably behind locked doors in their own homes.

The *Star* had a crafty method of getting rid of reporters who were suspected of drinking heavily. The paper had a fleet of staff automobiles. They would assign one of these staff cars to a suspected drinker, confident that his drinking would lead him into a driving accident which would provide a reason for his dismissal.

Despite the gloomy prophecies of my Vancouver friends, I joined Press News, settled down quite happily in Toronto and began to explore the city. Beneath its somewhat pious facade, Toronto was a wide-open town for gamblers and drinkers. There were four racetracks: Woodbine, Thorncliffe, Dufferin Park and Long Branch, all within the boundaries of what is known now as Metropolitan Toronto.

The gambling clubs, although officially illegal, were operating full blast. They remained in tolerated operation until 1942 when George Drew's Conservative Party swept the Ontario legislature. During his election campaign, Drew had promised to close the gambling clubs and curb bootlegging. After the Conservatives were elected, the gaming operators were forced to "float" from one temporary location to another, but booze continued to flow uninterrupted in hundreds of blind-pigs around Ontario.

Among the big gambling establishments which were operating very profitably before the Drew election was Abe Orpen's club on the Toronto lakeshore, just west of the Humber River. Davy Garrity and Ray Sullivan had a club directly behind Thorncliffe racetrack in Leaside. The most pretentious establishment, the Brookwood, was operated by Manny Feder in Etobicoke, on the western end of Queen Street. Morris Fishman and his partners operated the White House on the shores of Lake Ontario, just east of the city. A man certainly could find plenty of "action," just by asking any taxi-driver.

"Craps" was the favourite game among Torontonians, but you could play roulette, blackjack or almost any other game of chance which struck your personal fancy. The club owners were charmingly accommodating. At the opulent Brookwood Club, Manny Feder provided gratis chicken sandwiches and liquor for the better-known patrons. Newspapermen were permitted to partake of the sandwiches and booze at the Brookwood as long as they behaved themselves as proper little gentlemen.

The first night I was in Toronto, my friend Ralph Allen, the sports columnist at the *Globe and Mail*, took me to Sir Benjamin Stockley's combined gymnasium and unlicensed bar which was situated in a former church, one block north of Maple Leaf Gardens. Benny was a former carnival boxer from Birmingham, England, and he was a very popular figure on the Toronto sporting scene for more than 25 years. In his gymnasium he trained pugilists and provided rigorous courses in calisthenics, not only for clients from the business world but also for overweight members of the

Toronto police force and the Toronto Maple Leafs hockey team.

One section of the former church had been converted into living quarters for Mr. and Mrs. Stockley and their three sons. In the dining-room there was a large refectory table. After sweating off poundage in the gymnasium, Benny's clients would sit around this table consuming refreshing beer or schnapps which Benny sold to them at very reasonable prices.

Every evening a large crowd gathered around the dining-room table in the Stockley domain. During the between-period intervals at hockey games, parched representatives of the news media often would run one block to Benny's to assuage their thirst. For the most part, Stockley operated in the manner of a very proper publican. Precisely at 10:55 each night he would bang his fist on the refectory table and he would cry out, "Time, gentlemen, time! Ain't you got no bloody 'omes to go to?" Even his oldest and closest friends couldn't prevail upon Benny to serve another drink after that five-minute warning period had expired. The Stockley family wanted to go to bed.

Legal drinking in Ontario at that time was confined to those eminently forgettable establishments known as beer parlours. The beer parlours closed at 11:00 each night and there was no Sunday drinking.

Although he was disposed to play the publican role during the week, Benny felt, as a humanitarian, that a man should be able to get a drink on Sundays. Therefore, he served drinks around his dining-room table on Sunday afternoons and evenings although he refused to extend his customary 11:00 P.M. closing deadline.

When the beer parlours closed down at 11:00 P.M., Toronto was left with many all-night bootlegging establishments. Most of them were patronized by thirsty newspapermen, particularly members of the *Globe and Mail* staff who didn't get off shift before 1:00 A.M. There was Mrs. Gordon's oasis, in a house near the University of Toronto. There was Rosie's on Borden Street. There were several boozeries on D'Arcy Street within walking distance of all three newspapers, and, quite often, Benzy Benjamin and his tap-room manager, Mike Coleman, would open the back door of the Piccadilly Hotel to admit trustworthy members of the news media. Jimmy Drope didn't operate a drinking place but he was willing to deliver bottles of liquor at all hours of the day or night.

During my first couple of months in Toronto, I was boarding at the Delta Kappa Epsilon fraternity house on St. George Street. We ran out of liquor on the Sunday night of what is known now as the Civic Holiday weekend — the first weekend in August. In response to our telephone entreaty for supplies, Jimmy Drope replied that his car drivers were much too busy to make any deliveries. However, he gave a mid-town address where, if we had transportation, we could pick up a bottle or two.

It was still daylight on that August Sunday evening when we arrived at the address which was at the end of a cul-de-sac in a residential district which had known better days. The scene was unbelievable. The surrounding roadways were crowded by parked cars. The occupants of those cars were streaming in and out of the basement door of a large house; they were carrying money on the way in and they were carrying bottles on the way out. Jimmy Drope was doing as much business as the government liquor store does on New Year's Eve.

As the crowning touch, an unmarked police car was parked at the entrance to the cul-de-sac. The occupants of the police car weren't interrupting the illegal commerce. They probably parked there to be sure that none of Jimmy Drope's customers drove recklessly when they left the scene. Personally, I always found the Toronto police force to be very civilized and intelligent.

Bootlegging continued to flourish in Toronto until bars finally were legalized in 1949. Sir Benjamin Stockley, astute as always, had anticipated the changing times. A year before the bar-room sale of liquor was legalized by the provincial government, Benny folded his sinful operations in the old church and bought a little farm on the northeast outskirts of the city.

Ralph Allen had introduced me to Toronto night-life at Stockley's and he was to play a part in bringing me back to a daily newspaper; of course, our friendship had gone back to the Winnipeg *Tribune* days. With Ralph Allen leading me around Toronto, it didn't take me long to realize that as far as potential earnings were concerned, Press News held little opportunity for my advancement. Since the financial future wasn't bright, the obvious solution for me was to return to a daily newspaper where my ten years of experience would offer more promising rewards.

One Saturday night, Ralph Allen and Peter MacRitchie, the news editor of the *Globe and Mail*, took me with them when they went to gamble at Manny Feder's Brookwood Club.

While Allen and MacRitchie gambled unsuccessfully, I sat munching Manny Feder's chicken sandwiches and drinking his whiskey. The upshot of the evening was that, long after midnight, when he was well foxed with the grog, Peter MacRitchie offered me a job on the *Globe and Mail* rewrite desk at $60 per week.

I was more than happy to accept. I went to the *Globe and Mail* the next afternoon and stayed there for almost a full decade. Six months after I joined the staff, I was pulled off the rewrite desk and assigned to the job of writing a sports column, which appeared in the paper daily from Monday through Saturday.

Fortunately for me, George McCullagh, who owned the *Globe and Mail*, was a sports buff. He was a major shareholder in Maple Leaf Gardens and he raced a stable of thoroughbred horses. McCullagh was a striking personality in his publishing days. He was handsome, debonair, always immaculately turned out, and he moved with casual easy grace. When he smiled, which was frequently, his lopsided grin was infectious. People who worked for him liked him genuinely.

The *Globe and Mail*, in its magnificent new W.H. Wright Building, was the first Canadian newspaper to have its own cafeteria. On most weekday afternoons when he was in the city, McCullagh would drop in to the cafeteria, pull up a chair and spend half an hour gossiping with members of the staff.

George McCullagh was a good publisher who was involved passionately in the day-to-day operation of his paper. Although he had been a Liberal in his younger days, he hated the Liberal government of W.L. Mackenzie King and — in particular — he hated the prime minister.

When I became a sports columnist, I discovered quickly that next to the opportunities to skewer the Liberals, George McCullagh had a consuming interest in the sports pages of his newspaper. Fortunately, I was in the proper league because my main interests were hockey, horse-racing and Canadian football. McCullagh was deeply involved in hockey and racing and he was a supporter of the Toronto Argonauts because he liked Lew Hayman, who coached the Toronto team. The publisher never attempted to influence anything I wrote, but he could be slightly abrasive when a column which appeared in his paper conflicted with his own views.

One evening, I was sitting at my typewriter in the sports department attempting to compose some deathless prose. I was unaware that McCullagh had walked in from the newsroom and was standing behind me, reading over my shoulder. Soon I heard him saying in his genial growl, "Coleman, how much do I pay you every week for writing that crap?" Caught off guard, I blurted some inane response and mentioned the amount of my weekly stipend. "Good God!" cried the publisher, striking his forehead with his right hand. "I'd better make another appointment with my psychiatrist."

Nonetheless, George McCullagh was a warm, kind man with a deep understanding of human frailty. He had been a rambunctious drinker for many years but had forsworn alcohol before he became a newspaper proprietor.

He knew everything that was going on in the city and he was aware of those members of his staff whose off-duty antics were making them rather conspicuous in public. He called those revellers into his palatial private office occasionally, and related his version of their escapades to them. He didn't threaten them — he just wished to remind them that, after all, Toronto still was a rather small town.

Peter MacRitchie and I were called onto his mat once after Peter had thrown an ineffectual punch at a house-dick in the Royal York Hotel. MacRitchie was older and much bolder than I and, after listening to a couple of minutes of deserved reproval, he said, "Aw, c'mon George. I remember your drinking days and you always were pretty free with your dukes." The publisher didn't take offense. He just looked at MacRitchie with his lopsided grin and he said, "Ah, yes, my boy. But, don't forget that all those things happened *before* I became rich and pious!" It was on one of those trips to the private office that the publisher said to me presciently, "The trouble with you is that after you take your second drink, you believe that you've become invisible."

Another writer who profited from George McCullagh's devotion to the sports pages was Ted Reeve who, for a great many years, was sports columnist on the Toronto *Telegram*. When McCullagh, with the assistance of John David Eaton, bought the *Telegram*, he said at his first meeting with his new paper's staff, "I bought the *Telegram* so I could get Ted Reeve to work for me." He wasn't speaking entirely in jest.

Ted Reeve was a Toronto institution. He had been one of Canada's finest lacrosse and football players before his angular body became hopelessly crippled by arthritis.

When Reeve's Balmy Beach team met the Regina Roughriders in the 1930 Grey Cup Final, Ted insisted upon playing, despite having a dislocated shoulder. He wore a special harness that afternoon: his left arm was chained to a belt around his waist so that he couldn't lift that arm to shoulder level.

Nevertheless, when Regina was threatening to come from behind and seize the initiative in the second half, old Ted lumbered off the bench and, with his one good arm, blocked a Regina punt. At that point, the Roughriders lost their momentum and, unquestionably, the blocked punt was a major factor in Balmy Beach's eventual victory.

That Grey Cup Final was played on a Saturday afternoon. In his column in the *Telegram* on the following Monday, Reeve celebrated his feat with a bit of doggerel:

When I was young and in my prime
  I blocked kicks *all* the time.
But, now that I am old and grey,
  I only block them once a day.

He was a father figure to many young Ontario athletes and a living legend in the newspaper business. He loved nothing better than sitting up until three or four o'clock in the morning, exchanging stories with former teammates or old sporting friends.

Much of his afternoon drinking was done at the Toronto Press Club. Ted would occasionally leave the club in a state of considerable inebriation. One evening, he missed his footing as he took his first step down the stairway. He was a tall man and he windmilled all the way down the long flight of stairs, crashed right through the door, and lay sprawled on the Yonge Street sidewalk. Lying on his back, Reeve opened his eyes and looked up at a solicitous couple with a battered smile. He grunted amiably, "Think nothing of it! I *always* leave the club this way."

During the Stanley Cup playoffs each spring, Toronto sports columnists were expected to follow the fortunes of the Maple Leafs. On many of those playoff road trips, I had the good fortune to be assigned as Ted Reeve's roommate.

In 1947, the Maple Leafs went to Detroit for the third and fourth games of the Stanley Cup finals and Reeve and I were assigned to share a room on the twentieth floor of the Detroit Leland Hotel. It was an off-night between the third and fourth games and we were sitting at two desks in the bedroom, writing our columns for the following day's papers.

We had our room amply stocked with rum and I had been imbibing much too freely. Well, we were having a good time, cackling back and forth as we wrote what we assumed to be hilariously witty paragraphs. After an hour or so of this literary mayhem, Reeve called out to me, "Come over here. Take a look at this paragraph and tell me what you think of it."

Obediently, I lurched out of my chair, crossed the room to Ted's desk and, peering owlishly over his shoulder, examined the words which he had just typed. At that precise instant, the rum caught up with me and I was overcome by an acute attack of nausea. I rushed across the room to an open window and was actively ill into a Detroit thoroughfare twenty storeys below us.

I recovered immediately, but Reeve had turned in his chair and was glowering at me. He said sternly, "Young man, if that was intended to be literary criticism, it wasn't very damn subtle."

* * * * *

In those days, the *Globe* was the only morning paper and, of course, the morning paper was the daily publication which attracted the sports readers. The morning paper was always first on the street with stories about the hockey or baseball games and, most important, the results of the horse-races in Ontario, New York, Florida and California. There was a tremendous amount of bookmaking in Toronto and 90 percent of the bookmaking was conducted on horse-racing.

The *Globe and Mail* used to print an early edition called the Bulldog, and it was on sale on Toronto streets by 10:00 at night. There were two types of customers who were waiting at distribution points to buy the paper when it was dropped off by the circulation trucks at 10:00 P.M. Most of the eager buyers were looking for the race results. But another group was anxious to read the previous afternoon's closing stock-market quotations. The *Globe and Mail* catered to the sports fans but it also catered to the readers of the financial pages.

Working for a morning newspaper in a city as large as Toronto in those days could be hard on the health. Morning newspapermen were working when other people were socializing. By the time that a morning newspaperman finished his stint — anywhere from midnight to 2:00 A.M. — most of the people who held nine-to-five daytime jobs were sound asleep.

If a morning newspaperman had a wife and children, they would usually be sleeping when he finished work. Thus, among the more carefree members of the *Globe and Mail* staff, there was some disposition to go out to an all-night bootlegging establishment after work was finished. It was a vicious circle; stay out all night drinking and one was likely to report for work the next afternoon with a crashing hangover. Considering the circumstances, it was quite surprising that the *Globe and Mail* staff — while harbouring some rather dedicated drinkers — included very few active alcoholics. Some drinking members of the staff were lucky and the course of their lives was changed by a single incident which caused them to pull up short.

Frank Tumpane was one of the real stars of the *Globe and Mail* — highly intelligent, devoted to his family and to the Roman Catholic faith. He was an exceptionally talented writer and became a newspage columnist on the morning paper with a particular interest in the vagaries of civic government.

A short, very slender Irishman with a perpetually quizzical look, Frank had been quite a prominent drinker on the Toronto *Star* in his bachelor days. The *Star* got rid of him with their tried-and-true technique; they had assigned a staff car to him knowing full well that he was likely to get into an accident. Frank quickly obliged the *Star*; he was fired and spent a couple of years in exile on the Sudbury *Star*.

When the *Globe and Mail* reclaimed him from Sudbury and gave him the job of writing a newspage column, Tumpane really bloomed as a newspaperman. He invented a character named Alderman Mozart O'Toole who represented a mythical Ward Ten on the Toronto City Council. Alderman O'Toole was the anti-hero of a very large percentage of Frank's delightful columns.

His enthusiasm for drinking had moderated considerably, but there still were rare occasions when, quite unexpectedly, he drank himself into a stupor. Actually, it didn't take much to get him into a befuddled state because he weighed approximately 110 pounds and was so thin that when he turned sideways he was almost invisible.

One afternoon, Frank arrived in the newsroom in deplorable shape. How he got into that state so early in the day was a mystery which never was explained. He sat completely motionless and silent in front of his typewriter for 25 or 30 minutes before he put his head down on the machine and nodded off to sleep. When Frank's snores made him conspicuous, city editor Tommy Munns gave the signal to a couple of reporters who bundled Tumpane into a car and drove him to his house. Apparently, he didn't awaken until the next morning.

Meanwhile, it was necessary for someone to fill Tumpane's column space in the newspaper. Ken MacTaggart, the paper's senior reporter, sat down at the typewriter and wrote a typical Tumpane column about Alderman Mozart O'Toole's customary misadventures at City Hall. MacTaggart performed a magnificent job. And the column duly was printed in the next morning's paper under Frank Tumpane's byline.

The next afternoon, Frank Tumpane reported for duty in the newsroom. He walked in very slowly, wearing the unmistakable look of a man for whom the previous 24 hours have been a mystery. By agreement, all the other members of the staff greeted Frank very casually and no one made any reference to the previous day.

Tumpane walked over to the newsdesk and examined a copy of that morning's paper. His face was a study as he turned the pages slowly until he came to a column with the byline "by Frank Tumpane." Frank read through the column very slowly. Ken MacTaggart had imitated Tumpane's style perfectly, employing all his favourite phrases.

Tumpane closed the newspaper and, with a completely dazed look, walked back to his own desk and sat down heavily. His face clearly reflected what must have been going through his still-clouded mind: "That's my column, with my name on it. But I can't remember writing even a single word of it." By mutual agreement, the members of the editorial staff let Tumpane sweat for an entire day before, finally, Tommy Munns took him aside and explained that his column had been written by Ken MacTaggart.

That was the last occasion on which Frank Tumpane was drunk. As far as I know, he never touched the stuff again. He prospered at the *Globe* and when George McCullagh bought the *Telegram*, Frank moved over to that paper where he wrote his vastly entertaining columns for the rest of his natural life. He died of a heart attack one night when he was out for his regular evening walk.

For ten years, my newspapering was to be devoted almost entirely to sports. Although I became familiar with the city news staffs on the two evening newspapers, my most frequent companions were to be the athletes themselves and my colleagues in the sports news media.

Among regular news reporters, the sports department was regarded as the "half-world" of the newspaper business. There was a bit of intellectual snobbery and a certain amount of good-natured contempt for sports reporters who spent their time "writing about grown men who were playing children's games." Also, there was a bit of envy; sports reporters had free admission to the hockey, football and baseball games; they received passes to the racetracks and it was rumoured that members of the sports department received payola from professional promoters in return for publicizing the activities of those promoters.

In Toronto, at least, the sources of payola had dried up before my day. The newspapers had got around to paying the travelling expenses of writers who accompanied local teams on road trips. However, Maple Leaf Gardens still insisted on giving a small handout to all members of the media — radio announcers as well as newspaper writers — who accompanied the Toronto Maple Leafs hockey team on road trips. The handout wasn't much — $10 per day. Most of the media accepted it without cavil and spent the $10 on drinks or a steak dinner. One reporter always used his $10 to buy two new shirts when he was in New York, Boston, Detroit or Chicago. By the time that he retired from the hockey beat, he must have had the largest collection of shirts in Canada.

When I became a sports columnist, I was surprised to discover that in addition to two box seats for every Toronto

Maple Leafs home game, the *Globe and Mail* also provided me with a small expense account. It was made quite clear to me that I shouldn't plan any round-the-world tours, but for the first time in my newspaper career, I wasn't restricted to the office. I could follow the hockey team to four US cities and Montreal; I could go to football games in Ottawa, Montreal and Hamilton; I could go to the racetracks at Hamilton, Fort Erie and Niagara Falls. It was freedom which was new to me in newspaper work.

Although New York City, Boston and Chicago and even drab Detroit had their attractions for a sports columnist with a modest expense account, Montreal was the city which provided the greatest lure for Toronto sports writers. Montreal was vibrantly colourful and, before bars were legalized in Ontario, the freedom of access in Quebec was an extra inducement.

There were countless excuses for a Toronto sports writer to visit Montreal. The Toronto Maple Leafs played Les Canadiens in the Montreal Forum frequently every hockey season. The Baseball Maple Leafs went to Delormier Stadium frequently to play the Royals of the International League. And in 1946, Lew Hayman and Eric Cradock went from Toronto to Montreal where they established Les Alouettes as the most colourful football team in Canada.

Although Toronto prided itself on being the news media capital of Canada, it was a Montrealer, Elmer Ferguson, who certainly was the most widely known sports writer throughout the rest of Canada. He was a regular guest on "Hockey Night in Canada," which attracted the largest weekly listening audience in the history of Canadian radio. Every weekend, throughout the National Hockey League season, Elmer Ferguson travelled from Montreal to Toronto on the Friday overnight train so that he could be in Maple Leaf Gardens to appear on "The Hot-Stove League," the between-periods show which was an eagerly awaited feature of the hockey broadcasts.

Ferguson was sports editor of the Montreal *Herald*, a small noontime daily which was owned by the much larger Montreal *Star*. However, most of the *Herald*'s readers bought the paper to read Ferguson's columns which were bright, breezy and humorous.

Fergy, as he was known all across Canada by his media colleagues and the vast national radio audience, was a delightful cynic. He was the most influential sports writer in Montreal and he made no secret that his journalistic and political services were for hire — at the right price.

In his youth he had been a track sprinter of national prominence, despite the fact that a childhood accident in Moncton had left him with a withered left arm. He had fallen from a bridge; the arm had been badly smashed and the resultant surgical repairs had been botched. Nevertheless, he refused to be inhibited by his handicap. When he was typing his column, he used the fingers on his crippled left arm to moor himself to the typewriter as he hammered the keys with one finger on his right hand. The speed with which he typed was almost incredible; his admirers said that thin wisps of smoke drifted up from the red-hot keys.

Fergy had many sidelines. He shrugged off any implications of conflict of interest when he became a partner of Eddie Quinn, the Montreal wrestling and boxing promoter, in the operation of the very successful El Morocco Night Club. To compound the flagrancy of his association with Quinn, Fergy also was secretary of the municipally appointed Montreal Boxing and Wrestling Concession.

Jack Sharkey, former world heavyweight boxing champion, came to Montreal to promote a boxing show. Whenever Sharkey asked questions about the arena rental or appointment of ring officials, he received an unvarying reply: "Oh, you'll have to see Elmer Ferguson about that." After receiving this reply for the third or fourth time, Sharkey asked in exasperation, "Did Ferguson get his hand withered by always holding it out for a payoff?" Unknown to Sharkey, Ferguson was standing directly behind him. Completely unembarrassed, Elmer said coolly, "That's right, Jack. And I don't mind if I get the other hand withered the same way."

Although he was a cynical mercenary, Elmer Ferguson evoked genuine affection among his news media colleagues. He was a genial pirate utterly devoid of any pious pretension.

When, after many years as a footloose widower, Ferguson remarried at the age of 80-plus, the Montreal wags said with an irreverence Fergy must have appreciated, "He *had* to marry her."

Montreal had three English-language newspapers, the *Gazette*, the *Herald* and the *Star*. The Montreal wage scale generally wasn't as high as newspaper pay in Toronto but the Montreal newsmen never appeared to be short of money for after-hours entertainment. Next to Elmer Ferguson, the best-known English sports writer in Montreal was Baz O'Meara, the columnist on the *Star*. Dink Carroll was a popular columnist on the *Gazette*.

The two Montreal hotels most favoured by visiting sporting characters were the Mount Royal and the Windsor. Although you could fall through almost any doorway and find a bar, the favourite drinking establishment for visitors was Slitkin and Slotkin's.

Slitkin was Lou Wyman and Slotkin was Jack Rogers. Previously, they had managed prize-fighters of dubious distinction and their nicknames had been hung on them by Elmer Ferguson.

Slitkin and Slotkin had a "fix" with some compliant official in the Quebec liquor-licensing hierarchy. Also, the local constabulary never bothered them and they operated full blast at all hours of the night and on Sundays.

Over the years, Slitkin and Slotkin held forth at several sites in downtown-central Montreal, but they enjoyed by far their greatest prosperity when they were located in a two-storey restaurant and bar on Dorchester Street, about two blocks west of the Windsor Hotel. Officially, the name of this establishment was Chez Madame Henri but every night-sprite who came to Montreal knew it more familiarly as Slitkin and Slotkin's.

Never in the history of Montreal night-life was there another restaurant and bar which received as much unsolicited and free publicity as Slitkin and Slotkin's. Visiting New York newspapermen went home and wrote glowing testimonials to the steaks and other provender served at Chez Madame Henri.

Members of the US fight mob who were frequent visitors to Montreal also cavorted in the upstairs bar at Chez Madame Henri. Some of those fight mob visitors were, as the saying goes, "no better than God intended them to be." Two of them were notorious Philadelphians, Frank Carbo and Blinky Palermo, who were reputed to "own" the lightweight and welterweight divisions in the seedy world of professional prize-fighting. They were slightly uncouth chaps whose sense of humour ran to such hoary wheezes as "the hot-foot."

The particular butt of their humour was Paul Parizeau, sports editor of *Le Canada*. Paul was an effusively garrulous drinker, but there was no harm in him. Occasionally, he became so foxed with the grape that he couldn't have hit the floor with his own hat. In those circumstances, the fight mobsters picked on him.

One night in the crowded bar on the second floor of Chez Madame Henri, one of those tricksters dropped a couple of raw eggs into the two side pockets of Paul's jacket. As everyone milled around the bar, Parizeau was jostled deliberately until the interior of his jacket pockets resembled two uncooked omelets.

Our old friend Baz O'Meara of the Montreal *Star* was a gentle soul at heart, but when he was confronted with any evidence of injustice, he could become monumentally wrathful. When Paul Parizeau finally discovered the mess in his two jacket pockets, O'Meara immediately decided that the culprit was Blinky Palermo; in all probability he was correct.

Baz confronted Palermo at the top of the stairs and offered to punch him on the nose. Well-meaning friends attempted to restrain O'Meara, warning him that the Philadelphian probably was carrying a cannon beneath his bulging jacket.

It was that time of night when, along with almost everyone else in the bar, O'Meara had become rather unsteady on his feet. Nevertheless, scowling with righteous indignation, Baz threw a round-house right as he and Palermo stood at the top of the stairs. The punch missed — O'Meara fell head over heels down the long flight of steps. He didn't seem to miss one obstacle on the way down, and when he reached the bottom, he had a broken collarbone.

Baz went around Montreal with his arm in a sling for a week, but he received considerable local acclaim as the 60-year-old sports writer who had attempted to punch out the notorious Blinky Palermo.

In a truly shocking misapplication of frontier justice, Slitkin and Slotkin announced that Basil O'Meara was barred from their joint until he promised to refrain, in future, from throwing punches at US visitors.

While living in Toronto, I had become what — for the newspaper business — is not necessarily an uncommon combination: an alcoholic-workaholic. I wrote six columns per week, I worked on "Hot-Stove League" hockey broadcasts in the winter and I worked on baseball broadcasts in the summer. When I occasionally missed a day's production for the *Globe and Mail*, I sweated blood the next day to atone for my transgression. I managed to fill my allotted space 99 percent of the time, but there were occasions when my piffling prose was approximately as stimulating as cold mashed potatoes.

Obviously, I tested the tolerance of George McCullagh and Tommy Munns, who had become managing editor of the paper. Munns was quick with excuses for me when my column failed to appear. He told the switchboard to answer any calls for me by saying that I "was away for a couple of days of holidays."

Late one afternoon in 1950 I decided to get off my self-designed treadmill. I was sitting in the Paddock Tavern, owned by my horse-racing friend Morris Fishman. I went into Morris's private office, picked up the telephone and called Tommy Munns. I told him that I had decided to quit the newspaper business — just like that.

Munns was, as always, compassionate. He told me to go home and take a couple of days off. After all, there had been previous occasions when I had "resigned," only to crawl back later. But this time I was serious.

Two days later, I telephoned the paper and, muffling my voice, asked for Jim Coleman's office. Phyllis, the switchboard operator, replied smoothly, "He is away on holidays for a couple of days." Obviously, Munns was expecting me to return.

At that juncture, I put in a call to my friend Archie Macdonald, who sold advertising for the paper. I asked him to insert a small display-ad in the sports section. The advertisement listed my home telephone number and contained the information that I was seeking employment.

I can attest to the fact that the sports section of the *Globe and Mail* was an excellent advertising medium. That one-day ad elicited a rather flattering number of offers. It didn't take me any time at all to accept a job as public relations director for Thorncliffe Raceway, a new harness-racing operation which was due to open in Toronto.

Simultaneously, my old Edmonton *Bulletin* friend, Joffre Miville Dechene, who had become general manager of Canada Wide Feature Services in Montreal, gave me a deal whereby three days weekly I wrote sports columns which Joffre syndicated to more than 20 Canadian papers.

At that stage, the prospects filled me with glee. From my childhood and throughout my career on daily newspapers, horse-racing had been my consuming hobby. When I was with the *Globe and Mail* during the long summer thoroughbred-racing season, I had gone to the races almost every afternoon, returning to the office later to write my column.

Now, with the opening of Thorncliffe, someone actually was willing to pay me a salary to spend my days on a racecourse. I wasn't becoming wealthy but I was doing work which gave me a great deal of satisfaction.

Fortune continued to smile on me. In 1952, E.P. Taylor strode into the racing scene with an imaginative plan for improving the quality of the thoroughbred sport in Ontario. Under his leadership, the Ontario Jockey Club, which already owned the old original Woodbine, bought out Thorncliffe and the tracks at Hamilton, Fort Erie and Niagara Falls. Two years later, they would buy out two more Toronto tracks — Dufferin and Long Branch. With the completion of these purchases, they concentrated all of Ontario's thoroughbred-racing on three tracks: a magnificent new Woodbine, Fort Erie and the old Woodbine (which was renamed Greenwood).

When these purchases began in 1952, Mr. Taylor hired me to be the public relations director for all the thoroughbred-racing operations in Ontario. I couldn't believe my good luck. I looked forward to going to our tracks each morning; I worked hard and enthusiastically and I found it difficult to believe that anyone else in the country could enjoy a job as much as I enjoyed mine.

And I was dealing daily with my longtime friends of the sports news media. I spent the Jockey Club's money to get publicity for our tracks. Annually, we brought sports editors and columnists from all over Canada and from New York City to attend the running of the Queen's Plate, Canada's oldest and most important horse-race.

Under E.P. Taylor's leadership, it was a golden era of horse-racing in Canada. The quality of the sport in Ontario was on an upswing, and daily attendance and daily wagering at Woodbine, Fort Erie and Greenwood reflected the improvement in the quality of Canadian-bred horses.

Although we raced six days a week from April to November, I still found time to perform a couple of outside jobs. My deal with Canada Wide Feature Service terminated in 1952, but for the next ten years I wrote a sports column which appeared every Saturday in the Toronto *Globe and Mail* and the Winnipeg *Free Press*.

And a year or two after the CBC opened its television operations, I was hired to do an eminently forgettable weekly sports interview show which was sponsored by Buckingham Cigarettes.

Our show, on the full CBC network, filled the gap between the conclusion of the regular "Gillette Friday Night Boxing Show" and 11:00 P.M. "The Buckingham Show" couldn't be planned accurately because occasionally there were knockouts in the main event of the boxing. Sometimes we were left with only two or three minutes of air time. On other nights, when there was an early knockout, we were expected to fill the 25 or 30 minutes remaining until 11:00 P.M.

The CBC occasionally imported some high-profile guests to be interviewed on those dreary little Friday night shows, but the guests who were guaranteed to be non-conformists were those zanies from the world of professional wrestling.

Gene Kiniski, a former Edmonton football player who had become the designated world champion of the wrestling circuit, always was helpful. One night, while we were on camera, I asked him to comment on an article on Canadian football which had been written for *Maclean's* by Herb Capozzi. Gene scoffed, saying flatly, "Well, everyone knows that Capozzi is a complete idiot."

There was instant consternation in the studio. At the time, Capozzi was director of foreign-language broadcasts for the CBC. The producer of our show was furious — he feared that Capozzi would make an official complaint. Throughout the remainder of the brief show, the floor director kept circling in front of me, holding up a piece of paper on which he had written, "Apologize to Capozzi."

So, I waited until the studio director gave me a sign that only 15 seconds remained to finish the show. At that juncture, I faced the camera and I said smarmily, "You know, when Gene referred to our mutual friend, Herb Capozzi, as an idiot, Gene was only kidding." But before they could cut us off the air, Kiniski beamed into the camera and he bellowed genially, "That's right! I intended to call Capozzi an *imbecile*!"

Another wrestler, Bulldog Brower, was equally helpful. In the concluding 30 seconds of each show, I was expected to thank the guest for his appearance and, on camera, I would present him with a carton of Buckingham cigarettes.

After Brower, who always played the role of the deep-dyed villain, had been responding to my questions with his customary ranting and raving, the time came to bid him a grateful adieu. While thanking him for his important contributions to Canadian culture, I handed him the carton of Buckingham cigarettes. As the camera focussed on Brower's face, his eyes popped right out of his skull. He stood up, strode off the set, *threw* the carton of cigarettes at me and roared, "I don't smoke! I'm an *athlete*!"

The resultant mail left the impression that the television audience felt Bulldog Brower's performance was quite funny. The only ones who didn't appreciate the humour were the financial sponsors of the show — the makers of Buckingham cigarettes.

In 1958, my eighth year as a racetrack publicist, I was struck by a rare lightning-bolt of sanity. I joined Alcoholics Anonymous. My drinking had ruined one marriage and it was on the point of ruining a second marriage before that union had found a basis for permanence.

By 1962, my brains no longer addled by the fumes of fruity spirits, I decided that the time had come for another career change. I still loved my job at the Ontario Jockey Club, but some of the challenge had disappeared from it. We had made tremendous strides in ten years, but I had the feeling that we were due for a levelling-off period.

At 51, I had no clear idea of what I intended to do with the remainder of my life. I resigned from the Jockey Club in April 1962. Mr. Taylor asked me to stay on the job until the conclusion of the Woodbine summer meeting in mid-July. So, I was on the payroll for three months while I had the chance to ponder my next move.

Among the friends from whom I sought advice was Gillis Purcell, general manager of the Canadian Press. Our association went back a long way — to the time when he was a CP bureau chief in western Canada and Ralph Allen and I drank with him after football games.

Purcell was the most knowledgeable news executive that Canada ever has produced. I truly believe that Purcell, who lived until he was 82, knew at least "something" about every person who ever worked for any newspaper, radio-television station or news service in Canada. He saved the careers of countless newsmen. He could pick up a long distance telephone and find new employment for someone who had run out of options. In any event, it was Gil Purcell who suggested that I should go back to working for my original newspaper employers — the Southams.

Again, good fortune was smiling on me. The chairman of the Southam News Service was Tom Nichols, a friend from my boyhood and the oldest son of M.E. Nichols who had given me jobs on the Winnipeg *Tribune* and the Vancouver *Province*.

Tom Nichols convinced the Southam publishers that they should hire me to write three columns weekly for their newspapers. And when they sold my columns to outside papers such as the Toronto *Telegram* and its successor, the Toronto *Sun*, they gave me a generous share of the syndication rights.

I spent the next 21 years with the Southam organization. Since I no longer drank, they gave me carte blanche. I was permitted to travel all over the world in search of column material; possibly content with the knowledge that I would return from my assignments without landing in jail, they condoned my disposition to stay at the best hotels and dine in the better restaurants.

Therein lay one of the major benefits of being a sports columnist. Quite probably, our salaries weren't as large as some other members of the newspaper staff, but we flew to all the major sporting events; we were provided with the best seats in the house and, in our accommodations, we rubbed elbows with the rich and famous.

Bill Corum, sports editor and columnist for the old New York *Journal-American*, aptly described the sense of warm satisfaction which our jobs provided for us when he wrote: "I don't expect to *be* a millionaire, but I enjoy travelling *like* a millionaire."

There was only one occasion on which my expense-account elicited from head office a most diffident reproof.

In my ten years at the Ontario Jockey Club, I had been spoiled. E.P. Taylor made it plain that when officials of the Jockey Club travelled, he expected them to travel first class. Thus, whenever I was making a trip, my airline reservations were made by the general-manager's secretary. And always the secretary booked me a first-class seat on airplanes.

For almost a year after joining the Southams, I booked first-class seats on the airlines when I was travelling to hockey games, football games or any other sporting events. One day, when my annual budget was due for review, Brian Shelley, the secretary-treasurer of Southam, dropped into my office. Coughing politely, Mr. Shelley said, "In the year you've been with us, you've handled your expenses admirably. But I feel that I must give you a little tip: St. Clair Balfour, the president of this company, always travels economy class on airplanes. You might be embarrassed if you and Mr. Balfour happen to travel on the same plane." I accepted his friendly advice. Thereafter, I always booked economy class on domestic airlines.

If nothing else, those 21 years proved to me that my imagination didn't require alcohol for stimulation. I enjoyed every day, every week and every month, and, almost always, I sat down to my typewriter with a sense of eagerness.

When I reached the age of 72 in 1983, the Southams asked me to retire. They had been indulging me for seven years. The policy of the company was that even the publishers of their newspapers were expected to retire at 65.

I am grateful to the Southams for giving me those 21 years to add a few flourishes to a career which had begun on one of their own newspapers, 51 years earlier.

PART 3

CANADIAN FOOTBALL

FACT AND FANTASY

AFTER MORE THAN 60 YEARS OF ASSOCIATION WITH Canadian football, the things which I remember most affectionately are the oddities. After all, the totally unexpected often becomes the norm in any sport which is played with a hard ball which has two sharply pointed ends. A ball of that shape will take some really crazy bounces.

A Grey Cup flashback which I cherish concerns the two ceremonially bedecked sachems from Alberta's Sarcee Reservation — Chief David Crowchild and Chief George Runner — who were brought to Toronto in 1948 when the Calgary Stampeders won the national football championship for the first time.

Seated front and centre in the Calgary rooting-section at the University of Toronto Stadium, the two colourfully dressed chiefs were the hit of the off-field show. Throughout the game, they were leaping to their feet; beating tom-toms and whooping and yelling in response to every good play —

offensive or defensive — by the Stampeders. The two middle-aged warriors provided a display of cheer-leading, the like of which never had been seen before in a Toronto football stadium.

And when the Stampeders finally had defeated the Ottawa Rough Riders 12 to 7, the two Indian chiefs were hustled out of their seats by jubilant Calgarians. Still beating their tom-toms, Crowchild and Runner were swept along in the vanguard of hundreds of western celebrants who were preparing to parade from the stadium, down University Avenue to the Royal York Hotel.

Almost everyone who had watched the hyperactive pair in action throughout the game assumed that Crowchild and Runner were experienced football observers whose enthusiasm stemmed from the fact that they had wagered a couple of tons of pemmican on their Alberta team.

As the noisy fans surged out of the stadium into Devonshire Place, Sue Bell, wife of Calgary newspaper publisher Max Bell, found herself walking along between Chief David Crowchild and Chief George Runner. One of these supposedly football-wise sachems turned to Mrs. Bell and asked: "By the way, who won?"

Another story of the unexpected relates to Ray Bawel, a Hamilton defensive-backfielder in the 1957 Grey Cup Game at that same University of Toronto Stadium. For the first 55 minutes, Bawel had been experiencing the type of good fortune which causes unsung defensive players to dream of election to the Football Hall of Fame.

Already, he had scored a touchdown after intercepting a Winnipeg pass. Contributing also to Hamilton's comfortable lead over Winnipeg that afternoon was the fact that Bawel had recovered two Winnipeg fumbles.

Then, with only five minutes left in the game, Bawel scarcely could believe his continuing good fortune when he saw another errant Winnipeg pass coming his way. Bawel, playing wide-secondary on the western side of the field, was in full stride when the football sped unerringly into his hands. He saw that he had a clear path to the Winnipeg goal line, 65 yards away. There appeared to be no way he could be prevented from scoring his second touchdown of the Grey Cup Final. Hall of Fame, here I come! Bawel was sprinting confidently down the west sideline when a man in street clothes, who was standing in the vicinity of the Winnipeg bench, deliberately stuck out a foot and *tripped him*!

It was incredible. Here was Canada's greatest national sporting event, witnessed by a capacity crowd of more than 27,000, plus millions more on television. The man in street clothes — discovered later to be a Toronto lawyer — had been permitted to stand on the sidelines where he could trip a player who was running for a certain touchdown.

There was no rule covering a spectator intruding on the football field. But Referee Paul Dojack reacted quickly when he saw Ray Bawel lying on his face in the mud at the Winnipeg 42-yard line. The referee gave Hamilton a first-down on the Winnipeg 21-yard line — half the distance to the goal line. Dojack explained his ruling by saying that there was an "outside chance" that some Winnipeg player might have caught Bawel. Fortunately, Hamilton went on from the 21-yard line to score another touchdown and won the game, 32 to 7.

Canadian football's annual showcase games were plagued by that type of nonsense. The men behind the Grey Cup Game courted a Big League image, but quite often some unscheduled buffoonery left the spectacle with a Bush League discolouration.

Inadequate crowd control provided recurrent problems. Canadian football officials were rather slow to realize that they must hire hundreds of security police to prevent spectators from encroaching on the playing field.

Even three years after Ray Bawel was tripped by that addle-pated lawyer in Toronto, there was an equally embarrassing conclusion to the 1960 Grey Cup Final in Vancouver's Empire Stadium.

With only 36 seconds to play, the Ottawa Rough Riders— who were leading the Edmonton Eskimos 16 to 6 — called for a "time out" in the Edmonton end of the field. The two teams huddled in their respective areas while the field officials held their own private conclave about five yards from the line of scrimmage.

While the players and the field officials were thus preoccupied, a young man wearing a Cowichan wool sweater ran onto the field from the stands at the south end of the stadium. Displaying a good turn of speed, the young man plucked the football from the field, ran back into the stand and disappeared through an exit, running in the general direction of East Hastings Street.

The intruder's theft of the football was the signal for an outbreak of mass idiocy. Within ten seconds, hundreds of spectators were charging onto the football field. Within two minutes, at least 3,000 spectators were milling around, tugging at the football players, taunting the pitifully understaffed security force which attempted to remove them.

The 1960 Grey Cup Game never was completed. Realizing the hopelessness of the situation, Referee Seymour Wilson blew his whistle and ordered both teams to their dressing rooms.

Grey Cup competition has produced its own legends and not all of them have withstood the test of time. There was the case of the big, droll man with the improbable name of Eagle Keys, who came from a small town with the even more improbable name of Turkey Neck Bend, Kentucky.

Legend has it that in the 1954 Grey Cup Final Eagle Keys ignored a broken leg and gallantly permitted himself to be assisted onto the field to snap the ball for Bob Dean's winning convert, as the Edmonton Eskimos defeated the Montreal Alouettes, 26 to 25. That was the historic game in which Jackie Parker of Edmonton scooped up Chuck Hunsigner's fumble and ran 95 yards for the touchdown which tied the score at 25 to 25, with less than three minutes to play. In the general hysteria surrounding those last-minute histrionics, no one in the press box checked the number of the player who snapped the ball for Dean's winning converts. It was just assumed that Eagle Keys was the hero.

Since Eagle Keys has long been one of my favourite football men, I regret deflating his legend. He had suffered his broken leg in the first quarter, and throughout that bleak, cloudy afternoon, he had been limping (with support from teammates) onto the field to make the long snaps for Edmonton punts.

But by the time that Parker scored his dramatic touchdown, the pain had become so intense that, even with assistance, Eagle couldn't stand on the broken leg. Bill Briggs rushed onto the field to snap the ball for Dean's convert.

In any event, Eagle Keys didn't need that legend to insure his enshrinement among the immortals in the Canadian Football Hall of Fame. He achieved his greatest distinction in 1965 when he became the first man in history ever to coach the Saskatchewan Roughriders to a Grey Cup victory.

The Eagle was a player with the Montreal Alouettes and the Edmonton Eskimos for a total of six years. Later, he was a head coach in the Canadian league for 15 years.

Another hardy legend which resists deflation concerns the Calgary Stampeders. A generation of Canadians grew up believing that the Grey Cup Final didn't become a sporting event of national significance until the Calgary Stampeders and their trainload of 200 supporters invaded Toronto for the first time in 1948. Nonsense! The Football Final became a truly National Event as early as 1935 when Winnipeg was the first team from western Canada to win the Grey Cup.

It is true that the Stampeders with their horses, their trainload of boisterous fans in cowboy regalia, and their parade up Bay Street en route to the stadium brought a brand new dimension to the football game and signalled the beginning of annual weeklong celebrations which became known as the Grey Cup Festival. But 13 years before that, Winnipeg's 18-to-12 victory over the Hamilton Tigers had caused an explosion of chauvinistic emotion in western Canada. The country never was the same again after Winnipeg's victory in 1935.

The western team had been *attempting* to win the Grey Cup intermittently since 1921. But Canadian football didn't come of age until the afternoon of Saturday, December 7, 1935, at Hamilton when Fritz Hanson became the game's first media darling.

Hanson was only one of eight Americans in the Winnipeg lineup, but his performance in that game made him an enduring national superstar. With Winnipeg clinging to a 12-to-10 lead late in the third quarter, Hamilton's Huck Welch punted a low-bounding ball to the Winnipeg 32-yard line. Hanson picked up the ball and he sprinted 78 yards for the game-settling touchdown without a Hamilton player laying a hand on him.

Hanson's running over the slippery field completely frustrated the Hamilton Tigers throughout that afternoon. The stocky little halfback from North Dakota State University ran back punts and kickoffs for an astonishing total of more than 300 yards.

While Winnipeg's victory opened a bright new era for Canadian football, few people had anticipated the outcome of the game. It was a very cold, wet Saturday afternoon and only 6,405 spectators ventured into the old Hamilton stadium. And get this! The total gate receipts were only $5,583.92.

The Winnipeg team had spent a week in eastern Canada, travelling first to Windsor, in the hope of finding weather conditions which were somewhat milder than Manitoba's. Winnipeg hadn't played a game for three weeks and they wanted to do some hard scrimmaging on a snow-free field to prepare for the Grey Cup Final.

The winner's share of the gate receipts covered only a small fraction of Winnipeg's expenses — in fact, it didn't come close to bailing them out of the Royal Connaught Hotel where they had been staying in Hamilton. Les Isard, a member of the club's executive, cashed his personal cheque to pay the hotel bill and provide meals for the football players on the train ride back to Winnipeg.

Very few Westerners were in Hamilton for that 1935 game. Few Westerners could afford to make that trip in the middle of the Depression. However, for the first time in history, the Grey Cup Game could be *heard* in Winnipeg on a special radio broadcast. There was a snafu which was fairly typical of radio in those days — the broadcast didn't get on the air until several minutes after the start of the game; by that time, Winnipeg already was leading, 5 to 0.

There was a tremendous increase in fan support for western teams at Grey Cup Finals after 1935. Most of the travelling fans came from Winnipeg because the Blue Bombers was the only team to represent the West from 1937 until 1948.

Despite Calgary's claims, the first mass-scale football invasion of Toronto was provided by Winnipeggers in 1941. The two national railways operated special trains to Toronto. More than 2,000 noisy fans arrived from Winnipeg and took over the major hostelries — most particularly, the Royal York, which was the team hotel. In 1941, Winnipeggers didn't have those white Stetson hats which the Calgarians made nationally fashionable in 1948, but their exuberant behaviour raised the eyebrows of the usually staid Torontonians. The Ontario Liquor Commission reported record sales.

Two special trains arrived on Friday morning, more than 24 hours prior to the game. On Friday afternoon, the Royal York management removed the furniture from the main lobby of the hotel to provide more room for the boisterous football fans. The Friday afternoon removal of the Royal York furniture became a Grey Cup ritual in subsequent years.

The arrival of the Winnipeg team supporters generated infectious excitement in Toronto. The news of the non-stop merrymaking in the Royal York spread through the city, and soon curious Torontonians were converging at the hotel.

On Saturday afternoon, the football game at University of Toronto Stadium attracted a Canadian record crowd of 19,065. Extra seats had been erected to handle the last-minute appearance of a Winnipeg infantry unit which had come down from Camp Borden on overseas embarkation leave.

And, after Winnipeg had defeated Ottawa 18 to 16 that afternoon, the soldiers rushed onto the field and dismantled the goal posts at the north end of the field. Then, led by a band, they marched down University Avenue, surged into the Royal York and re-erected the goal posts in the hotel lobby.

Certainly, the Calgarians added many colourful new features to the football celebrations in 1948 — but that Winnipeg invasion of the Royal York in 1941 set the tone for future sporting visitors to Toronto.

The annual excursions of western football fans in the early days were little more than an excuse for prolonged drinking parties. Divorces still hadn't become commonplace in Canada in the 1930s or early 1940s, but unquestionably those annual Grey Cup trips placed a considerable strain on family relations.

* * * * *

Two events which changed the face of Canadian football were the formation of the Montreal Alouettes in 1946 and the emergence of the Calgary Stampeders in 1948.

Lew Hayman, who came to Canada from Syracuse University, coached the Toronto Argonauts from 1933 until he joined the RCAF as a sports officer in 1942. His Argonauts won the Grey Cup three times and his RCAF Hurricanes from Toronto won the national championship in 1942.

When Lew was demobilized, he expected to resume his former job with the Argonauts. However, the men who controlled the Argonaut Rowing Club had hired Teddy Morris to coach the football team. Hayman was understandably surprised, but he recovered quickly. He went to Montreal where, with the financial assistance of Toronto stockbroker Eric Cradock, he bought the Montreal Hornets of The Big Four.

Hayman was the first genuinely imaginative promoter to appear in Canadian football. For a long time, he had recognized that the game's inability to establish a successful franchise in Montreal resulted from the fact that nothing had been done to excite the support of the predominantly French population of the province of Quebec.

Lew solved that problem very quickly. He changed the name of the team to Les Alouettes and persuaded Leo Dandurand — by far the most popular French sportsman in Montreal — to be president of the reorganized club.

Les Alouettes were instantly a smash hit — not only in Montreal, but when they played road games in Toronto, Ottawa and Hamilton. Hayman put together a team which played wide open, highly exciting football. In their very first season of operation, Les Alouettes finished in a first-place tie with the Toronto Argonauts.

When Hayman was assembling his team in the summer of 1946, Jackie Robinson had become the first black player to be admitted to organized baseball and was assigned to the Montreal Royals of the International League. Robinson was wildly popular with Montreal's baseball fans and Hayman was convinced that his Alouettes must have some black football players.

Montreal's first two black recruits were Herb Trawick and fullback John Moody, graduates of colleges in the United States. Trawick, who spent his entire professional career with the Alouettes, was a superb two-way lineman and he was the first player in the history of the Eastern Conference to be selected for the All-Star Team *seven* times. John Moody, who resembled a small, high-speed tank in action, was a delightful personality.

The office of the Montreal Alouettes was situated in the basement level of Leo Dandurand's famous Mountain Street restaurant, Café Martin. Dandurand conducted his business from that building, and Hayman was provided with a football office.

Hayman was fond of recalling his first sight of John Moody in Montreal. John rolled through the office door carrying his "luggage" which consisted of one cheap suitcase. John left the suitcase open after he had gone into it to find a letter of reference from his college coach. After a brief discussion, Hayman sent Moody into another office to be weighed and assessed by the team trainer. In a moment of curiosity, Hayman walked over to the window seat and looked into Moody's open suitcase. John's "luggage" consisted of shirts, socks, underwear shorts and *four* large bottles of American gin.

Despite his limited wardrobe, John Moody was a resounding success in the uniform of the Montreal Alouettes.

Football had been revived in Calgary immediately after the Second World War, but it wasn't until 1948 that they assembled a team that electrified Canada. Tom Brook, an aggressive promoter of oil stocks who had come to Calgary from the United States via Toronto, took over the presidency of the

Stampeders. His first move was to hire a new coach: Les Lear, a Winnipeg-raised lineman who had gone to the National Football League to play for Cleveland, Los Angeles and Detroit.

After settling in Calgary, Lear brought in four imports: quarterback Keith Spaith, two-way end Woody Strode, two-way lineman Johnny Aguirre and centre linebacker Chuck Anderson. Those four imports had a very odd history. The previous year they had played professionally for the Honolulu Warriors, a farm club of the Los Angeles Rams. In their league championship game, the four players had bet *against* their own team.

To their embarrassment, their team *won* the playoff and the four idiots lost the money which they had wagered. News of the botched betting coup became public and the four were barred from professional football in the US. However, the Canadian Rugby Union, which still supervised football in this country, was blissfully unaware of the suspensions.

Anxious to ease their own consciences, the four imports played magnificently in Canada. And Lear, who was well known from his playing career in Canada, assembled an outstanding squad. He even recycled a couple of pre-war stars: fullback Paul Rowe and Fritz Hanson — the same Fritz Hanson who had become a national celebrity with his Grey Cup Game performance 13 years earlier.

With the super-tough, clever Lear inserting himself into the lineup occasionally to bolster his younger players' morale in moments of crisis, the Stampeders had a season of unparalleled success. In 1948, they established a record which never has been equalled in Canada. They went unbeaten through the entire season — recording 14 wins and one tie.

The Stampeders were the first team ever to travel to the Grey Cup Final by plane. They arrived in Toronto six days before the game and they moved into a motel in Bronte,

25 miles west of Toronto, where they could practice in comparative seclusion on the grounds of Appleby School at Oakville.

Meanwhile, the C.P.R. ran a "Football Special" out of Calgary, arriving in Toronto on Thursday morning, two days before the football game. It was an unusual train, consisting of 16 cars, one of which was set aside for a bar and barn-dancing. The 250 passengers included a western-style band. There was a special express car for 18 horses which would be ridden from the Royal York Hotel to the stadium.

Torontonians immediately were caught up in the hysteria as the visitors, wearing western regalia, cooked flapjacks on street corners, staged impromptu exhibitions of square-dancing and generally had one hell of a good time. The trip really had been planned as an advertisement for Calgary's great annual rodeo — the Calgary Stampede — but it became the blueprint for the annual Grey Cup Festival of future years.

When Toronto Mayor Hiram McCallum and other Ontario dignitaries caught the bug, they expressed a desire to ride horses in the parade to the stadium on the day of the game. Riding-stables in the Toronto area suddenly were enjoying an unexpected rental business.

Meanwhile, Coach Lear deliberately was keeping his players out of town. As a player with Winnipeg in previous Grey Cup Finals, he was keenly aware that physical conditioning usually was the key to success in the national championship. He drilled them relentlessly in two-a-day practices at Appleby. The night before the game, Lear moved his team into the Royal York. Early in the evening, he called a team meeting in the twelfth-floor suite which had been placed at his disposal.

All week long at the Bronte motel, centre linebacker Chuck Anderson had been making a great show of limping around on a pair of crutches. Now, at the team meeting, Anderson moaned that his injured knee was so painful that it would be impossible for him to play on the following afternoon. Lear's response was swift and decisive. The coach strode across the room, ripped Anderson's crutches from his hands and hurled them through the open window from the twelfth floor of the hotel.

Anderson played 60 minutes in the Grey Cup Game as Calgary defeated Ottawa 12 to 7, and his limp wasn't noticeable.

President Brook and Coach Lear turned their players loose to celebrate on Sunday. They cancelled the team's plane reservations and persuaded the C.P.R. to add an extra car to the Calgary Football Special which was scheduled to leave for the West shortly before midnight on Sunday. They felt that the players were entitled to spend a few days on the train, roistering with the fans who had supported them so faithfully.

The Football Special's trip from Toronto to Calgary was memorable for all those who managed to survive it. It was memorable, also, for the sports nuts who turned out at every divisional-point on the main line of the C.P.R. to greet the triumphant Stampeders. This was the last weekend in November and the train was travelling through lands which were already in the grip of winter.

The star attraction for the settlers who came out in the dark and cold of night to greet the football team was Woody Strode, who later went on to a long, successful career in motion pictures. Woody would appear on the rear platform of the train, wearing a war bonnet which he had borrowed from Chief David Crowchild or Chief George Runner. Apart from the war bonnet and a white jockstrap, Woody was completely nude. The welcoming crowd cheered enthusiastically as Strode raised his right hand above his head and bellowed, "How!"

The Calgary Stampeders of 1948 established a precedent by travelling to Toronto by plane. Although fans continued to travel on trains to the Grey Cup games each November, the football teams switched to the airways in the 1950s.

The transition from rail to air was not made smoothly by the football teams. Even on relatively short flights, the healthy athletes became bored and restless. The railways had some mixed feelings about the changes in transportation habits. They were happy to carry the football fans, but were not sorry to be rid of the football teams whose high-spirited horseplay annoyed other passengers and created problems for the train crews.

There was a period in the 1960s when flight attendants on Air Canada "booked sick" if someone tipped them off that they had been assigned to a flight which was carrying a football team. It seems that when a flight attendant leaned over to deliver a food tray to a passenger in a window seat, she was in danger of being bitten on her exposed flank by a football player who was sitting in a seat across the aisle. One flight attendant took the precaution of wearing a wire-reinforced girdle.

These assaults, after becoming epidemic at one stage, came to an abrupt halt in 1966 after Rudy Reschke of the B.C. Lions displayed just a bit too much enthusiasm for incipient cannibalism.

Rudy and Lion teammates were sitting around a table in the Admiral Hotel beer parlour in the Vancouver suburb of Burnaby. The football players were being served by Paula Russell, a college student who was a part-time waitress. It should be explained that all the waitresses in the Admiral wore costumes which displayed every inch of female thigh which the law permitted.

The football players bet Rudy $5 each that he wouldn't dare to bite Miss Russell on her bare buttock. Rudy won his bet but Miss Russell was not amused. Claiming that she had suffered severe injury to "her right lower dorsal region," she sued for damages.

Allan McEachern, Q.C., later to be Chief Justice of the British Columbia Court of Appeals, was counsel for the football team and arranged for an out-of-court settlement. However, the incident in the Admiral Hotel received nation-wide publicity. Commissioner G. Sydney Halter of the Canadian Football League warned all nine teams that such assaults no longer would be tolerated. After that, football players in Canada kept their teeth to themselves.

ON THE PRAIRIES, FOOTBALL WAS A STATE OF MIND

FOOTBALL WAS A RUDE, PRIMITIVE GAME WHEN I WAS first exposed to it in Winnipeg. An effete Easterner, who happened to attend a Winnipeg-Regina playoff, shook his head and he said, "Out here, football isn't merely a game — it's a state of mind." One of my Winnipeg newspaper colleagues described the sport as "the manly art of modified murder."

While my presence still was being tolerated rather coolly by the management of McGill University, I covered my first Grey Cup Final in 1931. I persuaded Paul Warburg, sports editor of the Winnipeg *Tribune*, to permit me to write the game story when the Regina Roughriders came east to challenge the Montreal Winged Wheelers. The *Tribune* subsequently sent me a cheque for $5. Probably I was overpaid.

Montreal whipped Regina 22 to 0, on a frozen field on the afternoon of Saturday, December 5, 1931. That game was remembered chiefly for an extracurricular incident. As the teams were trudging to their dressing rooms at the conclusion of hostilities, Red Tellier, the Montreal centre, punched George Gilhooley, the Regina centre. Gilhooley was knocked from his feet; as he fell his head struck a mound of frozen snow on the sidelines. He suffered a severe concussion and spent five days in the Royal Victoria Hospital.

The Canadian Rugby Union acted swiftly. Tellier, who was given a life suspension from football, felt that there was some justification for his assault. In that era, a single football was provided for the entire game. Every time that he came out of the Montreal huddle to make the snap that afternoon, Tellier discovered that someone had been spitting on the football.

On a dirty day, the frequent applications of saliva made the ball difficult to handle. Since Gilhooley was the Regina player facing him throughout the game, Tellier came to the not-unreasonable conclusion that Gilhooley was the culprit.

The game facilities for football in the early 1930s left much to be desired in my hometown of Winnipeg. The sport was just on the verge of emerging from the Dark Ages, and there was a good deal of expectorating, punching and cursing as the players of the two teams resorted to brute force — rather than subtle strategies — on the field.

There was a raffishly informal three-team local league composed of Winnipegs, St. John's and the Garrison. They played their games on Saturday afternoons in tiny Wesley Park which now has become part of the Portage Avenue campus of the University of Winnipeg. Wesley Park was also the local baseball facility and it had uncovered bleacher seats for 1,500 or 2,000 spectators.

Football crowds seldom were large enough to tax Wesley Park's modest capacity. Fanny Mogul, sister of Lou

Mogul who played for the Winnipegs, operated a bootlegging establishment in an apartment block overlooking the football field. On some cold, wet Saturday afternoons, the crowd in Fanny's apartment was almost as large as the crowd in Wesley Park.

The rough-and-tumble encounters at Wesley had the earmarks of longstanding neighbourhood feuds. Conventional wisdom had it that "there's a football game in Wesley Park on Saturday afternoon, and then there's a replay later on Saturday night in Child's Restaurant at the corner of Portage and Main."

The situation began to improve in 1932 when Carl Cronin, a second-strong backfielder from Notre Dame University, was imported to play coach and quarterback for the Winnipegs. Simultaneously, the St. John's team imported Russ Rebholz, a triple-threat backfielder from the University of Wisconsin. Rebholz soon was joined by Greg Kabat, who had been a Wisconsin teammate.

By 1933, the men who sponsored the Winnipegs and St. John's realized the folly of their ways. For years, they had been battering themselves into exhaustion in their own league, only to produce a surviving team which, invariably, lost to Regina in the inter-provincial playoff. A Manitoba team hadn't managed to beat Regina since 1925.

So, the Winnipegs and St. John's amalgamated for 1933. They managed to beat Regina that year, but in 1934 Regina imported five Americans and the Roughriders were too strong for Winnipeg. All this shifting and building was setting the scene for the West's first Grey Cup triumph in 1935.

The man who was largely responsible for assembling the 1935 Winnipeg team was Joe Ryan, one of the main architects of football in Canada. The team, which had *eight* imports in the lineup, ended the East's long domination of the national championship.

Those early Americans who came to Canada to play football were, in most cases, attracted by the promise of a permanent off-field job. During the Depression, jobs in the American Midwest were as scarce as they were in Canada.

The principal beneficiary of Winnipeg largesse in 1935 was Fritz Hanson, the hero of the Grey Cup Final.

When he graduated from North Dakota State, Hanson was offered $125 per game to play for the Detroit Lions of the National Football League. Ryan moved in and offered Hanson $150 per game to play for Winnipeg, but what really clinched the deal was the fact that Hanson would have an off-field job, working for Melady-Sellars on the Winnipeg Grain Exchange for a salary of $100 per month.

Hanson's total earnings for the winning season of 1935 were $2,300; at the time, this was a decent income for a kid just out of college.

His living expenses in Winnipeg were very modest. He shared accommodations in a Balmoral Avenue boarding-house with Bob Fritz, who had come from Concordia College to play coach and quarterback of the team. Hanson and Fritz paid $35 each — for a full month's room *and* board.

Fifty-five years ago, football prospered on the Prairies because it was an outlet for fierce, inter-city rivalries fanned by indiscriminate consumption of alcoholic beverages. Visitors from the East, who happened to drop in on a western football game, always were surprised by the passions which were aroused in those strange inter-tribal conflicts. No one viewed those games with intellectual objectivity — the Home Team was composed of the Good Guys and the Visiting Team was composed of the Enemy.

It is true that, in those same years, the supporters of the Hamilton Tigers had no difficulty in generating a noisy antipathy for the Toronto Argonauts. But those tiffs in the East were Sunday School stuff compared with the genuine hatred which marked football clashes between Winnipeg and Regina.

Regina was only one-quarter the size of Winnipeg, a circumstance which was reflected in the average Regina sporting fan's loathing for the Manitoba capital.

Reginans had been reasonably content with the state of affairs between 1925 and 1934 when they regularly defeated Manitoba teams in football. But when Winnipeg won the Grey Cup in 1935, football men in Saskatchewan were determined that some drastic changes must be made immediately.

In the period of Regina domination, most of their teams had been coached or managed by Al Ritchie, a gentleman who was widely accepted as the local sporting genius. Ritchie, an affable, talkative man, held court every morning at the coffee counter in the Balmoral Café. He used sugar cubes to illustrate football plays which, he vowed, would confound opposing teams. Al was such a pleasant man that no one bothered to question his right to be regarded as the final authority in all athletic matters. At least no one bothered to question his wisdom until Winnipeg's victory in 1935.

At that juncture, the executives of the Regina Roughriders imported 23-year-old Dean Griffing, a graduate of Kansas State University. Griffing became playing coach of the Roughriders for 1936. Not only did he play, but he was the *entire* coaching staff. He was the offensive centre when Regina had the ball. When the opposing team had the play, Griffing played middle linebacker with ferocious efficiency.

Griffing upgraded the entertainment level of football on the Prairies. With his neatly clipped moustache, his swarthy good looks and his practiced sneer, he could have earned a fortune playing the villain's role on the World Wrestling Federation's weekly shows. He genuinely enjoyed playing the part of the Bad Guy and he delighted in goading the Winnipeg players and the Winnipeg spectators when the Roughriders invaded Manitoba.

By this time the Winnipeg team, with the new nickname of Blue Bombers, had moved from Wesley Park to Osborne Stadium which, while slightly more commodious than its predecessor, still had ground level seats which were only about 15 feet from the sidelines. This close contact with the spectators gave Griffing plenty of opportunity for acts of provocation.

One day, just before the second-half kickoff, Dean led a group of his players up and down the sidelines, thumbing their noses at the angry Winnipeg spectators. It was childish, but don't forget, this was only an inter-city football game — it wasn't a performance by the Metropolitan Opera Company. One Winnipegger, swathed in a raccoon coat and exuding the fumes of alcohol, became so abusive that Griffing invited him to come down to the field. Mr. Raccoon Coat was stupid enough to accept the invitation. Griffing knocked him flat with one punch.

In that 1936 season, the Bombers went into Regina to play the Roughriders at Park De Young. After the game, Winnipeg's Greg Kabat complained that he had been bitten on the leg. He displayed what appeared to be teeth marks on one bare calf and expressed a suspicion that Dean Griffing had been the hungry assailant. When he read in press reports that he was being accused of incipient cannibalism, Griffing was scornful. He described the Winnipeg players as "cry babies."

More than 20 years later, I was interviewing Griffing on a network television show from Toronto and I asked him if, after the passage of so much time, he was prepared to acknowledge that he had bitten Kabat on the leg. "I couldn't have bitten him," said Griffing, "for the simple reason that, even at the age of 23, I had false teeth. And before going onto the field, I always left my false choppers in the dressing room." Then, with a malicious twinkle in his eye, he added, "Of course, I may have *gummed* him a little."

As the football rivalries escalated on the Prairies during the Depression, it became fashionable for the most devoted fanatics to accompany their team on road trips — most specifically, the Winnipeg-Regina trip which was only an overnight jaunt by railway.

Regina did not take kindly to football visitors from Winnipeg. In fact, Winnipeg civilians were rated as very poor insurance risks when they accompanied the Blue Bombers to Regina for a Saturday afternoon game against the Roughriders.

When the Bombers travelled overnight to Regina, as many as 100 or 150 football zealots would board the same train to provide alcohol-stimulated vocal support for their team.

On arrival in Regina, the football players would be taken to rooms at the Hotel Saskatchewan where, shortly before noon, they would don their gear and be taken by special bus to the stadium.

Meanwhile, the 100 or 150 Winnipeg camp followers, many of whom had been consuming raw spirits to ward off the autumn chills, would gather in the lobby of the Hotel Saskatchewan to give their football heroes an inspirational send-off to the playing field.

The Winnipeg fans would gather immediately in front of the hotel's bank of three elevators. As the door of each elevator opened — and uniformed Winnipeg players emerged — they were greeted with a salvo of cheers which must have warmed their hearts.

One Saturday morning, the throng of Winnipeggers who had gathered in the Hotel Saskatchewan lobby to hail their football players was infiltrated by a Fifth Columnist from Regina. As the door of one elevator opened to reveal Rosey Adelman, the portly and moustachioed Winnipeg centre garbed for football combat, the crowd in the lobby greeted him with a prolonged cheer. Rosey, his ample heart touched by such a display of affection, smiled benignly and raised both arms above his head to acknowledge the greeting.

At this juncture, the Regina Fifth Columnist inched his way to the front row of Winnipeg fans facing the elevators. As Rosey Adelman stood there — unsuspecting and completely defenceless with his arms upstretched — the Regina Fifth Columnist fetched him a round-house clout on the jaw and Adelman fell to the marble floor of the hotel lobby, semi-conscious. Then, the sneaky Reginan sped through the front door of the hotel, leaving the Winnipeggers in a state of righteous fury. Adding insult to injury, the Roughriders defeated the Blue Bombers later that afternoon.

The Winnipegs were the first football team to have a Booster Club, composed of die-hard supporters who shelled out $10 annually for the privilege of attending weekly meetings showing films of the team's recent games. The real attraction was the hilarious commentary supplied by Coach Reg Threlfall, who had come to Winnipeg after a colourful coaching career in several small US colleges. As a public speaker, Threlfall was a spellbinder.

Two of the liveliest members of the Winnipeg Booster Club were the McBean Brothers — Phillip McBean and his younger sibling, Atholl Oscar McBean. The McBean boys were incorrigible pranksters. Their father, a prominent grain merchant, had been entertaining a visitor, an airline vice-president from Minneapolis. The visitor expressed admiration for a black bear rug in the den of the McBean residence. The two younger McBeans, hospitable to a fault, offered to obtain another bear rug and ship it to the airline executive at his home in Minneapolis.

At this point, whimsy got the better of the McBeans. They put in a telephone call to a friend, a trapper in Northern Manitoba. But they didn't ask their friend to send them a bear *rug*, they asked for a bear *cub*. They reasoned that the cub would be a delightful surprise for the Minneapolis gentleman.

The following Saturday morning, the McBean brothers received a telephone call from a Winnipeg railway station, advising them that their "shipment" had arrived. The Blue Bombers were playing the Regina Roughriders at Osborne Stadium on the Saturday afternoon. So, in the normal custom of Winnipeg football fans, the McBean brothers were preparing for the game by having a couple of inspirational drinks.

They went down to the railway depot where they quickly discovered that their trapper friend had out-whimsied them. Waiting for them in the baggage room was a slatted crate which contained a six-month-old black bear, about the size of an Alsatian dog. The bear had a collar around its neck and attached to the collar was a chain. The bear had been in captivity since birth and it was relatively tame, but obviously it was too large to be shipped to Minneapolis by plane.

The ingenious McBean brothers recovered quickly. They decided they would take the bear to the football game and present it to the Blue Bombers as a mascot. Removing the bear from the crate, they tugged it by the chain and it followed them out of the station. They saw a vacant taxi parked on the cab rack. Phillip McBean got into the back seat of the taxi and pulled the bear up onto the seat beside him. Then, Oscar McBean got into the back seat and he sat on the *other* side of the bear.

The hack driver, who had been leaning against the exterior wall of the station smoking a cigarette, sauntered over to his cab. The driver was the celebrated Butch Dobrians who knew almost everyone in Winnipeg who was capable of renting a taxi-cab. Butch peered through the window of the back seat and he said matter of factly, "I know you two McBeans — but who's the old guy in the fur coat sitting between you?"

In his time, Dobrians had chauffeured many less-prepossessing fares. With a shrug, he agreed to drive his three passengers to Shea's Brewery, which abutted on Osborne Stadium. The bear was friendly and occasionally he leaned forward to lick the back of Butch's neck.

In preparation for the football game, the members of the Winnipeg Booster Club were whooping it up in the hospitality room of Shea's Brewery. The bear amiably followed the McBean brothers into the gathering and, thoughtfully, someone provided the bear with his own private pail of beer. When the pre-game festivities peaked, the McBean brothers made an official presentation of the bear to Les Isard, the president of the Blue Bombers.

In those informal days, the presidents of western football teams sat on the bench with their players. Accordingly, Isard sat on one extreme end of the bench and the new team mascot lay down on the ground beside the bench. At half-time, Isard stood up and gave a tug on the bear's chain. But the bear had begun to exhibit symptoms of an early hangover. Although he had been friendly up until this moment, suddenly he emitted a very surly growl.

Isard was no fool. He stood there quietly — but only after he had despatched a courier to put in a telephone call to the Winnipeg Humane Society. Before the game was concluded, the McBean brothers' gift to Canadian football had been taken away to a permanent home in the Assiniboine Park zoo.

Odd incidents occurred at Osborne Stadium. One afternoon, the official timekeeper stood at his table in front of the grand stand and he raised his pistol over his head to fire the shot which signalled half-time.

As the shot rang out, a chicken fell from the roof of the grand stand and landed at the timekeeper's feet. The chicken was dead but it bore no gunshot wound.

The McBeans weren't the only Winnipeggers who attempted to give an unwanted mascot to their football club. A couple of years later, some well-wisher brought a goat to a game at Osborne Stadium and, in an impromptu half-time ceremony, presented the animal to Scott Kennedy, the team manager.

Kennedy was stuck with the odoriferous goat throughout the second-half of the game. After the crowd had left, Kennedy and stadium manager Johnny Petersen took the goat with them when they dropped in to have a cup of coffee at Salisbury House, the fast-food restaurant which was situated next to the stadium gate.

Not unexpectedly, the little restaurant was jammed after the game. Kennedy surreptitiously tethered the goat to one of the stools in front of the coffee counter. Then he and Petersen quietly sidled out of the restaurant leaving the goat to become someone else's problem.

Looking back on it, I wonder why the two national railways competed so strenuously to obtain the travel business of western football teams, 55 or even 45 years ago. When a football party of 25 or 30 healthily rambunctious young men clambered about a train for a two-day road trip, there was a strong probabilty that they would become a pain-in-the-ass to other passengers who, having paid full fares, expected to travel in reasonable comfort and reasonable quiet.

In the late 1930s, the Winnipeg Blue Bombers played football chiefly for the fun of it. At best, they might expect a few dollars at the end of a successful season. They looked forward to the team's road trips. For them, a road trip was a *holiday* with all expenses paid. They slept between clean sheets on first-class passenger trains, stayed in first-class hotels, and received money to pay for their meals. For many of them who came from Depression-squeezed homes, a road trip was a picnic.

To say that the young Bombers occasionally became obstreperous on a road trip was an understatement. Fritz Hanson frequently was a ringleader in the horseplay. In 1989, still frisky at the age of 76, Hanson looked back on the antics of his Winnipeg playmates and said fondly, "They were rough, raucous and occasionally rowdy — but when it came time for the kickoff, they were *ready*!"

I was party to one particularly rowdy road trip when the Bombers travelled west to play back-to-back games in Calgary and Edmonton. The trip started inauspiciously when Ches McCance, the most energetic of the young homebrews, missed the train out of Winnipeg on a Friday morning.

McCance had gone to a party on Thursday night and, when the party went long past midnight, decided that it would be silly to go home. He reasoned that it would be more sensible to go directly to the C.P.R. station and sleep on a waiting-room bench until his teammates appeared.

When McCance woke, the train had left without him. A club executive managed to get him a seat on Friday night's once-daily Trans Canada Airlines flight which put him into Calgary in plenty of time for the Saturday night game against the Calgary Bronks.

McCance thoroughly enjoyed the first flight of his life, but Coach Reg Threlfall was not amused. As a disciplinary measure, he forced McCance to play the full 60 minutes of the Saturday night game in Calgary. McCance responded typically. The reporters in the Mewata Stadium press box selected him as "The Star of the Game."

Later Saturday night, things got out of hand. Les Lear, McCance and other Winnipeg free spirits left their lodgings at the Palliser Hotel and went across the street to the Alberta Hotel. The police were called to throw them out of the Alberta because the football players were wading barefooted in the ornamental fish-and-flower pool in the hotel lobby. The police, having had previous experience with Winnipeg footballers, didn't bother to toss them into the jug.

The next day — Sunday — Wally Brown, president of the Winnipeg club, devised a scheme to keep the players out of further trouble. He chartered a bus to take the team for a swim in the sulphur pool at the Cave and Basin in Banff, west of Calgary.

Settled down at the Cave and Basin, President Brown, Coach Threlfall and other civilian functionaries were taking their ease in deck chairs at the edge of the pool when their reveries were disturbed by an extraordinary outburst of noise.

They looked up to perceive that the noise had been created by Chester McCance, who was poised on the high diving board. McCance was wearing flaming red swimming trunks; he had a fedora hat perched atop his head and a lit cigar between his lips. With a jaunty wave of his hand, McCance dove gracefully into the pool, still wearing someone's good hat and smoking that large cigar.

After playing in Edmonton on the Monday afternoon (Thanksgiving Day), the Bombers, who had booked their trip via C.P.R. lines, were obliged to travel home via Calgary. Two football games in less than 48 hours had consumed only a small portion of the football players' excess energy. To mitigate their boredom as they travelled eastward, they collected all the waste-paper receptacles on the train and brought them into the washing-smoking room of their own coach.

With newspapers, they set fires in the waste baskets. Emitting war-whoops, they staged a war dance, circling the bonfires. When the smoke became a bit too dense, they opened a couple of windows in the speeding train.

Prairie farmers who lived close to the right-of-way must have been mildly curious about a Canadian Pacific train rushing across the landscape with smoke belching from the windows of one passenger coach.

The sleeping-car porter, who had been assigned to the Calgary-Winnipeg leg of the Blue Bombers' road trip, was physically and emotionally exhausted when the train reached its destination. The next day, he requested a transfer to trains which operated on a branch-line service between Winnipeg and Edmonton, via Saskatoon. Those two trains never carried football teams.

COACHES USUALLY GET THE CHOP

COACHING IN CANADA NEVER HAS BEEN A JOB FOR THE faint of heart. Reg Threlfall, who came from the United States to take over the Winnipeg Blue Bombers in 1937, said philosophically, "Coaching a football team is a high-risk profession. Just when you think that you're doing okay, some son-of-a-bitch saunters across the field and he pokes a sharp stick in your eye."

Threlfall was colourful; he was an exceptionally fascinating public speaker and an outstanding motivator of the young, locally born players who were the backbone of his Winnipeg teams which won the Grey Cup in 1939 and 1941. Unlike the generation of coaches who followed him in prairie cities, Reg didn't stay around to be fired. Firing is the inevitable fate of 95 percent of the men in that precarious profession.

There was a four-year period — from 1950 through 1953 — when the worst possible mistake which could be made by a western Canadian coach was to get his team into the Grey Cup Final — only to lose the Big Game!

In 1950, Frank Larson coached Winnipeg to the Grey Cup Final against the Toronto Argonauts. Toronto won. Winnipeg promptly fired Larson.

In 1951, Harry Smith coached the Saskatchewan Roughriders to the Grey Cup Final against Ottawa. It was the first appearance for a Saskatchewan team in the national championship in 25 years. Nevertheless, when Ottawa won, Saskatchewan fired Smith.

In 1952, Frank Filchock took the Edmonton Eskimos to the Grey Cup Final. They were the first Edmonton team to appear in a national championship in 30 years. However, when Edmonton lost to Toronto, Filchock was fired.

In 1953, George Trafton coached Winnipeg to the Grey Cup Final against the Hamilton Tiger-Cats. The Bombers lost to Hamilton. Trafton was fired.

In those gruesome circumstances, it isn't surprising that coaches occasionally took to strong drink. It was an exceptionally precarious existence.

Even in the less-frenetic East, coaches who came to town seldom bought a house with a long-term mortgage. Toronto became celebrated as "the Graveyard of Coaches" after the Argonauts fired Frank Clair at the end of the 1954 season.

In the ensuing 13 years, the Argonauts employed seven head coaches. One of those gentlemen, Leo Cahill, was so wildly misguided that he sought and accepted the same job *twice*. Accordingly, Leo has the distinction of being the only Toronto coach who was *fired* twice.

Critics of Hogtown sporting enterprises took much satisfaction from the fact that the Argonauts didn't win the Grey Cup again until 1983, 20 seasons after they fired Frank Clair.

Frank Clair was a hardy survivor, outwardly solemn and lugubrious. After his dismissal by the Argonauts, he turned to college coaching in Ohio for one season and then returned to Canada to coach Ottawa in 1956. Prior to Clair's arrival, the Rough Riders had put four coaches through the meat grinder in the previous five seasons. Clair continued to coach the Rough Riders for 14 years, after which he moved up to become general manager of the football club.

Frank compiled one of the most impressive coaching records in the history of Canadian football; he also acquired a public reputation for being delightfully absent-minded. Appropriately, his nickname in Canada was "The Professor."

One Saturday morning he told his wife, Pat, that he was going to drive down to the Ottawa football office to do some research work in preparation for the team's next game. As he left, he assured Mrs. Clair that he would be home "in time for lunch."

By 3:30 that afternoon, Frank Clair still hadn't returned.

Meanwhile, Mrs. Clair had the television set tuned to an afternoon football game which was being played in Toronto. Suddenly, her husband's face appeared on the television screen. He was in Toronto being interviewed at half-time in the football game.

Frank hadn't *planned* to go to Toronto. When he left home that morning, lost in thoughts about football, his car automatically bypassed his office and headed for the parking lot at the Ottawa airport. Clair bought a ticket for a Toronto-bound plane and, even at that point, forgot that he had told his wife that he would be home for lunch.

Clair managed to return to Ottawa that night in time to sleep in his own bed. Before retiring, he raided the refrigerator and ate his Saturday lunch. Mrs. Clair didn't comment on his 14-hour absence from home. Years of marriage had conditioned her for her husband's absent-mindedness.

Peahead Walker, who was brought from Wake Forest College

to coach the Montreal Alouettes in 1954, was a drawling Southerner with a laid-back attitude. He didn't *look* like a football coach. He wore a hat and a business suit on the sidelines and his belly bulged over trousers that appeared to be suspended from his hipbones.

His nickname of "Peahead" was a distinct misnomer if someone had coined it as as a snide reflection on his intellectual capacity. Walker, who adopted a pose of being profoundly indifferent to the events on the football field, actually was sharper than a steel trap. He took wry satisfaction from playing the role of the rustic in the Big City.

He always denigrated his own part in recruiting quarterback Sam Etcheverry, who proved to be the greatest passer in Canadian football. With a straight face, Peahead told Canadian reporters that he had "scouted" Etcheverry simply by studying Sam's photograph in a magazine which was devoted to US College football.

"I just found myself looking at this kid's picture," Walker drawled. "The longer I looked at it, the better I liked the cut of his jib. So, I just put in a telephone call to his college coach and told him I was ready to offer Etcheverry a contract."

Regardless of any unusual tactics which Montreal employed to "scout" him, Etcheverry proved to be the greatest single acquisition in the history of the Alouettes. For seven years, he led all quarterbacks in Canada in completed passes and in yardage gained on passes. And he was a 60-minute man, playing a defensive-halfback position when the opposing team was in possession of the ball.

Les Lear was brought back from the United States to coach the Calgary Stampeders in 1948. Lear was intensely combative and for him, football was warfare and his rival coaches were the enemy. He was an extremely tough disciplinarian, who insisted that his players must be properly dressed in public at all times — always wearing jackets and ties on road trips.

Lear had a vibrant personality. Even his detractors in rival western cities acknowledged he was a newsmaker. And the success of the Stampeders in 1948 aroused so much enthusiasm for football in Calgary that it was not unusual, in the next two or three seasons, for 1,000 or 1,500 Calgarians to gather in Mewata Stadium on an autumn evening — just to watch the Stampeders *practice*.

The coach had a voice which could be heard as far as the foothills of the Rockies. The language which he employed in supervising the team practices was, sometimes, colourfully vulgar and Calgary parents were advised to keep their impressionable children far from Mewata Stadium. Naturally, quite a few children ignored the ban and their vocabularies were augmented for the worse.

Edmontonians, piqued by Calgary's success in 1948, decided to re-enter a team in western football for 1949. The Eskimos hadn't fielded a team since 1939.

To coach their new team, the Edmontonians hired Annis Stukus, an extroverted Toronto newspaper reporter who had been a longtime player for the Toronto Argonauts. Stukus, who was known among his newspaper friends as the Loquacious Lithuanian, had coached a Navy service team during the war, as well as Balmy Beach.

The arrival of the garrulous Stukus in Edmonton provoked an immediate feud with Les Lear. The sporting citizens of Edmonton and Calgary have nurtured an inter-city rivalry since the 1920s. That antipathy, which often verges on outright hatred, is exemplified today by hockey's Flames-Oilers rivalry and the Stampeders-Eskimos rivalry in football.

This type of situation was deep-dish apple pie for Stukus, who thrived on a bit of controversy. Stukus soon proved to be an irritant to Les Lear who had a remarkably low boiling point.

In his rookie season as Edmonton's head coach, Stukus discovered that the Eskimo roster didn't include a reliable kicker of field goals. Stukus had been an all-round backfielder with the Argos and he had been an exceptionally proficient kicker of field goals and converts.

Stukus promptly inserted himself into the Edmonton playing roster. He wore a football uniform while he prowled the coaching box on the sidelines. However, he didn't encumber himself by wearing shoulder pads. When it became necessary for Edmonton to kick a field goal, Stukus clapped a helmet on his head and went onto the field to perform the job.

Stukus's airy disinclination to wear shoulder pads offended Lear. But what drove Lear into an absolute fury was the fact that Stukus, when he went onto the field, wore an expensive wristwatch. The sight of that innocent wristwatch was just too much for Lear.

Soon, every football fan in western Canada was aware of the fact that Lear had a standing offer of $50 for any of his Calgary players who, in the course of action, managed to smash Stukus's watch.

The stormy relations between coaches in western Canada were exacerbated by the arrival of George Trafton to take over the Winnipeg Blue Bombers in 1950. When he arrived, Trafton was equipped with the most impressive football credentials of any man who ever had come to Canada. Some indication of his celebrity in his own land can be taken from the fact that he was only the eighteenth man ever to be voted into the US Football Hall of Fame at Canton, Ohio.

George had attended Notre Dame but was booted out of college when it was discovered that he had sneaked off the campus to play a game of semi-professional football. With his academic career aborted, George joined George Halas in playing professional football for the Decauter Staleys in 1920.

The Trafton family played an important role in the birth struggles of the National Football League. It was George's mother who put up the money to finance the Bears' first year of operation after Halas moved the team into Chicago. For this and other reasons, George Trafton always deferred to the wishes of his autocratic mother.

For 12 seasons, Trafton anchored the line of the Chicago Bears as centre on offence and middle linebacker on defence. He was rough and tough and given to extolling his own prowess to a degree which irritated his opponents. Stout Steve Owen, the legendary lineman and coach of the New York Giants, referred to Trafton as "The Biggest Wind from the Windy City."

There was a good deal of on-field slugs and fisticuffs in the early years of the NFL, and despite the scoffing of Stout Steve Owen, Trafton had acquired a national reputation as "the toughest man in professional football."

Coincidentally, a reformed alley-fighter named Art Shires was an infielder with the Chicago White Sox of the American Baseball League. Shires had acquired a reputation as "the toughest man in professional baseball."

An importunate Chicago promoter made an offer to Trafton and Shires to engage in a boxing bout at Chicago Stadium, with the winner being hailed as "the Toughest Man in Professional Sports."

Although he was a public blow-hard, Trafton was very much under the domination of his strong-willed mother. Among other things, Mrs. Trafton held the purse strings for her son. Mrs. Trafton quickly made it clear that she didn't wish to see Georgie-boy indulging in any vulgar fisticuffs. Reluctantly, she had accepted the fact that her son was something less than a Little Lord Fauntleroy on the football field, but the thought of him engaging publicly in pugilism was unnecessarily demeaning.

For one of the very few times in his life, George decided to ignore his mother's wishes. After all, he was a born ham and he couldn't resist the world-wide publicity which the proposed bout was attracting. This bout, involving two large men who had no real claim to pugilistic eminence, drew a huge crowd to Chicago Stadium and was covered by the major North American news services: Associated Press, United Press and International News Service.

Trafton didn't keep the spectators in suspense. Football, after all, is a game which requires more physical toughness than baseball. Trafton knocked out Shires in the very first round.

Later that night, George picked up his cheque from the promoter and, proudly, carried it home to be shown to his mother. Mrs. Trafton defrosted very quickly when she examined the numerals on the cheque. She patted her large son affectionately and said: "George, I think you should give up professional football and concentrate on boxing."

After his retirement as a player, Trafton became a line coach with the Cleveland Rams, who later moved to the Pacific Coast where they were known as the Los Angeles Rams.

When Les Lear, an unknown rookie from Canada, appeared in Cleveland, the younger man's controlled violence caught George's attention. Lear quickly became Trafton's protégé and the Old Pro taught him all the tricks of this very rough game. There was a very strong bond between the two men.

However, when George Trafton came to coach in western Canada where Les Lear already was well established, their friendship developed some love-hate aspects. The mutual respect and affection were still there, but since they were coaching rival teams in the same league, some jealousy inevitably emerged.

First of all, Trafton up-staged Lear — although, perhaps

it wasn't intentional. When he heard that Lear was offering $50 to any Calgary player who smashed Annis Stukus's wrist-watch, Trafton announced that he was offering $100 to any Winnipeg player who demolished the offending timepiece. But Lear was hypersensitive and thought that his old mentor was trying to make him look like a cheapskate.

The truth is that George Trafton never was really happy unless he was embattled constantly. Very soon, he involved himself in feuds with the Winnipeg news media. And even the ticket-buying supporters of the Winnipeg Blue Bombers quickly found themselves battling with their local coach.

During the first of Trafton's three seasons in the city, the football team still was playing in little Osborne Stadium, where the spectators' seats came right down to within 15 feet of the Blue Bombers players' bench. Some of the spectators, who were season ticket holders, spent a good deal of their time heckling Trafton and loudly criticizing his coaching strategies.

George never professed to being a polished gentleman. He responded to the heckling with grinning vulgarity. Even while a play was in progress, Trafton would turn around to face the spectators and would raise the middle finger on his right hand high above his head in an unmistakable gesture.

Almost effortlessly, Trafton won the cordial dislike of the fans in Calgary, Edmonton and Regina. Also, he delighted antagonizing the news media in those three cities. Remarkably, he was welcomed cordially in eastern Canadian cities when the Blue Bombers played pre-season exhibition games. The news media of Toronto in particular loved George's exuberant American b.s. and his inexhaustible supply of colourful football anecdotes. He was a character.

However, the feuding of the coaches and the incessant quarrels between the executives of the rival clubs were threatening to tear apart the Western Canada League in

1951. In the emergency, the four teams put aside their individual complaints and appointed a commissioner, Professor Kent Phillips of the University of Saskatchewan. They hoped that Professor Phillips would be an impartial arbiter since he resided in Saskatoon, a city which didn't have a football franchise.

The fourth Western coach at this time was Harry "Blackjack" Smith of the Saskatchewan Roughriders. Despite his formidable nickname, Smith was really an ardent pacifist and spent most of his time shaking his head in bewilderment as he observed the lunatic antics of his rivals in the other three cities.

Finally, the quarrels between the clubs had intensified to the extent that Commissioner Phillips felt obliged to call an emergency meeting of his four head coaches at the Palliser Hotel in Calgary. From the very outset, the meeting was doomed — at least two of the men with whom Phillips was dealing were in an utterly unreasonable mood. Phillips had reserved a tenth-floor suite for this important parley; almost immediately, it became evident that even a suite wouldn't be large enough to contain those explosive temperaments.

Lear and Trafton quickly united in vocal assaults on Stukus. Blackjack Smith just sat there, trying to escape the notice of the verbal combatants. Finally, the assault became physical. Trafton and Lear jumped from their chairs, wrestled Stukus across the room, and threatened to toss him from the window.

Commissioner Phillips, appalled by the spectacle, was vainly shouting for order. Coach Smith finally lurched out of his chair and attempted to dissuade Lear and Trafton from committing manslaughter. In frustration, Commissioner Phillips banged a large glass water jug onto a silver tray on the table in front of him. The jug shattered with a loud crash.

Brought to their senses by the noise, Trafton and Lear released Stukus. Snarling over their shoulders, the two malcontents stomped out of the suite and drove to Lear's little spread on the southwest outskirts of Calgary. In keeping with the disposition of its owner, the Lear spread was listed officially as The Bar-None Ranch. In the next half-hour, they destroyed a 26-ounce bottle of rye, after which their good humour was restored.

Thirty-seven years later, Stukus was recalling the sorry incident for me and said, "In my heart, I knew that Lear and Trafton would stop short of shoving me through that window. But you never could be *sure* about those two — they were crazy enough to do almost anything."

Western Canadian football became considerably more decorous after those three coaches left the sidelines. The Calgary Bronks fired Lear after the 1952 season. Trafton was dumped by Winnipeg after his Grey Cup defeat in 1953. Stukus left Edmonton of his own volition in 1952 but he resurfaced as founding coach and chief promoter of the B.C. Lions. Stukus refutes any suggestion that he was fired by the Lions at the end of his second season of coaching in 1955. "I wasn't fired," Stuke says hotly. "They just failed to renew my contract!"

The most entertaining football in Canada, in my view, was played in the 1950s. Nothing else matched the excitement of those three wild, high-scoring games in which the Edmonton Eskimos defeated the Montreal Alouettes for the Grey Cup in 1954, 1955 and 1956.

Edmonton's victory over Montreal in 1954 was dramatic — chiefly because it was almost completely unexpected. After all, no western team had been able to win the national championship for the previous five seasons — since the Calgary Stampeders of 1948.

The Alouettes were heavily favoured at odds of 3 to 1 in 1954. With Etcheverry at quarterback throwing to such great receivers as Hal Patterson, Red O'Quinn and Joey Pal, they had set a Canadian record by scoring 341 points in a 14-game schedule.

But the result of the 1954 Grey Cup Game was a stunner. Montreal was leading 25 to 20, and in the closing minutes, they were down on the Edmonton 10-yard line, from where it would have been a simple matter to kick another field goal.

Incomprehensibly, the Als decided to go for another touchdown which, in the circumstances, appeared to be unnecessary. Chuck Hunsinger started on a sweep to his left, but he was tackled by Rollin Prather and he fumbled. The ball was scooped up by Jackie Parker who sprinted 95 yards to score the tying touchdown. Bob Dean kicked the winning convert. (In 1954 a touchdown was worth only five points in Canadian football.)

The Alouettes, feeling that they had been robbed, pointed towards meeting Edmonton again in the 1955 Grey Cup Game which was the first ever to be played in Vancouver. However, Pop Ivy's Eskimos whipped them again, 34 to 19.

In 1956, Montreal and Edmonton were back at the University of Toronto for their third successive Grey Cup meeting. The Eskimos made their domination of Montreal "official" that time — they won handily, 50 to 27.

One Les Lear story always will stay with me. In 1951, Lear imported an American centre named Mel Embree. In the opinion of everyone who watched him, Embree "dogged it" on the football field from the first moment he arrived in town.

Finally, one evening while 1,500 civilians were watching the Stampeders practice at Mewata Stadium, Coach Lear and Embree got into a public shouting match.

In the course of the shouting, Embree made one of the more serious mistakes of his young life; he called Coach Lear a "liar."

When the practice was finished, Lear summoned Embree to his little office at one end of the Stampeder locker-room.

Assistant Coach Ed Champagne, a huge former lineman from the Chicago Bears, stood in front of the door, preventing any interruptions while Coach Lear remonstrated with Embree.

Subsequent court evidence left the strong impression that Lear remonstrated with at least one hand and, possibly, with both hands.

Against the charge of aggravated assault, Lear was defended by Harold Riley, a colourful Calgary counsel who later was elevated to the Bench.

Mr. Riley called Ed Champagne as a defence witness.

Champagne had attended Louisiana State University before he played professional football, but possibly he hadn't majored in English.

In the course of his examination, defence counsel said: "Now, listen to my next question very carefully, Mr. Champagne. When Mr. Embree called Mr. Lear a liar, did Mr. Lear become exercised?"

Champagne blinked twice; then, with his noble brow corrugated by the effort of concentration and recollection, he replied in a slow drawl: "I don't know about *that*! But he sure was pissed off!"

Case dismissed!

PART 4

HOCKEY

THE ALL-STARS

IF A CANADIAN IS WRITING A BOOK WHICH INCLUDES some references to hockey, it is almost obligatory to provoke a bit of controversy among prospective readers by selecting an All-Time, All-Star Team.

I have been watching hockey for more than 70 years and I have been writing about it for more than half a century. Consequently, I go back all the way to the era when professionals were reputed to be sturdier than oak trees and tougher than pemmican. I'm old enough to remember the apocryphal story of the primeval Ottawa player who, during a game, had a finger severed from his hand. And he didn't notice the loss of the digit until the following morning when he went to the cashier's wicket and experienced difficulty in counting his pay.

The passing years lend enchantment, but the feats of the oldtimers still are engraven indelibly on my brain-pads. Were those oldtimers really as great as we believed them to be?

Well, I have no hesitation in selecting Howie Morenz as one of the centremen on my All-Star Team. I saw him playing when I was attending my first Stanley Cup Finals: in 1925 when the Victoria Cougars defeated the Montreal Canadiens. And I saw him in his greatest years when I was attending McGill University from 1929 through 1932.

Morenz was more than the quintessential hockey player of his day. He was the type of athlete whose superb ability transcended the years — he could have been just as outstanding in today's hockey as he was in the era when forward passing wasn't permitted.

King Clancy, another of hockey's legendary heroes, is my authority for the selection of Morenz as an All-Star centre. Clancy had been playing for the Ottawa Senators for two years before Morenz broke into the NHL. And Clancy continued to be actively involved with the NHL right up until the month he died at the age of 83.

King Clancy always maintained that Howie Morenz was the best he ever saw. And who am I to question the opinion of Francis Michael Clancy?

The recollection of Morenz in flight still makes my scalp tingle. The words "in flight" are appropriate because Howie skated so swiftly and so gracefully that he appeared to be soaring about two inches above the surface of the ice.

Then there was his shot! Morenz was left-handed. When he was preparing to shoot, he had the puck cradled on the blade of his stick which he was dragging slightly behind his hurtling body.

At the firing point, he would pull his stick level with his left thigh, and with a powerful twist of his wrists, he'd let the puck go as it slid along the face of his stick blade.

It wasn't merely a shot — it was a rocketing missile.

Because it was travelling so swiftly, and because he had such power in his wrists, the puck performed some strange manoeuvers on its way to the target. A goalie couldn't be certain where Morenz's shot was going. Sometimes it ducked upwards and to the left; other times, it took a sharp, downward twist to the left. I doubt that even Morenz could be sure where it was going.

I sat behind the Montreal Maroons' net one night in The Forum. I was about ten rows above the ice level and directly behind the goal. Morenz fired a shot from just inside the Maroons' blue line.

From my vantage point, I saw the flying puck take a "break" upwards and to Morenz's left. The puck "moved" in such extraordinary fashion that Maroon goalie Clint Benedict was unable to react. The puck struck him in the face and fractured his right cheekbone.

Historians usually credit Jacques Plante of the Montreal Canadiens with being the man who introduced the goalie's mask to professional hockey.

But the truth is that Clint Benedict donned the first mask when Jacques Plante still was wearing diapers. After missing only one game, Benedict came back to guard the Montreal net, wearing a crude leather mask which had been improvised for him by Bill O'Brien, the Maroons trainer.

Probably an entire generation of hockey spectators has grown into comfortable middle-age without being aware that — prior to 1960 — the slapshot was only an improvisational rarity. Up until then, the wristshot was the principal weapon of offence.

The first practitioner of the slapshot was Cliff Pennington, a graduate of the St. Boniface Juniors who went up to play for the Hull-Ottawa team on the Eastern Professional League in the 1960-61 season.

Pennington received a lot of attention with the Hull-Ottawa team when he raised his hockey stick above his shoulder before he whacked the puck at the net.

However, Pennington's other hockey talents weren't startling. He wasn't particularly successful in two seasons with the Boston Bruins and he drifted into minor league hockey, leaving behind him the slapshot which, with improvements and embellishments by superior hockey players, has made life a living hell for two generations of shell-shocked goaltenders.

Having rewritten hockey history to suit myself, this is an appropriate moment to select my All-Star team. When one reaches the age of 79, caution long since has been thrown to the winds. So, with nothing further to lose, the following are some of the best players I've seen in action in my lifetime.

Centres: Howie Morenz, Wayne Gretzky, Phil Esposito, Mario Lemieux.

Right-wingers: Gordie Howe, Maurice Richard, Bill Cook, Mike Bossy.

Left-wingers: Bobby Hull, Ted Lindsay, Toe Blake, Sweeny Schriner.

Defencemen: Eddie Shore, Bobby Orr, Doug Harvey, Red Kelly.

Goalies: Chuck Gardiner, Terry Sawchuk, Glenn Hall, Ken Dryden.

All these selections are eminently defensible. It should be pointed out that Chuck Gardiner was only 29 when he died from peritonitis in 1934. The NHL didn't begin to name All-Star teams until the 1930-31 season and Gardiner was the All-Star goalie in three of those first four years. It should be pointed out further that Gardiner was the one shining star of the Chicago Black Hawks. He provided credibility for the team and he led them to a Stanley Cup victory, just a few months before his unexpected death.

There are other players who could have been included in my All-Star team if I had been willing to increase the roster. For instance, Milt Schmidt and Jean Béliveau would have been powerful additions at centre ice.

In prodding my memory, I was surprised to find that, apart from Hull and Lindsay, very few men had dominated the left-wing position in the NHL. I made Schriner one of my left-wing selections because Conn Smythe always said that Sweeny was the best man ever to play that position for the Toronto Maple Leafs. And, although I included my old friend Toe Blake, there are many of their living contemporaries who will tell you that little Doug Bentley of the Hawks was Blake's equal.

I probably could have added King Clancy and Babe Pratt to my group of defencemen. Smythe always said that Pratt was the best defenceman ever to play for Toronto. This was an odd statement in view of the fact that, when Smythe was attempting to build his first championship team, the key to the success of that team was the purchase of Clancy from the Ottawa Senators. Looking back on it, it's regrettable that Clancy and Pratt weren't in the same age brackets. I would have loved to watch them playing as a defensive pair; the combative little Clancy with his on-the-puck leadership and the tall, super-smooth Pratt controlling the play in his own end of the rink.

In my early years on the hockey beat, NHL players still deigned to treat hockey writers or radio commentators as more or less social equals. In those days, NHL players and newspapermen were in the same annual salary range. The team owners had an agreement limiting top salaries to $7,000, although there were some stars who received considerably more than that — but under the table.

I remember that when Frank Boucher was coaching the New York Rangers, he used to bring bottles of Myers' Rum from New York for Vern DeGeer and myself. He insisted that we accept the rum as a gift.

Then we discovered that Boucher was making only $5,000 per year as coach of the Rangers. This was considerably less than DeGeer and I were being paid at the *Globe and Mail.* Nonetheless, we had quite a battle with Boucher before he would permit us to pay for the rum which he had bought in New York and which he had smuggled through Canada Customs.

Mind you, Boucher had made as much as $10,000 a year when he was a player with the Rangers. But Lester Patrick had some fascinating theories about money, and incredibly, he convinced Boucher that he should take a dramatic cut in salary in order to have the privilege of coaching the New York hockey club. Some of his former players, who still are around today, will tell you that Lester would go to extraordinary lengths to save money for the owners of the Rangers.

Alex Shibicky recalls that, when he outscored all the other right-wingers in the league with 24 goals in the 1938-39 season, he was surprised when he wasn't selected for the first All-Star Team — or even the second All-Star Team. At that time, the All-Star Teams were chosen by the coaches.

Shibicky did some investigating and discovered that Lester Patrick, his own coach, hadn't voted for him because Lester didn't want to put the Rangers to the expense of paying Shibicky a bonus of $1,000, which had been promised to him if he was named to either of the All-Star Teams.

Over fifty years ago, in a relatively underpaid and carefree era, professional athletes and reporters from the news media drank together, partied together and were aware of each other's weaknesses and peculiarities. Some of my hockey friendships began with my childhood hero-worship and they were ended only by death. Two of those friends who had been my boyhood heroes — Red Dutton and King Clancy — lasted until this book was being written. Clancy died late in 1986 at the age of 82 and Dutton died less than six months later when he was 88.

Babe Pratt and King Clancy were born to be blood-brothers, although King was 13 years older than the towering Babe. Clancy had become a distinguished NHL referee by the time that Pratt was playing for the New York Rangers and Toronto. Both were compulsive yappers and they had some cornball repartee on the ice. One night, Pratt barked at Referee Clancy: "You make me so damn mad I could bite your head off." Clancy snapped back: "In that case, all your brains will be in your stomach."

Pratt came out of Winnipeg with a wave of young athletes which included football's Ches McCance and Les Lear and hockey's Alex Shibicky, Joe Cooper, Jake Milford and Rudy Pilous.

Pilous didn't make the NHL as a player but he coached the Chicago Black Hawks to their last-recorded Stanley Cup victory in 1961. And among hockey men, he is revered for his philosophical dicta, such as "you can slide a lot farther on bullshit than you can slide on gravel."

Pratt, Cooper and Milford all played junior hockey for the Kenora Thistles before they turned professional. Milford, like Pilous, never made the Big League as a player but went on to be general manager of two NHL teams. Furthermore, Jake always has been the butt of an in-house anecdote. When Owner Eddie Shore decided to drop Milford from his Springfield Indians, he traded Milford to Buffalo for a set of goal-nets. Jake always bridled at the suggestion that the goal-nets for which he had been traded were "second-hand."

Pratt still was eligible for junior hockey when Lester Patrick first took him to New York to play for the farm club, the Rovers. And Pratt was playing in the NHL by the time that he was 20.

Babe took to the bright lights of Broadway as a moth takes to the flame. He was big, handsome and gregarious. The Big Apple was his dish. His size, his skill and his beaming personality made him an instant favourite with the fans at Madison Square Garden. But there were occasions when his youthful impertinence got him into trouble with the ice officials.

Francis J. "Mickey" Ion had been a referee in the Pacific Coast League for many years before he joined the NHL staff in 1927. Mickey was one of those hardened oldtimers who loved a drink, and there were occasions on which he sipped a bit too freely before he went onto the ice.

Mickey was handling a Ranger game at the Garden. Pratt, due to his height and strength, had been designated by Patrick to take most of the face-offs in the New York end of the rink. On each of those face-offs, Mickey would place one hand on Pratt's shoulder to brace himself before he dropped the puck.

After one of those face-offs, Ion blew his whistle loudly. He waved Pratt from the ice with a ten-minute misconduct penalty. When Lester Patrick asked Babe to explain why he had been penalized for ten minutes, Pratt gave some vague, evasive explanation. But, later to teammates, Babe explained that he had said politely to the referee: "Mr. Ion. Will you please lean on the *other* guy for a few of these face-offs. I'm getting an early hangover from your breath."

Pratt loved his beer and, for the most part, Patrick was exceedingly tolerant where the drinking activities of his talented young defenceman were concerned. However, when the Rangers broke camp at Winnipeg in the autumn of 1940 and they headed east, Babe's drinking got him into trouble when the team stopped at Fort William to play an exhibition game.

The team's railway coach was parked on a siding at Fort William and, when Pratt staggered aboard about three hours after the exhibition game, Lester was waiting up for him. Patrick, for one, was genuinely angry. He told Pratt that he was going to fine him $1,000. However, Patrick told Pratt that he would rescind the $1,000 fine if Babe didn't take another drink before the end of the coming season.

In those days, $1,000 was one hell of a chunk for Pratt — particularly as a member of the poorly paid Rangers. So,

Pratt went on the wagon, but his hockey ability suffered. He struggled along, having an absolutely horrible season. Although he was as sober as a judge, he wasn't playing worth a damn.

In the crisis, his Ranger teammates held an emergency meeting. Ten of the players agreed to kick in $100 each to pay Pratt's $1,000 fine — on the condition that he'd start drinking again.

Assured that he wasn't going to lose $1,000, Pratt went back to drinking his beer in the final month of the season. His play improved dramatically. The slumping Rangers pulled up their socks and, with a belated rush, made the playoffs. Some of the Ranger players who have survived until today insist that, privately, Lester Patrick threw his own $100 into the pot to persuade Pratt to resume his love affair with beer.

In 1942, Lester made one of the worst deals in his long career as a manager of hockey teams. Weary of Pratt's increasingly publicized peregrinations on The Great White Way, Patrick decided to trade his multi-talented defenceman to the Toronto Maple Leafs. However, it proved to be a great trade for the Maple Leafs. As a reconstruction move, it ranked right up there with their acquisition of King Clancy from the Ottawa Senators 12 years earlier.

In addition to playing hockey, Pratt was working in railroading which was listed as an "essential industry" during the Second World War. He was employed by the C.P.R. as a switchman and he worked a daily shift in the Toronto Terminal Yards. In my column in the *Globe and Mail*, I referred to him as "The Honest Switchman" — because he never had stolen a boxcar.

Whether or not Babe was an expert switchman is open to question. He was refreshingly modest concerning his talents for sending boxcars crashing into long lines of more boxcars. He acknowledged that, on many occasions, he had clambered aboard an empty freightcar, bedded himself down in a dark corner and slept off a slight hangover.

Years later, I attended an annual meeting of C.P.R. pensioners. I was introduced to a gruff gentleman who had been the C.P.R. switching foreman in the years when Pratt was playing for the Maple Leafs.

In all innocence, I asked the retired foreman: "What kind of a switchman was Babe Pratt?"

"Pratt!" the old gentleman replied in a genial shout. "That big son of a bitch couldn't switch the Pope out of a Protestant parade!"

Pratt always was the good-natured playboy; eventually, it caught up with him. When he arrived in Toronto, he was adopted immediately by the members of the sporting-gambling fraternity, who were more than happy to buy his beers in exchange for the conviviality of his company. Babe's association with the gamblers among his drinking friends precipitated his speedy departure from the National Hockey League.

Meanwhile, Babe had made a big hit with the Toronto sports fanatics and, as far as the public was concerned, he may have been the most popular athlete in the city. In 1944, he became the first Toronto Maple Leaf ever to win the Hart Trophy, which is awarded to the most valuable player in the NHL. When the Maple Leafs won the Stanley Cup in 1945, Pratt was the individual star of the playoffs and scored the winning goal against Detroit in the seventh game of the Stanley Cup Final.

But less than eight months later, the entire Canadian sporting world was shocked when President Red Dutton of the National Hockey League announced on January 30, 1946, that Walter Pratt had been suspended indefinitely — for betting on a hockey game. The fact that Pratt's bet had been made on his own team — the Toronto Maple Leafs — was beside the point.

For some months, the NHL had become hyper-sensitive on the subject of players making bets *of any kind*. Down in the United States, some key players in the National Football League had been expelled for being involved in possible wagering coups. The irony of the situation was that one of Pratt's "friends" among the Toronto gamblers had pipelined the betting incident to Dutton's attention.

For Pratt, the extrovert, the suspension was a bewildering experience. During the weeks while Dutton and the NHL governors were investigating his case, Pratt was barred from Maple Leaf Gardens. He was under orders to stay away from his teammates and he conducted lonely skating practices by himself in a Toronto suburb.

Finally, Dutton and the governors decided to reinstate Pratt. But by that time, the Maple Leafs had been deprived of the services of their star defenceman for nine league games and — one year after winning the Stanley Cup — they were going to miss the playoffs. At that point, Conn Smythe decided to dump Pratt. Before the next season, he was shunted off to the Boston Bruins.

There was a curious double-standard where Smythe was concerned. Smythe condoned gambling on hockey games in Maple Leaf Gardens. The large concession area behind the "Blue" section on the east side of the Gardens was known as "The Bull Ring." Before every game, almost all well-known bookmakers in Toronto would be in "The Bull Ring," where they would be quoting odds and accepting public bets on that evening's game. Furthermore, all those bookmakers subscribed for season tickets at Maple Leaf Gardens.

However, when Pratt was suspended, the management of Maple Leaf Gardens suffered from a belated onrush of piety. Police suddenly arrived to clear out The Bull Ring although, not surprisingly, the Gardens didn't offer to refund the money which the bookmakers had paid for season tickets.

Pratt's fall from grace was precipitous. He played less than one full season in Boston and he was demoted to their farm club, the Hershey Bears. It became painfully obvious that Babe was "blacklisted" — no other NHL club was going to salvage his career.

Alex Shibicky came to Pratt's rescue. Shibicky, who had been Babe's teammate in the Ranger days, was coaching the New Westminster Royals in the Western League. Alex persuaded club owner Ken McKenzie to pay $1,000 to buy Babe's release from Hershey.

Pratt had an immediate rebirth in New Westminster. The Royals surged to the finals of the Western League playoffs against San Diego. This championship final was a reunion, of sorts, for three old friends from Winnipeg. Rudy Pilous had taken over the coaching of San Diego.

Shibicky, who had saved his old buddy from the hockey scrap-heap, was bemused by what happened next. In justice to Pratt, no one had bothered to tell him that it was Shibicky who had induced McKenzie to extricate him from Hershey.

So, unaware that Shibicky was his *real* benefactor, Pratt went to McKenzie and applied for the job of playing coach of the Royals for the next season. The suggestion appealed to McKenzie, who, in that situation, wouldn't have to pay a salary to Shibicky. Suddenly, Alex was out and Babe was in.

Pratt prolonged his career for five years as player coach in New Westminster. Despite his gaudy lifestyle, he could control the flow of any game from his position on the defence.

Max McNabb, later to be general manager of two NHL franchises, tells a story about the Detroit Red Wings sending him to the New Westminster Royals. McNabb arrived in town just in time to don a uniform for a home game. After they came off the ice, the players were lounging in front of their lockers and Coach Pratt was making inroads into a case of beer which sat on the floor in front of him.

McNabb was accustomed to the militaristic regime in Detroit, where everything was minutely scheduled. The players were expected to be in their dressing room at 8:30 A.M. — and the practice began promptly at 9:00 A.M.

So, turning to the Royals player sitting next to him, Max asked quietly: "What time do we practice tomorrow morning?"

The player nodded in the direction of Pratt and replied: "We practice approximately half-an-hour after Babe decides to roll out of bed."

Pratt went out of professional hockey not with a bang but with a burp. Cut adrift by New Westminster, he was induced to play one final season with the Tacoma Tigers, coached by Muzz Patrick, his beer-drinking playmate from the New York Rangers.

Babe's lifestyle changed after he stopped playing hockey. He also stopped drinking — but not before the night he was stopped by a motorcycle policeman when he was driving home. The policeman ordered Pratt to step out of his car and he asked: "Have you been drinking?" Always cheerful, even in moments of crisis, Pratt roared: "If I *haven't* been drinking, there's a bartender in this city who just cheated me out of $15."

At this point, a successful British Columbia lumberman took a hand in Pratt's life. With the promise of a job, he induced Babe to enroll in the B.C. Government's demanding course for log-scalers. Applying himself to the books for the first time in his life, Pratt passed the course with exceptionally high marks. Thereupon, he became established successfully in the lumber industry.

When the Vancouver Canucks were admitted to the NHL in 1970, the new club hired Pratt as assistant to the vice-president. Actually, his duties were in the area of public relations, and for the final 19 years of his colourful life, he was the goodwill ambassador for the hockey team.

King Clancy and Babe Pratt were kindred spirits. Although they worked for individual teams — Clancy for Toronto and Pratt for Vancouver — they were, actually, ambassadors-at-large for the entire sport of hockey.

Clancy didn't take a drink in his entire lifetime. And Pratt didn't take a drink in his final 30 years. Never in the history of hockey have there been two other men who, through the sheer charm and warmth of their personalities, made so many lasting friendships. And when they departed, a great deal of happy laughter went out of this world.

To the very last, Pratt was the cheerful fatalist. He had one warning heart attack in the autumn of 1988. This did not deter him from representing hockey on the rubber-chicken circuit, where he told dinner audiences: "I've reached the stage of my life where I no longer buy green bananas. In fact, I'm not even buying long-playing records."

Death came for him in an appropriate setting. He was watching a Canuck home game at the Pacific Coliseum when he had his fatal heart attack.

Babe would have liked it to end that way. He died in a hockey arena which, in the opinion of his many friends, really had been his spiritual home since he was a small boy.

There is a widespread conception among observers of the game that if hockey players all were obliged to undergo psychoanalysis, the most fascinating case-histories would be provided by goaltenders.

Among goaltenders, I have known many wildly disparate personalities. They range from the cerebral Ken Dryden to the easy-going Gerry Cheevers, and from Frank McCool (whose duodenal ulcers occasionally compelled him to leave the ice and visit the bathroom in the middle of a game) to hard-drinking Red McCusker, the only professional netminder of my acquaintance who held an opposing team scoreless through 60 minutes when he was drunker than a hoot owl.

The first goaltender whose mild idiosyncrasies came to my attention was Norm "Heck" Fowler, who played for the Victoria Cougars before he went to the Boston Bruins in the NHL. Among other minor peculiarities, Fowler was a fire-buff.

When the Cougars came to my hometown of Winnipeg to play a pre-season exhibition game, the fire engines (with bells ringing in those days) passed the Fort Garry Hotel just as the Victoria hockey players were emerging from the lobby to get into taxi-cabs.

It was a November night and the fire engines were driving slowly and carefully because there was a new fall of light snow on the ice-covered streets. As one of the fire engines slowed in front of the hotel, Heck Fowler jumped on the back step of the fire truck and was carried away to the scene of the conflagration.

I remember the incident clearly because the next day's Winnipeg papers reported that the start of the hockey game had been delayed for 25 minutes because Victoria's goalie was watching a fire.

For all-round irascibility, there never was another goalie to match the immortal Red McCusker. He played for Regina and Portland back in the days when the Western Canada League and the Pacific Coast League challenged the NHL for the Stanley Cup. Later, he had a brief stint in the NHL before playing for the Edmonton Eskimos when the Western Canada League was revived in the 1930s.

On New Year's Eve, 1936, McCusker was living temporarily in the Selkirk Hotel in Edmonton. His wife was staying with her family in Vancouver and Red missed her badly on this traditionally most festive of evenings.

As New Year's Eve progressed, the lonely McCusker decided that he must phone his wife. There was a pay phone on the first floor in the Selkirk Hotel. Repeatedly, McCusker attempted to get through to Vancouver, but all the long distance lines were busy.

After more than an hour of fruitless attempts to complete a call to his wife, Red became so angry that he ripped the pay telephone off the wall of the hotel. The night manager of the hotel decided that it was not a propitious moment to remonstrate with the raging McCusker. It was wiser simply to ignore the uprooting of the telephone.

On New Year's Day, the Edmonton Eskimos were booked to play a home game with the Portland Buckaroos. When Red arrived at the Eskimo dressing room at the old Edmonton Arena, he was in terrible shape. He had continued drinking after his aborted efforts to reach his wife by telephone. He had done little or no sleeping and was higher than a Georgia pine.

In that era of financial stringency, Western League teams were operating with a basic roster of only 11 players: six forwards, four defencemen and one goalie. No team could afford the luxury of having a spare goalie. In the circumstances, McCusker was compelled to play, sober or drunk. There was no one to replace him.

His teammates helped him to don his uniform, his heavy pads and his skates. With two of his teammates steadying him, Red lumbered uncertainly from the dressing room to the gate, leading to the ice.

When Red put his first skate on the ice, he knew that he was in trouble. He kept one hand on the sideboards until he was within groping distance of the net. He was weaving noticeably in his crease while an old 78-rpm recording blared the National Anthem on the arena's public address system.

After the face-off, the first time that a Portland player ventured over the Edmonton blue-line, McCusker let out a ferocious roar and waved his goal stick over his head menacingly. The alarmed Portland player shot the puck vaguely into the Edmonton zone and very quickly retreated to centre-ice.

What followed was one of the most amazing spectacles in the history of professional hockey. Throughout the entire 60 minutes, Portland didn't take more than a dozen harmless shots on the Edmonton net. The Eskimo players fore-checked and back-checked furiously to protect their alcoholically enflamed netminder.

All histories of unusual goaltending must include a reference to the night that Lester Patrick went in the New York Rangers' net when they won the second game of the 1928 Stanley Cup Final in the Montreal Forum.

The Rangers had been evicted from Madison Square Garden to make room for the annual visit of Ringling Brothers, Barnum & Bailey Circus. The hockey team elected to play the entire three-out-of-five games final series in Montreal.

The Montreal Maroons won the opening game, 2 to 0. Two nights later, early in the second period, New York goalie Lorne Chabot was badly injured. The Rangers didn't have a backup goaltender and, unsportingly, the Maroons wouldn't permit them to use Ottawa's Alex Connell, who was a spectator in the Forum.

In the emergency, Coach Patrick donned the big pads. Odie Cleghorn, of Pittsburgh, volunteered to replace Lester behind the bench. Lester didn't approve of drinking hockey players, but on this occasion, he settled his own nerves with a couple of slugs from a flask of whiskey which Ranger trainer Harry Westerby had smuggled into the dressing room.

With silver-haired Patrick guarding the goal, the Rangers won the second game, 2 to 1. Patrick spent a good deal of the final two periods scrambling around on his hands and knees. But as his confidence increased, he was shouting at his players: "Make them [the Maroons] shoot! Make them shoot!"

Patrick's bold sentiments weren't shared by his players. On the bench, Cleghorn and the Ranger subs were shouting: "*Don't* let them shoot! *Don't* let them shoot!"

Considering the ungracious manner in which the Maroons had reacted to Chabot's injury, justice was served ultimately when the Rangers won the Stanley Cup, three games to two.

Jacques Plante, who saved a lot of surgical stitching for his brethren when he defied convention and insisted upon wearing a face mask in every game, was a brilliant netminder, but like many of the best of them, he had his little oddities.

In his off-ice hours, Jacques whiled away the time with needles and a ball of wool as he knitted toques. He also suffered from mild hypochondria; when his team visited Toronto, he insisted upon staying at a hotel near Maple Leaf Gardens instead of being billeted at the Royal York with his teammates. He argued that the Royal York's proximity to Lake Ontario had a deleterious effect on his bronchial condition.

The goalies who have survived without emotional scars are those who, superficially at least, don't appear to take life too seriously. High on the list of those robust survivors must be Gerry Cheevers and Gump Worsley.

Gerry had a magnificently equable disposition. He tended goal professionally for 16 years and he sauntered cheerfully through another three years as coach of the Boston Bruins. When the Bruins dropped him he became publicist for a New England racetrack and he has been very successful as a hockey colour-commentator on television.

There is an anecdote which illustrates Gerry's aplomb in the face of adversity. One night, the Boston Bruins were whomped 2 to 8 by the New York Rangers. Hap Emms, the Boston general manager, stomped into the dressing room and strode over to Cheevers, who was sitting nonchalantly in front of his locker. Emms, puffing furiously on his pipe, glowered down at his goalie and demanded: "What the hell happened out there, Gerry?" With a gentle smile on his face, Cheevers replied:

"Roses are red, violets are blue;
They scored eight and we scored two!"

Gump Worsley was the archetypical non-conformist. He refused to wear a protective mask, even after they had been adopted by everyone else in the NHL. And he had strong doubts about the future of aviation. He travelled by train when his teammates were travelling by much speedier planes. Gump, like Cheevers, believed that once off the ice, life should be enjoyable. He drank a lot of beer and generally was in a merry mood.

Before he was rescued by the Montreal Canadiens, Gump had spent five or six seasons in the employ of the hapless New York Rangers. While he was still toiling in New York, a newspaper reporter asked him that most fatuous of all questions: "Which team gives you the most trouble?" Gump replied promptly: "The New York Rangers."

Coaches of my acquaintance usually treated goaltenders as special cases. The coaches acted as if they *expected* a goalie to be moody or withdrawn or to harbour some hitherto unobserved tic.

One Saturday morning, I was in the lobby of the Royal York Hotel when the Pittsburgh Penguins were visiting Toronto. Red Sullivan, the Pittsburgh coach, edged over to me. "We have a new goalie, Les Binkley, with us on this trip," Sullivan said in a half-whisper. "I suggest that you walk over to where he's sitting and have a little talk with him. You're going to be really surprised. Binkley doesn't act or talk like a goaltender. He sounds just like a normal human being."

THE LIGHTER SIDE OF BIG LEAGUE HOCKEY

IT IS HIGHLY IMPROBABLE THAT TODAY ANY NEWSPAPER-man would have the opportunity to leave a healthy domestic duck swimming in the bathtub of the hotel suite occupied by the president of the National Hockey League.

The two most recent presidents of the NHL — the late Clarence S. Campbell and John Ziegler — wouldn't have taken too kindly to discovering a web-footed intruder cavorting in their tubs.

However, Mr. Campbell's immediate predecessor — Mervyn "Red" Dutton — was a chap with a merry heart. Mr. Dutton was a very effective president of the NHL, but his elevation to the League's highest position didn't cool the warm friendships which he had established with members of the sports news media during his long career as a professional hockey player and manager-coach of the Brooklyn Americans (formerly the New York Americans). When Vern DeGeer was sports editor of the *Globe and Mail* and I was sports columnist for that paper, we had an open invitation to visit Dutton's suite at the Royal York Hotel when hockey business brought him to Toronto.

For more than a year, Dutton had been boasting of the large numbers of ducks, prairie chicken and Canada geese which he and his Calgary friends shot during the Alberta hunting season. Always he was promising that "on his next trip east," he would bring half a dozen ducks for DeGeer and me from his deep freezer in Calgary. Regrettably, he forgot about those annual promises when he returned to Calgary at the end of each hockey season, so DeGeer and I decided to jog Dutton's memory.

When the Detroit Red Wings came to Toronto to play the Maple Leafs in the 1945 Stanley Cup Final, President Dutton invited us to visit his suite on the afternoon prior to the Saturday night game. On our way to the Royal York, we made a stop at a poulterer's and purchased a lively looking duck. Before we entered the hotel, DeGeer tucked the duck under the front of his overcoat. The duck's head protruded from the coat, just beneath DeGeer's chin. As we rode a crowded elevator to the eleventh floor of the hotel, several passengers were rather disconcerted to see a duck staring at them beadily from the aperture of an overcoat worn by a short, stout, merry-faced man.

The logistics of the operation were simple. We were accompanied in the elevator by our friend Bill Anderson, an assistant manager of the Royal York, who carried a pass key.

While DeGeer and Anderson remained out of sight, I went to Dutton's sitting room and joined a lively afternoon party. The assemblage included Lester Patrick of the New York Rangers, Arthur Howey Ross of the Boston Bruins, John Digby Chick, the perpetual vice-president of the American Hockey League, and Reg Jennings, Dutton's construction business partner from Calgary.

"Where's DeGeer?" Dutton asked as he steered me towards the bar.

I explained that DeGeer had been delayed in the lobby talking with Jack Adams, the manager of the Red Wings.

Meanwhile, using the pass key, Bill Anderson was letting DeGeer into the bedroom of the presidential suite. As Anderson withdrew discreetly, DeGeer put the duck into the bathtub. Then, DeGeer ran about two inches of water into the tub so that the duck would be comfortable. Finally, he drew the shower curtain so that the duck could swim and preen unseen. DeGeer went back into the eleventh-floor corridor, knocked on the sitting room door and was admitted to join the party.

Later President Dutton announced that he was going to shave in preparation for the hockey game. He excused himself; in the sitting room, the party continued.

Approximately five minutes later, there was an uproar in the corridor outside the suite. We could hear the high-pitched cries of a startled woman.

Lester Patrick flung open the door and looked out. A hotel chambermaid was in flight down the hotel corridor, followed by a quacking, waddling duck which, in turn, was pursued by the president of the National Hockey League, clad only in his underwear shorts, socks and shoes, his face covered with shaving lather.

Dutton got the point. Not a bit embarrassed for frightening the maid in his underwear shorts, he announced firmly that "on his next trip from Calgary" he'd bring some ducks for the DeGeer and Coleman dining-room tables.

DeGeer greeted Dutton's promise with a derisive razzoo. He raced down the corridor to rescue the duck and, ostensibly, took it away to put it in his car in the hotel parking lot.

An hour later, the freshly shaved, handsomely clad President Dutton announced that it was time to go to the coffee shop for a snack, before going to Maple Leaf Gardens. Grabbing our topcoats, we strode away to prepare for watching the Red Wings and the Maple Leafs.

But DeGeer hadn't really taken the duck to the parking lot. From the desk telephone in the elevator vestibule of the eleventh floor, he had called another of our assistant manager friends, Reg Cooper.

DeGeer had induced Cooper to bring his pass key and admit him to the room assigned to John Digby Chick in the west wing of the eleventh floor. DeGeer put the duck into Mr. Chick's bathtub, ran a couple of inches of water into the tub and pulled the shower curtains, concealing the puzzled bird.

After the hockey game, John Digby Chick went from Maple Leaf Gardens directly to Red Dutton's hotel suite. It was only in the small hours of Sunday morning that Mr. Chick lumbered away to his own room.

When he arrived in his own bedroom, Mr. Chick stripped down to his underwear shorts and decided that he must yield to a call of nature before going to bed. He had seated himself on the toilet when he heard a hissing sound coming from behind the shower curtain.

Mr. Chick pulled back the shower curtain and was surprised to see a duck staring up at him. By this time, the duck was becoming hungry and it attempted to nibble on Mr. Chick's ample left flank. Indignantly, Mr. Chick arose and stomped out to the room telephone to call the house detective.

When the detective came on the line, John said: "This is John Chick in Room 1105. There's a duck in my bathtub. Come on up here and get rid of the damn thing."

It was 2:00 A.M. or 3:00 A.M., and the house detective, who had previous experience with the nocturnal drinking habit of Mr. Chick, said brightly: "Now, you just go to bed, Mr. Chick. We'll get rid of the duck in the morning."

John Digby was not amused. Straining himself to keep his voice under control, he blurted: "Listen, if I had a girl in my room you would have been up here pounding on my door hours ago. Now I'm telling you that I have a duck swimming in my bathtub and you won't do anything about it." The duck was finally retrieved and taken to the hotel kitchens.

In that era, the general managers, coaches and players of NHL teams made themselves readily accessible to the news media in the cities which they visited. In Toronto, the headquarters for visiting clubs was in the Royal York Hotel. In Montreal, all teams stayed at the Mount Royal Hotel on Peel Street.

If a sports columnist sat in the lobby of the Royal York about noon on the day of a hockey game, he could collect enough material to keep him in business for half a week.

I recall those years as the era of the Hockey Raconteurs and also the era of the Hotel Lobby-Sitters. It was customary, after a leisurely breakfast, for the members of the visiting team to sit in the lobby of the Royal York for a couple of hours, many of them puffing contentedly on large cigars. Occasionally, other hotel guests or lobby visitors would ask them for autographs which they would sign in rather lordly fashion. NHL players were Canada's most visible celebrities. Acknowledged as league champions among the Lobby-Sitters were the Detroit Red Wings who, for some unknown reason, were almost 100 percent addicted to cigar smoking.

Most of the oldtimers who had risen to the management level in the NHL were compulsive and engaging raconteurs. Particularly sought-after by Toronto sports commentators when they came to town were Dutton, Art Ross of the Boston Bruins, Tommy Gorman of the Montreal Canadiens and Lester Patrick of the New York Rangers. Patrick sometimes was a bit standoffish — leaving one with the distinct impression that he had *invented* professional hockey, but when he had a couple of drinks under his belt, he would tell some wonderful stories about the early days of the sport.

Among Toronto hockey writers of the period — particularly among those who enjoyed a drink with their conversations — the most popular hockey visitor was Frank Boucher, coach of the New York Rangers.

Frank was a charming Franco-Irishman from Ottawa, a member of a family of hockey players. One of his brothers, George "Buck" Boucher, had been a famous defenceman with the Ottawa Senators and the Montreal Maroons. Another brother, Billy Boucher, enjoyed his greatest fame as a right-winger for the immortal Howie Morenz in the lineup of the Montreal Canadiens.

Frank, for his part, was the most famous of all the Bouchers. He came to the New York Rangers after starring for the Vancouver Maroons. With the Rangers, he was selected three times as the centreman on the NHL All-Star team. He was also a seven-time winner of the Lady Byng Trophy, awarded to the most gentlemanly and effective player in the NHL.

Boucher loved to sing, he loved a drink and he loved to tell stories. When the Press Club first was formed in Toronto, Frank was a regular visitor to those premises when the Rangers came to town. And when Toronto hockey writers followed the Maple Leafs to New York City, they rushed to file their post-game stories because they were anxious to join Boucher in his favourite estaminet, which rejoiced in the name of Hogan's Irish House.

The Boucher story which, for me, always has been most memorable was concerned with the first training camp of the New York Rangers when Conn Smythe was assembling the team for admission to the National Hockey League in the autumn of 1926.

Two of the oddly disparate personalities selected by Smythe to attend the first Ranger training camp were

Frank Boucher and Ivan "Ching" Johnson. Strangely enough, although they had been playing hockey for years, they hadn't met until someone introduced them in the lobby of Toronto's King Edward Hotel the day before they were to report to Smythe. Frank had been playing for Vancouver while Ching Johnson, a prematurely bald Winnipegger, had been playing for the Minneapolis Millers in the American Association.

Boucher and Johnson hit it off immediately — particularly after Johnson invited Frank to his room in the King Edward Hotel where, in his club bag, he had three bottles of New Jersey Applejack. This drink, also known as "Jersey Lightning," wasn't necessarily lethal, but it had an exceptionally high octane rating. To Frank's delight, he discovered that Ching shared his fondness for singing. After a few belts of Jersey Lightning, they were harmonizing with gusto.

Smythe had given written orders to all prospective Ranger players that he expected them to be bedded down at the Queensberry Hotel before midnight on Saturday. He had selected that establishment as their headquarters because it was situated in a northwest suburb of Toronto, close to the Ravina Rink, but far from the city's bright lights.

As the afternoon wore on, Boucher and Johnson were becoming fast friends at the King Edward. They were pleased to discover that, on many matters concerned with professional hockey, they shared the same robust opinions.

They discovered quickly that they had a mutual antipathy for curfews and other militaristic strictures for Smythe's proposed training camp at the Queensberry Hotel and the Ravina Rink. Shaking hands and vowing eternal friendship, they expressed vehemently the mutual opinion that Smythe's proposed training regimen was a crock.

The midnight deadline passed while Frank Boucher and Ching Johnson still were harmonizing cheerfully in the bedroom at the King Edward. It was approximately four o'clock, Sunday morning, when they decided to join their future teammates at the Queensberry Hotel. In his bag, Ching stashed his one remaining bottle of Jersey Lightning.

At the front door of the King Edward, they found a lonely cabbie who was more than happy to drive them to the Queensberry Hotel in remote suburbia.

No lights were showing in the Queensberry Hotel when they pulled up at the front door. However, the two hockey players paid off the hack driver and, as the cab disappeared, attempted to get into the little hotel, but the doors had been locked at midnight — on Conn Smythe's orders.

Boucher and Johnson weren't defeated. They found a fire-escape, the bottom rungs of which were about nine feet above the ground. Boucher climbed upon Johnson's shoulders; Johnson stood erect and Boucher was able to get a footing on the fire-escape. But when he climbed to the second storey of the hotel, he discovered that the door leading into the hotel from the fire-escape also had been locked.

For some reason, Boucher thought that this was hilariously funny. As he attempted to descend, he was chuckling so hard that he lost his footing and landed atop Johnson who was peering up at him.

Standing there in the darkness, hammered to the gills, the two hockey players attempted to assess their situation. There was no available telephone on which they could call for a taxi. The only alternative was for them to strike out on foot; hoping to find a well-illuminated main thoroughfare and, just possibly, a prowling cab.

They weren't very far from Bloor Street, one of the city's main east-west thoroughfares. Taking a restorative sip of Jersey Applejack, they walked along Bloor Street until they came to the Jane Street loop of the city tramways system.

Miraculously, they espied lights. Parked on the Jane Street loop was a tram car waiting to begin its 6:00 A.M. trip across the city from west to east.

The motorman conductor of the trolly must have been surprised to see two excessively cheery men staggering towards him through the darkness. However, he was delighted to welcome them aboard, particularly when they offered him an early morning jolt of Jersey Applejack. Boucher and Johnson still were in a mood for singing and they discovered that the motorman, after that first slug of Applejack, had an untrained but promising tenor voice.

The tram was scheduled to leave the Jane Street loop at 6:00 A.M., but it didn't leave until 6:15 that particular morning.

When it took off, Boucher, Johnson and the motorman were clustered around the motorman's seat at the front of the tram. The bottle always was within easy reach. As he eased the car onto the Bloor Street tracks, the motorman asked his new-found friends: "Where do you want to go?"

Boucher and Johnson told him that they'd like to go back to the King Edward Hotel where, they felt quite certain, the management would permit them to bed down for a few hours.

"Well, it's a bit off my regular route," the motorman conceded. "But don't worry — I'll get you there."

The motorman wasn't kidding when he said that the King Edward Hotel was a "bit off his regular route." He was going to take a detour of at least five or six miles. The motorman eventually stopped the tram directly in front of the main door of the King Edward. Boucher and Johnson thanked their benefactor effusively before they lurched happily into the lobby of the hotel.

Most of professional hockey's legends have been created within the span of my own lifetime. Stories such as The Moonlit Ride of Frank Boucher and Ching Johnson were told to newspapermen by the actual participants and were absorbed into the folklore of the game.

The circumstances of my employment gave me the opportunity to spend many hours in the convivial company of some of hockey's greatest raconteurs. I could fill an entire book with the personal recollections I heard from Newsy Lalonde, Cyclone Taylor, Red Dutton, Frank Boucher, Tommy Gorman, ex-referee Mickey Ion, King Clancy and Babe Pratt. The feats of individual derring-do never diminished with the passage of time. As King Clancy was fond of saying: "The older we *are* — the better we *were*!"

Most of the legends that have survived until today have been concerned with major figures in the sport — the Super-Stars of the NHL or, at least, the Stars.

Eddie Shack had considerable accomplishments as a player. After all, Eddie spent 14 seasons in the NHL and ten of those seasons were in the old Six-Team League, before the original expansion of the autumn of 1967.

Shack, who was nicknamed "The Entertainer" in his two separate stints with the Toronto Maple Leafs, was equipped with some tremendous natural ability. He was very strong and he could outskate 98 percent of his contemporaries.

There were occasions, however, on which he acted as if he was a nuclear warhead which had gone off-course after being blasted from the launching pad. When he was in full flight, if someone had opened the gate behind the goal at the north end of Maple Leaf Gardens, Shack probably would have hurtled right through the end of the building without stopping until he reached Lake Simcoe.

Shack is remembered for his crowd-pleasing antics, but the facts are that he was good enough to appear for more than 900 games in the NHL and he played for four of Toronto's Stanley Cup-winning teams.

On the other hand, Jean Pusie played only parts of three separate seasons in the National Hockey League. He appeared successively in the colours of the New York Rangers, the Boston Bruins and the Montreal Canadiens.

But Pusie spent most of his hockey career in the Minor Leagues where his often-ridiculous antics didn't offend his former Major League coaches: Lester Patrick in New York, Art Ross in Boston and Sylvio Mantha in Montreal.

Jean Pusie had many of Shack's attributes. He was big, compared with hockey players of his era; he could skate like the wind and he had a tremendously-hard wristshot — always, he kept it within six inches of the ice surface.

Pusie was a tough-looking, lantern-jawed defenceman, but his ferocious mien was a fraudulent facade. Although Jean precipitated scores of on-ice melees in his Minor League career, he was seldom around for the finish of any of those imbroglios. At heart, he was a pussy cat and pugilism wasn't among his strong points.

Actually, Jean Pusie was a buffoon — possibly the most amusing buffoon ever to play professional hockey. Unfortunately, he was born about 40 years too early — if he had been in his prime in 1972 when the World Hockey Association was beginning to struggle for recognition, his antics would have filled an arena for a couple of those WHA clubs.

He was hockey's consummate showman — a born ham. I can attest to the magnificence of his buffoonery because I know him personally and watched him in action.

Jean was twice a winter resident of Vancouver when he came to the Pacific coast city to play for Vancouver's minor league franchise. First he was playing for Regina in the early 1930s and, when the financially depressed Saskatchewan capital failed to support them adequately, the team was moved to Vancouver. After his three separate stints in the NHL — which were punctuated by demotions to the Canadian-American League — Pusie returned to Vancouver in the autumn of 1939 to play for Guy Patrick's Vancouver Lions in the Pacific Coast League.

It was in the old Vancouver Arena and in the slightly less ancient Vancouver Forum that I had the opportunity to appreciate Jean Pusie's comic talents. To watch him taking a penalty shot for his team was worth the entire price of admission.

Pusie would watch the referee intently as the official placed the puck on the face-off circle at centre ice. Occasionally, he would ask the referee to pick up the puck and remove any dirt or moisture. Then he would take a warm-up whirl around the entire outer circumference of the ice surface, skating at tremendous speed and often waving his stick in response to the derisive cheers of the crowd.

Pulling up in a blizzard of snow at centre ice, he would pause momentarily, as if lost in thought. Then he would skate slowly to the opposing goaltender, who would be yelling at Pusie impatiently from his net. Sportingly, Pusie would offer to shake the goalie's hand, after which he'd give the goalie an encouraging pat on the back. This was only Minor League Hockey and the referee was prepared to go along with the histrionics.

After encouraging the goalie, Pusie would make another complete circuit of the rink at high speed. While he was in full-flight, he'd pick up the puck at centre ice and bear down on the net, grimacing fiendishly. When he was about 20 feet from the net, he'd fire his projectile. If he scored — which was frequently — he'd circle the rink in triumph, holding both arms aloft. When he missed — which I am sure he did deliberately on a few occasions — the puck would scatter the spectators who were sitting ten or 12 rows behind the net.

After scoring on a penalty shot, Pusie occasionally gave an extra fillip to his victory circuit of the ice. Sometimes, he would skate down to the beaten goaltender and, very ostentatiously, offer the netminder his condolences.

One night in Vancouver, he pulled this particular act on the wrong goaltender, Andy Aikenhead of the Portland Buckaroos.

Aikenhead had been netminder of the New York Rangers in 1933 and — as a former Major Leaguer — didn't appreciate anyone taking liberties with him in the ill-paid Western Hockey League. After beating Andy on a penalty shot, Jean Pusie made his usual circuit of the rink, acknowledging the applause of the Vancouver crowd. Then he skated down to Aikenhead, and in rather condescending fashion, he offered to shake the goalie's hand. Aikenhead exploded indignantly. He raised his goal stick over his shoulders and thumped Pusie on top of his head. Pusie retreated at full speed.

During the Depression years, Pusie was a great attraction in the cities of the American Hockey League. He would provoke brawls on the ice; he would engage in verbal brawls with the spectators, and on several occasions, he was lugged off to the local police cells for causing a disturbance in a public place. All this, of course, attracted considerable publicity and assured a good crowd the next time that Pusie's team came to town.

The most innovative performance of his career was provided when he was playing for St. Louis and his team played a road game in Tulsa. A Tulsa spectator, sitting in a rail seat next to the ice surface, had spent the evening heckling "The Great Man," as Pusie modestly described himself. Finally, feigning complete rage, Jean jumped right over the boards and landed in an aisle a few feet from the heckler's seat. The heckler fled. He ran from his seat to a corridor which led into the lobby of the Tulsa rink.

Pusie, clumping along on his skates, brandishing his hockey stick and shouting threats of violence, followed the heckler into the corridor. The spectator, badly frightened, ran along the corridor and into the lobby. Pusie, caught up in the spirit of the thing, was right behind his prey. The spectator, genuinely frantic by this time, charged through a lobby door and went right out into the street. Pusie, howling vengefully, was right behind him.

Actually, the pursuit ended at the door leading into the street; once again, Pusie was arrested for causing a disturbance. But legend has it that, clattering along the pavement on his skates, Pusie continued to pursue the heckler for a full block — before he noticed the welcoming door of a bar-room and dropped in to have what they used to describe as "a short bee."

I must admit that I prefer the legend.

My final meeting with Jean Pusie came after he had abandoned hockey and embraced professional wrestling. We met at Toronto's Maple Leaf Gardens on a Thursday night when Pusie appeared in a preliminary bout on a regular weekly wrestling card promoted by Frank Tunney.

Late that night, the wrestlers and several members of the news media were drinking in Tunney's suite of offices on the main floor Church Street side of Maple Leaf Gardens. One of the wrestlers, Rudy Paytek, was an accomplished accordionist and was entertaining his fellow-wrestlers on the squeeze box as they waited to be called into Tunney's inner office to receive their individual shares of the night's box-office receipts.

Finally, from behind his office door, Tunney bawled out, "Pusie!" As he arose from his chair, Pusie tapped the accordion-player, Rudy Paytek, on the shoulder. "Come with me," Pusie said to Paytek. "I like to listen to music while I'm getting screwed."

TOMMY GORMAN AND THE CHICAGO SNOW JOB

WHEN COMPARING CLUBS BASED ON THEIR STANLEY CUP victories, the two least successful franchises in professional hockey have been the New York Rangers and the Chicago Black Hawks. Each of those clubs has won the Stanley Cup only three times: the Rangers in 1928, 1933 and 1940; the Hawks in 1934, 1938 and 1961.

At the same time, the Rangers and the Black Hawks have been enormously successful financially. This leads to the reluctant conclusion that, in professional hockey, championships aren't essential as long as the local team continues to attract capacity crowds.

A cynic might point out that this condition isn't exclusive to a couple of US franchises in the National Hockey League. The once-mighty Toronto Maple Leafs haven't won the Stanley Cup since 1967, but the Maple Leafs have continued to play their home games in the presence of a full-house.

When the Rangers were admitted to the National Hockey League in the autumn of 1926, Coach Lester Patrick, who had gone to New York after selling his Victoria Cougars, had a team of first-class players at his disposal. One of the reasons for the successes of the Rangers in their early years of NHL membership was continuity of top-grade personnel.

Patrick was manager-coach of their first Stanley Cup-winning team in 1928. The mainstays of that brilliant squad were Bill Cook, Frank Boucher, Bunny Cook, Ching Johnson and Taffy Abel.

When they won again in 1933, Boucher, the Cook brothers and Ching Johnson still were playing and Patrick still was behind the bench.

Even when the Rangers won for a third time in 1940, there were some important holdovers. Frank Boucher had become the coach, but Patrick always was lurking close to Boucher's shoulder. And gnomish Harry Westerby had been the trainer of the Rangers ever since Conn Smythe hired him in 1926.

Continuity on the ice, behind the bench, and in the dressing room contributes importantly to the success of professional sports franchises.

There was another factor which contributed to the eminence of the Rangers in that 1926-1940 period. They had been the first NHL team to develop a farm system. They had scouts in eastern and western Canada; they operated an annual pre-season training camp at centrally located Winnipeg. At the conclusion of each camp, after selecting personnel for the Rangers, Patrick and his advisors would assign other promising young players to their farm teams: the Philadelphia Ramblers and the New York Rovers.

The Rangers had a monopoly of most of the young hockey talent in Canada and their grip on that market wasn't broken until the outbreak of the Second World War. At that point, Lester Patrick moved upstairs to the executive suite and, thereafter, exhibited a curious compulsion to cut operating costs for Madison Square Garden Corporation. He became Scrooge-like in paying salaries to players; the farm-club operations were curtailed but the annual training camp at Winnipeg survived.

In contrast with the Rangers, the Chicago Black Hawks joined the NHL with a rag-tag collection of Western League veterans in 1926. The older Hawks had been great players in their prime, but several of them were members of the Over-the-Hill Gang. In their second season of operation, the Hawks won only seven games in a 44-game schedule.

Initially, the Hawks were regarded by hockey purists as something of a joke. Much of the derision resulted from the peculiar manipulations of Major Frederic B. McLaughlin, the mercurially dispositioned president of the hockey club. Major McLaughlin was a bull-headed martinet who hired and fired hockey coaches on whim. Incredible though it may seem, the Chicago Black Hawks had 13 different coaches in the first 12 years of the franchise's existence.

An additional problem was caused by Major McLaughlin's autocratic wife. Mrs. McLaughlin was the former Irene Castle; she and her brother Vernon Castle had been one of the most famous ballroom-dancing teams in the United States.

Mrs. McLaughlin became an instant expert on professional hockey. She and the major sat directly behind the Black Hawks players' bench and, from that vantage point, the imperious lady enunciated her opinions in a loud, clear voice.

Mrs. McLaughlin's proximity to the bench resulted in the omission of Gordon B. "Duke" Keats's name from the long list of men who coached Chicago.

Late in their first season of operation, the major had made up his mind that he was going to fire Coach Pete

Muldoon and replace him with Keats. However, just before the change was to be made, Keats, who was sitting with his teammates on the bench, heard himself being addressed quite unmistakably by the haughty Mrs. McLaughlin. The dear lady was telling Keats that she wasn't pleased by the manner in which he had played his last shift on the forward line.

Keats, who had been a star in hockey for more than ten years, rose majestically from the Chicago bench. He turned around, handed his hockey stick to Mrs. McLaughlin and told her exactly what she could do with it. The next morning, instead of being appointed coach of the Hawks, Keats was on his way to the farm team at Omaha.

Due to the unseemly haste with which they hired and fired coaches, the Black Hawks organization often was the butt of ridicule among sports commentators who covered the activities of the National Hockey League.

I confess to making my own contribution to the great mass of apocrypha connected with the Chicago franchise. One night at the *Globe and Mail*, I wrote a fictional story in my column about the unseemly dismissal of Pete Muldoon, the first coach of the Black Hawks, by the impatient Major McLaughlin.

According to my column — which was written 30 years after Muldoon disappeared from the hockey scene — Major McLaughlin summoned Pete to his office. It took only a couple of minutes to fire the coach, after which Pete rose from his chair and — according to my imaginative prose — pointed at McLaughlin and said: "I place The Curse of the Muldoon on this team. It is my curse that the Chicago Black Hawks never will finish in first place as long as you own this hockey club."

To my embarrassment, several of my US colleagues revived the story of "The Curse of the Muldoon" when the Hawks, after 44 years of operation, finally finished in first place in the 1966-67 season. I felt obliged to write a disclaimer, but my explanation was ignored; in the sports world, legends often are more entertaining than facts.

In the 12 years from their formation in 1926 — through 1938 — the Hawks were coached by 13 men. Five of those coaches — Barney Stanley, Hugh Lehman, Herb Gardiner, Dick Irvin and Tommy Gorman — subsequently were installed in the Hockey Hall of Fame. Tommy Gorman was the *third* man to coach the team in the 1932-33 season of 48 games.

Gorman, a red-haired Ottawa Irishman, was, in the context of his times, the quintessential Canadian sports promoter. He was quick-witted, ingenious, as mischievous as a leprechaun and magnificently agile in leaping from success to success — his feet barely clearing the yawning chasms of potential disaster.

Thomas Patrick Gorman, the ever-ebullient sporting gadfly, coached the Chicago Black Hawks to the first Stanley Cup triumph in the history of their franchise. That feat alone would entitle a man to be memorialized at considerable length, but for Gorman, it was only a pit-stop on a lifelong joy ride.

The fascinating thing about Gorman was the fact that he usually managed to be in the right place at the right time. He began as a pageboy in the House of Commons. Quickly, he became sports editor of the Ottawa *Citizen*. He was only 28 when he left journalism and formed a partnership with Ted Day to purchase the Ottawa Senators hockey club, a charter member of the National Hockey League.

The Senators, who were bought by Gorman and Day for a piffling $2,500, went on to win the Stanley Cup three times — in 1920, 1921 and 1923 — with Gorman listed as manager-coach. Gorman said later: "I didn't bother to do much coaching. When the players wanted to hold a practice, they took up a collection and sent me out to a movie."

Despite his gift for wry self-deprecation, Tommy was smarter than most of his hockey contemporaries — although they would have refused to acknowledge that fact. As an example of his foresight, Gorman decided late in 1924 that the cities of Ottawa and Hull wouldn't have enough combined population to continue to support an NHL franchise when US cities began to clamour for admission to the League. He guessed, correctly, that the expansion to Boston and New York — and later to Chicago and Detroit, was not far away. Ottawa had been good to Gorman — but the time had come for him to move.

On January 24, 1925, Gorman sold the Ottawa Senators to Frank Ahearn, the proprietor of the Ottawa hydroelectric system. It was an extremely lucrative deal. Gorman received $35,000 for the hockey club which he had bought for $2,500. But that wasn't all! In addition to $35,000 in cash, Gorman received Ahearn's stock in the Connaught Park racetrack, in the Hull suburb of Aylmer, Quebec. Sixty-six years later — in 1990 — Connaught Park still is being operated by T.P. Gorman's descendants. It is the scene of a lengthy annual harness-racing meeting and produces a comfortable annual profit.

Gorman didn't stay around to savour the success of his transaction. Two days after he sold the Ottawa Senators to Frank Ahearn, Tommy became assistant to Tex Rickard at Madison Square Garden in New York City. Officially, Gorman was the manager of the New York Americans, the second US team to be admitted to the NHL. (The Boston Bruins were the first.)

Although he quit the newspaper business when he was 28, Gorman never travelled without his portable typewriter. He maintained a voluminous correspondence with sports editors and sports entrepreneurs in all corners of the continent.

When Gorman had been in New York for slightly less than three years, Sunny Jim Coffroth was completing the construction of the great new Agua Caliente racetrack at Tijuana, Mexico. Coffroth had been receiving letters extolling the virtues of a man named Thomas P. Gorman. Not surprisingly, Coffroth hired Gorman on Christmas Day, 1928.

At that time, horse-racing with pari-mutuel betting wasn't permitted in the State of California. Consequently, members of the Hollywood motion picture colony, loaded with pre-Depression dollars, were regular clients of Agua Caliente, which was just across the border from San Diego. Agua Caliente received a tremendous amount of international publicity because it was the first track in the world to offer a purse of $100,000 annually for a horse-race — the Agua Caliente Handicap.

Agua Caliente racetrack was a thriving establishment for four years, but in 1932, there were two occurrences which shaped Gorman's future. First of all, the California Legislature passed a bill legalizing betting on horse-racing. A great new California track, Santa Anita Park, was under construction and would be ready for operation in 1934. With Santa Anita operating in their own backyard, the well-heeled film stars and their playmates no longer would have to cross the border to enjoy thoroughbred-racing.

Coincidentally, the 1932 renewal of the Agua Caliente Handicap had been won by Phar Lap, probably the best horse ever bred in the Antipodes. Phar Lap was a giant of a thoroughbred and outclassed the US steeds which ran against him at Agua Caliente.

Gorman, sensing that the best days of Agua Caliente were numbered, hit upon a brilliant scheme. He signed a contract with Phar Lap's owner to take the Australian "wonder horse" on an exhibition tour of the major tracks in the United States. It was a "can't miss" plan because

Phar Lap had generated tremendous curiosity among US sports enthusiasts; with the exception of news-reel clips in motion-picture houses, more than 200,000,000 Americans hadn't seen the "Champion from Down Under" in action. (This was almost 20 years before horse-races were televised.)

Gorman and the horse's owner were expecting to split a juicy melon. They had guarantees of more than $200,000 from eastern tracks. Then, something disastrous occurred — Phar Lap died!

Just before the tour was to begin, the horse was grazing on some grass outside his barn at Menlo Park, California. The barn had been spray painted the previous day and some of the paint — which contained arsenate of lead — had blown onto the grass. Phar Lap died of lead poisoning.

This catastrophe would have destroyed a lesser man. But Gorman barely broke stride. Even while he was cooking up the Phar Lap deal, he had been sending a few letters to Major Frederic B. McLaughlin, president of the Chicago Black Hawks. Some of those letters purported to be written by sports editors or hockey men in US cities, but all of them contained the same general message: if Major McLaughlin wished to improve his hockey team, he should obtain the services of Thomas P. Gorman. The major was seduced by the unsolicited mail which came to his desk.

Gorman took over as coach of the Chicago Black Hawks on January 14, 1933. He knew what he needed to convert the Hawks into winners. Immediately, he made a trade to obtain veteran defenceman Lionel Conacher from the Montreal Maroons. Neither Gorman nor Conacher had any illusions about their relationship. Conacher, taking a regular shift on the ice, was going to be the team's playing coach while Gorman walked up and down behind the bench, taking all the bows.

Gorman had been absent from the NHL for five years, but very quickly, his players became aware that he was a multi-talented man who had friends in every newspaper office throughout the entire league. One afternoon, when the Hawks were on a road trip to Montreal, Paul Thompson, the team captain, was sitting in the lobby of the Mount Royal Hotel, reading the sports pages of the Montreal *Star*.

Gorman, who was making one of his customary high speed circuits of the lobby, paused in front of Thompson's seat. Paul looked over his newspaper and said admiringly: "This paper has a very flattering write-up about you. This story says that, in all probability, you're the most astute manager in professional hockey." "Indeed! Indeed!" said Gorman in his staccato fashion. "Well, I'm really not surprised that the Montreal *Star* has such a keen appreciation of my talents. After all, I wrote that particular story myself."

Under the Gorman-Conacher aegis, the Black Hawks showed steady improvement, and 15 months after Gorman arrived in town, Chicago won the Stanley Cup on April 10, 1934.

In that 1933-34 season, Charlie Gardiner had performed magnificently in the Black Hawks nets. Lionel Conacher, who had been reputed to be washed up when he was traded by the Maroons, was a superb ice general and surprised everyone by scoring ten goals and picking up 13 assists in a 48-game schedule. In that particular season, the leading scorer in the American Division of the NHL had 27 goals.

The Black Hawks completed the regular schedule in second place in the American Division. In the playoffs, they eliminated Montreal Canadiens from the opening round. Then they eliminated Montreal Maroons from the semi-finals.

In the Stanley Cup Finals, Chicago defeated the Detroit Red Wings three games to one. The star of the playoffs was

Chuck Gardiner, who had given up a total of only 12 goals in his team's eight playoff games.

The sports fanatics in Chicago celebrated enthusiastically. The Hawks had won the championship of the world of professional hockey in only their eighth year of operation. Gorman, Conacher, Gardiner and the other Black Hawks players became civic heroes overnight.

The only person who wasn't entirely satisfied was Major McLaughlin. For the past six months he had become increasingly nettled by the fact that Gorman was making executive decisions without bothering to consult the president of the hockey club. So — although the Hawks had won the Stanley Cup — McLaughlin had decided that Gorman would be replaced by Clem Loughlin to coach the Black Hawks for the next season.

As usual, Tommy was several jumps ahead of everyone. For some months, he had been conducting a correspondence with Senator Donat Raymond, president of the Canadian Arena Company in Montreal. The Canadian Arena Company owned two NHL teams — the Montreal Maroons and the Montreal Canadiens.

Before the victory champagne had gone flat in Chicago, Gorman was on his way to Montreal to be coach of the Maroons. With him he took Lionel Conacher who had been the ice engineer behind the Black Hawk success.

Once again, the Gorman Magic worked immediately. The Maroons finished second in the Candian Division at the end of the 1934-35 regular schedule. With a fine touch of irony, they eliminated the Chicago Black Hawks from the first round of the playoffs. Then they eliminated the New York Rangers from the semi-finals. And, in the Stanley Cup Finals, they beat the heavily favoured Toronto Maple Leafs, three games to none.

Thomas Gorman had accomplished a hockey feat which never has been duplicated. He had coached two hockey teams — in two different cities — to Stanley Cup victories in two successive seasons.

To no one's surprise, Gorman soon became general manager of the Canadian Arena Company. Financial retrenchment during the Depression led to the disbandment of the Maroons, and Les Canadiens became Montreal's only NHL team.

In the summer of 1940, Gorman made one of his most astute moves when he hired Dick Irvin to coach Les Canadiens. Irvin had become increasingly restive in eight years of coaching the Toronto Maple Leafs for the autocratic Conn Smythe.

Superficially, there were similarities in the public personalities of Smythe and McLaughlin, but Smythe was — by a million light-years — the smarter hockey man.

By the spring of 1946, Les Canadiens, coached by Irvin, had won the Stanley Cup twice within three years. After 12 years in Montreal it was time for Gorman to move on. In addition to managing the Forum, he had been managing the annual thoroughbred-racing meetings at Montreal's Blue Bonnet tracks, and receiving a fee for his services. If you count Gorman's three youthful triumphs in Ottawa, he had been coach or manager of seven teams which won the Stanley Cup.

He left Montreal but retirement was far from his mind. He returned to his hometown of Ottawa and bought the Auditorium, the local ice arena, for $50,000. He operated the Ottawa team in minor league professional hockey and conducted horse-racing at Connaught Park.

Even those activities didn't entirely satisfy his restless spirit. After Barbara Ann Scott, Canada's world champion figure skater, had completed her contract with US promoters, Tommy conceived the idea of starring Miss Scott in an ice show which would tour every Canadian city — including many smaller cities which, up until then, never had seen a major ice show.

To the surprise of Gorman's critics (and, indeed, he had managed to acquire many of *those* in his colourful career), the ice show was a resounding success. It was reputed to have earned more than $200,000 for Miss Scott and her mother over a period of 30 weeks.

Gorman always was engagingly coy about revealing his share of the profits from any promotion. All he would say about the ice show was: "Oh, we did quite well! Quite well indeed!" He was a character — he deserves a special niche in Canada's Sports Hall of Fame.

Let us return to the sorry saga of the unfortunate men who coached the Chicago Black Hawks.

Clem Loughlin succeeded Tommy Gorman and managed to retain the support of his employer for three seasons. Then, in the autumn of 1937, Major McLaughlin once again stunned the hockey world when he hired Bill Stewart to coach the Black Hawks.

Stewart was unusual in several respects. First, he was an American. Second, he had achieved his greatest fame as a longtime umpire in the National Baseball League. Third, he was an NHL referee when Major McLaughlin decided that he had the qualifications to be a hockey coach.

Stewart's appointment occasioned a lot of derisive laughter around the National Hockey League. But grumpy Bill confounded his traducers. In Stewart's second season as coach, the Black Hawks won the Stanley Cup.

In the spring of 1938, the Hawks eliminated Les Canadiens from the opening round of the playoffs. They went on to eliminate the New York Americans from the semi-finals and then they whipped the over-confident Toronto Maple Leafs, three games to one, in the Stanley Cup Final.

Less than a year after his team won the Stanley Cup, Bill Stewart was gone — replaced by Paul Thompson.

The Black Hawks didn't win the championship again until 1961. By that time, Major McLaughlin had gone to join his ancestors and the Chicago franchise was being operated by James D. Norris and William Wirtz.

The third man to coach the Hawks to a Stanley Cup victory was, in his own way, quite as unusual as Tommy Gorman and Bill Stewart.

Rudy Pilous was born in Winnipeg of Bohemian parentage. He was a lifelong hockey man but he never played in the NHL. He had coached successfully in the Minor League professional ranks and was the founding manager-coach of the St. Catharines TeePees, one of the most successful junior clubs in Canadian history. When the Teepees produced such players as Bobby Hull, Stan Mikita, Pierre Pilote and Elmer Vasko for the Chicago Black Hawks, Norris and Wirtz moved in to buy the St. Catharines franchise. And they began to toy with the idea of giving the effervescent Pilous a chance to coach in the NHL.

Midway through the 1957-58 season, Pilous was brought up to coach the Hawks. From being perennial tail-enders, they improved to third-place finishes in the NHL in 1959 and 1960.

Then in the spring of 1961, they hit the jackpot, winning the Stanley Cup. Glenn Hall provided magnificent goaltending, and Coach Pilous was handling a well-balanced team which appeared capable of staying close to the top of the heap for several years.

Co-owner Norris was charmed by Rudy's success and intrigued by Rudy's gift of the gab. This happy relationship chilled slightly in the spring of 1962 when the Black Hawks lost the Stanley Cup to the Toronto Maple Leafs.

When the Hawks were blown out of the semi-finals in 1963 — only two years after winning the championship — Pilous realized that he soon would share the fate of the 21 men who had preceded him in the Chicago coaching job.

Ultimately, Pilous was the victim of an insurrection. A group of senior Black Hawks players got the ear of Jim Norris and complained that Rudy wasn't treating them with the deference due to wealthy professionals.

Norris, to his discredit, listened to the players and dumped Pilous. Rudy was crushed, but he managed to crack: "I don't know where I went wrong. This season, I have been opening and shutting the gate to the players' bench exactly the same way I was doing it when we won the Stanley Cup two years ago."

Possibly, they haven't been much worse than other NHL clubs but the Black Hawks acquired a reputation for giving rather shabby treatment to longtime employees when the time came to get rid of them.

I was fantasizing when I wrote in the *Globe and Mail* that Pete Muldoon put a "curse" on the Chicago Black Hawks when he was discharged. But, 63 years later, I'm beginning to suspect that Old Pete really *did* subject the hockey club to The Curse of the Muldoon.

I remember now, that when Vern DeGeer was sports editor of the *Globe and Mail*, he took a rather cynical view of NHL club owners. DeGeer used to say: "Hockey *must* be a great game because it continues to prosper, despite the worst efforts of the men who run it!"

PART 5

RACETRACK REPRISE

MORNING ON THE BACKSTRETCH

I HAVE A RECURRENT DREAM ABOUT SADDLING A WINNER of The Queen's Plate. I realize that it must be one of my very old dreams because it's in black-and-white. I'm 79 now but this same dream persists. In fact, the older I am, the more I dream — although not always about the racetrack. In all those dreams, I'm a very active participant — not merely a spectator.

Many of my night-time flashbacks are wide-screen stuff in living colour. These technicolour retrospectives feature disastrous drinking parties, long-dead playmates, former girl-friends and even world-class politicians, most of whom I knew only by reputation. For instance, last night, Rt. Hon. Lester B. Pearson and I were sharing a seat in an Ottawa Airport bus which drove us right to the front door of the Parliament Buildings. Well, I *did* know Mr. Pearson but not well enough for him to mention me in his autobiography.

Some night, before I go to the Big Press Box in the sky,

I'm going to reach a satisfactory conclusion to my recurrent dream about The Queen's Plate. So far, all the pieces haven't fitted together. I dream that I'm saddling an entry in Canada's most famous thoroughbred horse-race, but I've never been a properly licensed trainer. And always I awaken before the race is completed. On a dozen occasions, my horse has been charging along with a comfortable lead, deep into the homestretch, but always the film runs out before we reach the finish post. The dream never will be complete until I'm in a bank, cashing the cheque for more than $200,000 which the Ontario Jockey Club issues to the owner of the winner.

Many of us who aren't perfectly sculptured human beings have found fantasy to be preferable to reality. Even today, in the era of instant global communications, the racetrack is one place where, still, you can escape from the real world.

There is something about the racetrack which reaches out and clings to me forever. With each day's bright dawning, I hear the siren call. If I was younger, I'd slip out of bed quietly, don some old clothes and get into my car to drive to the track. You don't bother to shave when you're going directly from bed to the track — just a waste of time in the backstretch where scruffiness is a carefully nourished conceit.

When you show your pass at the stable gate, you're ready to enter a world of silent acceptance. No one asks questions, apart from a politely non-committal, "Are you okay?"

As you pass acquaintances standing outside the open door of a tackroom, they offer you a drink. It is a normal gesture of hospitality. They know that you quit drinking years ago, but they are aware, also, that the path of human abstinence is full of pitfalls. There never can be any absolute certainty that this won't be the morning when a man changes his mind; his wife may have left him for a television preacher, the bank may have foreclosed on his loan, his daughter may have been impregnated by a defensive halfback from the University of Southern California.

So, the offer of a post-dawn drink is declined politely, but somehow it's comforting to know that a well-wisher is keeping your franchise open.

This oasis in the land of escapism is familiar territory for me. For the first 46 years of my life, I was in flight from reality. I'm not going to bore you with an explanation of my conduct, but my particular form of schizophrenia could have been diagnosed quickly by any shrink into whose hands I tumbled. As it was, I didn't seek help until it was almost too late. I lived two lives: one, the newspaperman who drank too much but who usually managed to complete his work; the other, the escapist who spent much of his time in a dream world populated by horses, horsemen, gamblers, bookmakers, touts, carnies, stock hustlers and oddball sports promoters, most of whom were no better than the Good Lord intended them to be.

I was addicted to the racetrack and the sports world in general long before I got into the newspaper business. I was a privileged intruder on the backstretch at Whittier Park and Polo Park in Winnipeg in my early teens.

Those were the days when you could do anything you were big enough to do and horse-racing in our section of the land still was conducted under "Hudson's Bay Rules."

There were no film patrol cameras to pry into the illegal riding practices of some strong-armed jockeys. There were no saliva tests or urine tests to ascertain whether a horse's performance had been improved by a slight shot of cocaine or heroin.

Of course, these were the days when *horses* were the only athletes who received drug injections. No one yet had thought of the possibilities of injecting human sprinters or weight lifters with steroids.

In Toronto, the introduction of film-patrol motion pictures and drug tests had put a distinct crimp in the activities of some of my friends among the horse trainers and jockeys.

Toronto immediately provided widened scope for my alcohol-fuelled imagination. I found myself intrigued by the activities of local citizens who rejoiced in such pseudonyms as Charlie Snakes, Joe the Goof, The Good Kid, The Mad Russian, Slow, Little Slow, Whitey the Pest, Maxie Chicago, The Senator, Toothpick Tommy, Chicken-Pie, Banjo-Jack, Centrefield-Willie, Break-the-Bed Louie and Johnny Come-Lately.

Many of those colourfully named gentlemen lived semi-normal lives. Even those who were involved in slightly larcenous activities had wives, sired children and tipped their wide-brimmed hats to ladies on the city's walkways.

None of my acquaintances in that assemblage had any use for Break-the-Bed Louie. His nickname stemmed from the excessive enthusiasm with which he embarked upon his amatory adventures. Louie's behaviour was so widely deplored that, one night, several chaps stabbed him full of holes and stuffed his body into the trunk of their car. They buried him in a huge snowdrift alongside Highway 27, on the way to Toronto International Airport. He wasn't found until spring when the snowdrift melted.

I don't recall that Louie's passing caused any mourning. In fact, some persons mentioned, without emotion, that it reminded them of the circumstances under which Whitey the Pest left Toronto.

Whitey had an argument with a bookmaker and, jumping into his car after the tiff, ran over the bookie in a laneway in a quiet working-class neighbourhood. Then, just to be sure that his message would be understood, Whitey put his car into reverse gear and *backed* over the fallen bookie.

Around Toronto, conventional wisdom had it that, because the bookmaker had cheated Whitey in their business dealings, the bookie deserved to be scrounged. But when

Whitey *backed* his car over the bookie, he was going too far. There was general agreement that Whitey the Pest deserved to be exiled to the United States — where he fled.

At first I found Ontario horsemen slightly reserved in comparison with the more carefree characters I had known in the West. Ontario tracks already subscribed to the repressive legislation which had been introduced to the sport in major North American racing jurisdictions. East of the Great Lakes, banditry had been outlawed!

It was time to re-educate myself. Out west, I had known trainers whose skill with a hypodermic needle and mixture of drugs could inspire a slow horse to run a hole in the wind. I still can remember some trainers on the prairies who, with a single injection, could persuade a horse to climb into the branches of a nearby tree and sing "The Star-Spangled Banner" in a clear Irish choir-boy tenor.

I discovered that there were Ontario horsemen who knew more tricks than Harry Houdini. But with "The Coming of the Law," trainers were obliged to become more sophisticated. All of them managed to present a public appearance of such piety that it was virtually impossible to distinguish the unrepentant knaves from the genuine church wardens.

On one of my first visits to the backstretch at Old Woodbine, I overheard a practicing veterinary surgeon, much respected in his profession, telling a couple of trainers about a new "powder," imported from Mexico, which was guaranteed to make even a slow horse run very speedily.

Many trainers still were on the lookout for any stimulant which couldn't be detected by the drug-testing equipment. So, it was only natural that one of the trainers should ask the veterinarian how the "powder" could be administered to a horse.

"Well," said the veterinarian, "you pour the powder into the palm of your left hand. Then you face the horse, head-on. And you take a firm grip on his halter with your *right* hand.

When you've got him settled down, you reach up with your right foot and you give the horse a solid kick in the nuts. When the horse opens his mouth to scream, you blow the powder down his throat."

The veterans among the trainers on the Ontario racing circuit were, for the most part, a close-mouthed group. Obviously, they had their little secrets which they didn't choose to share with the entire world.

E.P. Taylor, later to become the most influential man in the history of Canadian horse-racing, was making his first appearance on the Ontario tracks, racing under the nom-de-course Cosgrave Stable. His trainer was Bert Alexandra, one of the shrewdest horse conditioners in all of North America.

Alexandra, who was English-born of Greek heritage, had become "rich and pious" by the time he was training for E.P. Taylor, but in his younger days, Bert was reputed to exercise an intellect which was keener than a Toledo blade.

Alexandra deserves nomination to the Racing Hall of Fame if only for the unique success which he enjoyed as the trainer of an equine rogue named Carefree. Although many other men attempted to train Carefree, Bert was the only man who could persuade the horse to win.

This scatty thoroughbred gelding lived up to his name. He performed some amazing capers on the track. On two occasions, while leading comfortably in the homestretch, he dug his front feet into the ground, came to a dead stop and whimsically watched his rivals rush past him to the finish post.

Alexandra didn't worry about running Carefree in cheap claiming races because most rival horsemen had learned that there was no point in claiming the gelding. Those other trainers simply couldn't persuade the horse to *win*. Within a week or so after claiming Carefree, the disgusted new trainer would be asking Bert to take the old horse off his hands.

The record books of the North American turf reveal that Carefree won a total of 67 races. For 66 of those wins, he was saddled by Bert Alexandra. All the other men who owned the eccentric animal combined to win *only one race*.

Bert Alexandra knew something about Carefree, a secret which never was discovered by any of the other men who attempted to win with the horse. Bert never shared his secret. A contemporary said: "Bert never was upset when someone claimed his old horse, because Bert kept the horse's 'prescription' locked in his personal safety-deposit box."

In my time, I've seen many other examples of a "one-man horse." For instance, Colonel K.R. Marshall, the president of the Ontario Jockey Club, bred a horse named Big Fish.

Colonel Marshall turned over Big Fish to two or three different trainers in an attempt to make the horse run fast enough to win a race. A couple of the most astute trainers in Canada tested Big Fish thoroughly — but they couldn't persuade him to win. So, utterly disgusted, Colonel Marshall sold Big Fish for only $500 to a struggling young horseman named Bill Raines.

Over the years, Big Fish won 39 races for Bill Raines. Other trainers claimed the horse from time to time, but they couldn't persuade him to win. As was the case with Bert Alexandra and Carefree, Bill Raines was the only man who knew Big Fish's secret prescription — and the horse went to the equine Valhalla without any rival trainers having seen his hole-card.

Bert Alexandra was a loner and wasn't particularly popular with other trainers. In his younger years, he had displayed slightly unbecoming enthusiasm for "claiming" horses from his rivals. No one was immune when Bert saw what he believed to be a horse which was entered below its true value. One trainer told me, with more than a touch of bitterness, that Alexandra would claim a horse from his own mother.

Another reason for Alexandra's slight unpopularity may have been his biting sarcasm. He was quick to needle any trainer who had committed an obvious error in judgment. I had occasion to be the butt of his wit.

I owned a three-year-old named Broom Time, which my father had bought for me as a yearling. I brought him to Ontario where he won a race as a two-year-old and then he won two more races at three — but always he was running at a cheap claiming price. He was running for a $1,000 claiming price in his third win and an old farmer named Tom Frost paid the $1,000 to claim him.

Three weeks later, Frost ran Broom Time in the Breeder's Stakes. The Breeder's had a purse of only $5,000 in those days, but the winner's share of $3,500 was considerably better than a kick in the butt. To my understandable chagrin, Broom Time — which I had permitted to be taken away from me for only $1,000 — *won* the Breeder's Stakes.

My sorrow and embarrassment were mitigated to some extent by the fact that I bet $50 to win on Broom Time, which paid $56.10. I collected $1,402 — but I knew that, behind my back, people were having a sardonic laugh at my expense.

Bert Alexandra was waiting for me as I walked swiftly through the paddock. Without a word, he shoved something into my right hand — it was a gift-wrapped match box.

I was alone in a cubicle in the washroom of the Club House before I dared to take the gift-wrapping off the match box. The match box contained two aspirin tablets.

Although drugs weren't a subject for public discussion round the tracks when I arrived in Ontario, there were many trainers who still surreptitiously used "joints" — tiny hand batteries — to stimulate their horses. It's amazing how a sluggish horse can become instantly animated when the business end of a battery is pressed against his skin.

Discussions of drugs were taboo, but you could joke about "joints" with comparative immunity. After the stewards suspended a groom who was found carrying a hand battery in his raincoat pocket, I wrote in my *Globe and Mail* column that "around Woodbine, you could find enough batteries to provide electric light for the entire city of Oakville." The written comment didn't elicit any rebuttals from the racing authorities. They knew it, too.

One day, I was sitting on the outside rail at Dufferin Park, watching the runners going to the paddock for the next race. As one horse pranced past me (he was acting quite frisky), I thought that I recognized Stand Easy, a veteran selling plater whose performance always was sparkling if he had received some pre-race electric energizing.

So I asked the groom who was leading the horse: "Is that Stand Easy?"

"Yes, sir," the groom replied genially. "It's the old Presto-Lite Kid in person."

I had discovered the fantasy world of the racetrack when I was a small boy in Winnipeg. I was unaware then that it would become my refuge when I grew older and acquired the vices which were to cause so much emotional turmoil for my family and me.

Fifty-five years ago, the backstretch of a Canadian racetrack was exclusively a male domain. The trainers, the jockeys and the grooms were all men.

A woman on the backstretch was a rarity. At Old Woodbine, there was Mrs. Belanger, whose husband, Leo, operated the track kitchen. It would be more accurate to say that Mrs. Belanger operated the kitchen while Leo gassed with the customers. There was Judy Johnson from Baltimore, who became the first woman trainer on Ontario tracks when she shipped in with a stable of horses for the steeplechases and the hurdle races. There was Peggy Major, who assisted her husband, Jack Major, with the chores around the barns.

Before I left the West, there had been Babe Barnes, the wife of Stub Barnes who trained on the prairie tracks. But Babe, as she sat in front of the tackroom with a cigarette dangling from her mouth, looked so tough that she could have been mistaken for a man.

Earlier, there had been dear old Jessie Mackenzie on the British Columbia tracks. Jessie was the first woman to be licensed as a trainer in western Canada and she was unique. Whenever one of her horses was running, she'd stand in the infield, shaking her Mackenzie tartan skirt vigorously and singing one of her hit songs from her youth on the stage of British music halls.

It wasn't until the 1950s that trainers began to hire women to gallop and groom their horses. It had taken many years for trainers to recognize the obvious fact that women were much more satisfactory and reliable than men as stable help. Women didn't drink as much as men. Women were neater and cleaner than men.

Male grooms were inclined to dress in the same old pants and rough shirts for weeks at a stretch and took few shower-baths. The older grooms, whose only home usually was a tackroom at the end of the barn, were notorious for the griminess of their apparel.

It is safe to say that the standards of personal cleanliness on Canadian tracks improved about 500 percent when trainers began to hire female grooms and exercise women. Simultaneously, most of the larger tracks built dormitories to house the increasing population of female employees.

Looking back on the all-male population of the backstretch in the distant past, I am inclined to believe that many of them were confirmed misogynists.

Some grooms — usually the more ambitious among them who hoped, some day, to become trainers — were married.

They had homes and children. When the horses were racing at Toronto tracks, they went home each evening and returned to the track about 6:00 the following morning. However, when racing shifted to the tracks at Hamilton, Fort Erie or Niagara Falls, those married men left their homes for weeks on end and slept in tackrooms at the tracks.

Many of the oldtimers among the grooms appeared to have no homes other than the racetrack. When the Canadian racing season closed down for the winter, those old gaffers signed on with some trainer who was taking a carload of horses to tracks in the southern United States. Or a trainer who was wintering his horses on an Ontario farm might take one of the veteran grooms to the farm for the duration. They were a strange but dedicated crew — those old coots, such as Coleman O'Flaherty, Bohunk Shorty, Centrefield Willie and Skippy Lawrence.

Skip Lawrence epitomized those career grooms who didn't appear to have any home but the racetrack. He worked for my friend Morris Fishman. If Skip had kith or kin, he kept that information a closely guarded secret.

When ladies came around the barns at the track (usually they were the wives or girlfriends of some of Morris's racing patrons), Skip would beat a quick retreat, busying himself at the far end of the barn and grumbling aloud to himself.

Once, Skip took up residence at Morris Fishman's farm where the trainer was wintering his horses. Possibly, the effects of living in a cottage and sleeping between real sheets had thawed Skip's personality, but I damn nearly fell off my kitchen chair when, one afternoon, I saw the old misogynist actually *winking* at a woman.

Six of us were sitting around the kitchen table, drinking rye. The lady in question was in her prime and elegantly dressed. I happened to look round just in time to see Skippy staring at her, his right eye closing and opening again in a wink. The lady was a dear. Concentrating on Skip as if he was the only man in the room, the lady winked right back. It must have given old Skipper his jollies for the entire winter.

I've always suspected that there is a special God who looks after children and drunken racetrackers. Old Skipper Lawrence must have been among those who, from the cradle, were chosen for special care.

Fishman had been racing his horses on New England tracks one autumn. At the conclusion of a meeting, the horses were loaded into what was known as a "palace baggage car" which was attached to a passenger train for shipment to Toronto via Buffalo. The grooms, including Skip, rode in the palace car with the horses. They slept on camp cots. Before turning in, they knocked off a couple of bottles of rye in anticipation of a long, boring train ride to Toronto.

In the middle of the night, Skip was awakened by an uncontrollable urge to have a pee. He staggered out of his cot and opened the sliding middle door on the baggage car as the train rocketed through the night at more than 60 miles per hour.

As Skip was in the middle of his proceedings, the train lurched around a fairly sharp curve. Skip, who was far from steady on his feet, toppled through the open door and disappeared from the train as it sped on its mission of commerce.

It wasn't until some time later that one of the other grooms woke. He saw that the baggage car door was open. And he saw quickly that Skip's cot was empty.

Any sober man who fell through the open door of the train, travelling at 60 miles per hour, would have been maimed at the very least — if he hadn't been killed outright.

However, that special God had his eye on Skippy Lawrence. Skip landed in a dry ditch beside the railway right-of-way. Both his legs were broken, but he wasn't even knocked unconscious. The night was black. Skip, lying there helpless, began to hoot and holler, but the odds against anyone hearing him were approximately 100 to 1.

Miraculously, someone *did* hear him. An hour or so earlier, two convicts had escaped from a minimum security state penitentiary and, in order to avoid probable road blocks set up by the police on the main highways, had been walking along the railway tracks.

Just before the locomotive headlight picked them up, they had taken refuge in the dry ditch beside the right-of-way. They were hiding less than 50 yards from the spot where Skip landed when he fell through the door of the train.

These two men were convicted felons but they weren't hardened criminals. They could have walked away, but their humanitarian instincts got the better of them. They picked up Skip who, after all, didn't weigh much more than 110 pounds, and carried him to a nearby farm house. Then they sacrificed their own bid for freedom when they asked the farmer to telephone the State Police to send out an ambulance to take the injured racetrack groom to hospital. There's a doubly happy ending to the story. The judge, before whom the two convicts were arraigned for jail-breaking, suspended sentence on them and granted them an early release from prison.

Skip Lawrence was back on the job at Fishman's barn within six weeks. When he became too old and crotchety to be a nursemaid to horses, the Ontario Jockey Club invented a nice, cushy job for him as gateman at the entrance to the Woodbine training track.

Those old guys keep coming back to me in my recurrent dream about The Queen's Plate. They never age a bit, although 20 years must have passed since last I saw Skip Lawrence leaning on the gate to the Woodbine training track. They loom up there in the swirling mist, fresh and sassy and always thirsty. I don't know how much whiskey we consumed around the shed rows in those early years in

Toronto, but it was more than enough to float the entire Atlantic Fleet of the US Navy.

Long-forgotten persons and incidents are reproduced in my nocturnal adventures in film land. Only a couple of nights ago I was dreaming about Amos, Frank Stocker's big black dog, and Tansey the Tout.

Stocker was assistant track superintendent at Thorncliffe, the now-forgotten one-mile track in the Leaside area of Toronto. The track concessionaire at Thorncliffe, Eddie Washburn, had a chef named Andy, who carved the roasts to produce the beef or ham sandwiches which were sold at booths under the Thorncliffe grand stand. At the end of an afternoon of racing, Andy usually would give the remains of a hambone to Amos. The dog, which was a Newfoundland about the size of a polo pony, would lug the hambone to his kennel and gnaw on it all evening. Then, Tansey came along to crab Amos's act.

Tansey officially was listed as a "clocker", but really he was a tout, selling information about the morning workouts to gullible clients. Anyhow, Tansey persuaded Andy to give him a hambone at the end of an afternoon to take home to gnaw on in his rented room.

The first time that Amos saw Tansey disappearing down the roadway carrying a hambone, the big dog gave chase. Amos never would go any further than the Thorncliffe gate which opened into Laird Drive.

This race used to take place every evening during the Thorncliffe spring or summer meeting. The racetrack "regulars" used to gather to watch Amos making his nightly charge in pursuit of the fleeing Tansey. Amos could have *caught* Tansey any time he wished — but for the huge dog, it just became a daily game.

Then, one night, Tansey found a message waiting for him at his rented room. It was his draft call. So that night, Tansey went back to Thorncliffe and dropped over to Amos's kennel. "Big dog," said Tansey, "I've got to leave here tomorrow morning because President Roosevelt has asked me to look after a problem he's having with some Krauts. But as soon as I straighten out this war business, I'll come back to see you."

Tansey never returned to Toronto. A piece of shrapnel with his name on it caught up with him in the Ardennes.

The word about Tansey reached Thorncliffe the next spring when Tom "Longboy" Ellison checked in from Baltimore. While Tony Simms was conducting the draw for post positions for the opening day's program, Longboy told how Tansey's parents in Baltimore had received a letter from one of General Dwight D. Eisenhower's regimental commanders telling them that Tansey had done a hell of a good job for the Allies. Amos, the big black dog, was lying outside the open door of Tony Simms's office while Longboy was talking. That same day, Frank Stocker found Amos lying motionless on the grass just inside the Thorncliffe gate which opened into Laird Drive. He called to Amos — but Amos didn't answer.

I've always believed that Amos understood every word of the conversation which took place in Tony Simms's office. And the big dog simply decided that it was his own time to go, because without Tansey to chase, life would have lost most of its meaning.

Undoubtedly, that world of fantasy on the backstretch wasn't always as glamorous as I imagined it to be. The morning ingestion of alcohol heightened the cosy belief that we were inhabiting a different planet. It's amazing that we didn't contract every disease in the book. There would be ten or 15 of us drinking every morning, sharing the same three or four glasses which never seemed to get broken. We should have contracted the hoof-and-mouth disease or pyorrhea, but we survived, generally unscathed. It must have been the whiskey that killed all the germs.

Some of the characters from my night dreams keep popping up, quite unexpectedly, in real life. After the

Southams turned me out to pasture in 1983, I spent the next three years working as an over-aged publicist for the horse-racing department of the Calgary Stampede. Then I retired to Vancouver and, on my very first trip to the thoroughbred-races at Exhibition Park, I discovered that Gyp the Blood was still alive and frisky. Talk about deja vu! This was ridiculous! Gyp the Blood was a candidate for extinction more than 50 years ago!

George Starkell (aka Gyp the Blood) came into my life when I was a cub reporter on the Winnipeg *Tribune* in 1931. There he was, almost 60 years later, lounging comfortably in a box seat in the Club House of Exhibition Park, talking away in his familiar hoarse voice, sounding as if his throat was full of iron filings.

When I first knew Gyp the Blood, he was, by day, a hustler with headquarters in the Stag Poolroom, a Donald Street establishment owned by Squinchy Leib and Louie Silverman. By night, Gyp the Blood was a bootlegger, selling home-distilled rye and gin out of the office of the Blue Line Taxi in a garage behind the Canada Block.

I wasn't a client of the bookmaking establishment in the Stag Poolroom but in emergencies I bought bootleg gin or rye from Gyp at the garage in midtown Winnipeg. Even then, Gyp was acquiring a national reputation as a hustler. Whenever Bill Eddy, the chief of the Winnipeg Police Morality Squad, issued an order to "round up all the usual suspects," Gyp would have been offended if he wasn't included.

Looking at Gyp today, and recognizing the glint of larceny which still slumbers in his darting eyes, I am reminded of the story which a Winnipeg oldtimer told me about the afternoon when Gyp "laid" all the customers in the Stag on a horse named Pension, which was running in the seventh race at Regina.

In the great tradition of touting, "there's a story goes with it." No self-respecting tout would lay a client on a horse without providing some feed-box information which would justify complete confidence in that particular steed.

Gyp's story was a zinger. Gathering his clients around him in the Stag, he assured them that Pension was a gilt-edged certainty. The jockey had telephoned long distance from Regina that very morning to inform Gyp that he would be carrying a "joint" when he rode Pension — and it was common knowledge on prairie tracks that Pension was a horse that ran with amazing speed when he was stimulated electrically.

The seventh race at Regina was scheduled to go to the post at 5:45 P.M. But because the two cities are in different time zones, the race would start at 6:45 Winnipeg time. So, many of Gyp's clients risked the wrath of their wives by keeping dinner simmering while they awaited the result of the seventh race from Regina. Impatiently, they listened for the chatter of the teletype printer tapping out the result of the seventh.

Finally — after a long delay — the result came through. There was instant consternation — Pension had *not* won. In fact, Pension hadn't even finished in the first three at Regina.

Several disgruntled bettors picked up billiard cues and, with mayhem on their minds, looked around for Gyp the Blood. But Gyp had softshoed out of there at the first hint of trouble. He didn't even bother to occupy his customary booth in Jack Cancilla's Café later that evening.

The next day, as bold as brass, Gyp was back at his regular stand in the Stag Poolroom. He was ready with a story which completely placated even the most indignant bet-loser.

"Last night, Jockey Russell telephoned me at home to tell me why Pension didn't win," Gyp said smoothly.

"Shortly before five o'clock yesterday afternoon, Regina was hit by a cloudburst which was close to typhoon proportions. The racetrack was completely flooded. By the time the last field went to the post, the water on the track must have been close to three inches deep."

Gyp had them in his mitt by the time he reached this stage of his explanation. Then he hit them with the punchline. "Seeing all that water on the track, Jockey Russell decided that it was unsafe to use his battery — because he was afraid that he might *electrocute* the nice old horse."

DEACON ALLEN

APART FROM NEWS MEDIA FRIENDS, MY CLOSEST ASSOciates over the years have been racetrackers, professional athletes and professional promoters of all types.

The first promoter I knew was Ivan Mikailoff, who came from Toronto to stage professional wrestling shows in Winnipeg. He lived in a residential block — appropriately named the Ivan Apartments — and, when newspapermen visited him there, he served them his own favourite drink: a mixture of Benedictine and Scotch whiskey.

Mikailoff's concoction wasn't lethal, but it rattled the fillings in one's teeth. For short-fused explosive power it was surpassed only by the mixture which trainer Bob Ramsay injected into his race horses. Bob put great faith in his prescription of one and one-half grains of heroin, mixed with belladonna in a bottle of brandy.

When newspaper employment took me to Vancouver

from Winnipeg, the wrestling franchise in the West Coast city was operated by a large gentleman with the resounding name of Emil Klank. But there I also met John Finlay Allen, whose career as a boxing promoter already had resulted in some rather spectacular disasters.

History will record that, in his years as a sports entrepreneur, Allen went broke in Vancouver, Calgary, Edmonton, Winnipeg, New York City and Toronto. He said cheerfully: "I would have gone broke in Lethbridge, too. But in Lethbridge, I had a partner named Chippy Max who cheated me out of my share of the loss and he went broke all by himself."

Even when I first met him in 1933, Jack Allen appeared to be considerably older than his real age. It was his demeanor which fooled people. He dressed very soberly, usually in well-cut, dark suits. He wore thick spectacles which he described as "my cheaters." And he glided rather than walked.

He went to New York and became assistant matchmaker to James Joy Johnston (The Boy Bandit) at Madison Square Garden. It was Allen's habitually solemn air which inspired Damon Runyon to give him the nickname "The Deacon." The sobriquet stuck with him for the rest of his life.

Our first meetings in western Canada had been superficial, but we became close friends when I moved to Toronto and became a sport columnist at the *Globe and Mail*.

In Sacramento, Allen had grown up next door to Ancil Hoffman, who managed Max Baer to the world heavyweight boxing championship. Not far away lived Jack Kearns, the immortal manager of such immortal champions as Jack Dempsey and Archie Moore.

Kearns and Hoffman certainly were among the most astute of all fight managers of their or anyone else's time. Archie Moore, with awe in his voice, said of Kearns: "If you gave Jack a ball of steel wool, he'd knit you a stove."

The power of example provided by his famous neighbours probably lured Allen into the business of managing pugilists. Already he had discarded the thought of manual labour.

Allen seldom referred to his early schooling, but it was obvious that he had acquired some education because he could write his own press releases and was surprisingly well read. He was articulate and well mannered. His parents were Irish-Americans. His father had been a boomer telegraph operator for Western Union, jumping from city to city until finally he settled in Sacramento. It is probable that Allen inherited his lusty thirst from his roving father and most of his couth from his mother.

Occasionally, when we were drinking in his room at the Walsingham Hotel, Allen would show me the letters he was receiving from his mother, then living in Alameda. The Deacon was 60 and his mother must have been in her 80s, but her letters were written in a bold, educated hand. Even at that age, she still was worrying about her errant son. In her letters, she adjured him to dress warmly for Toronto's frigid winters and she mailed him woolen socks which she had knitted.

Jack must have inherited some strong strain of gentility from his mother because he was innately polite — even when he was so drunk that he couldn't move. He may have spent all his adult life cavorting with weird characters from the half-world of sports and entertainment, but his raffish charm seldom deserted him.

In his latter years, warm-hearted women always were inclined to feel protective of Allen. One night, a beautiful lady looked at the old reprobate and said fondly: "Jack, I'm going to have to find some really nice girl to marry you and look after you." "Why pick on me?" cried Allen, recoiling as if he had been bitten by a puff-adder. "I've already served *two* ten-year terms."

Allen first "burst into obscurity" — as he phrased it — in Fresno, California, in the early days of motion-picture theatres.

His initial venture was a partnership with the Great Morton, an acrobat. Morton would perform his death-defying feats on a tight wire, strung between the tops of two telephone poles outside a movie house. Allen would shout into a megaphone to attract a crowd to watch the Great Morton in action — four or five times daily before inducing them to go into the theatre to watch one of those new-fangled motion pictures. It was basic schlock, but after all, Californians weren't overly sophisticated in 1915.

On closing night, after they had played a full week in Fresno, the Great Morton persuaded Allen to pack their gear while the acrobat toddled over to the theatre box-office to collect their performing fee.

Allen still was rolling up their high-wire cable when he noticed the Great Morton clambering into their car and driving away. That was the last Allen ever saw of Morton or the car.

During a period of healing in Sacramento Allen was associated with Ancil Hoffman in promoting boxing shows. Emboldened to branch out on his own, he went across the border to Mexicali where he promoted boxing shows staged in the local open-air bullring.

Mexicali could be a bit too exciting in those days. The Mexican Army and rebel bands frequently exchanged shots in the streets, and the marksmanship of the combatants was notoriously inaccurate.

After a couple of near-misses, Allen decided to seek a colder climate in which to amass his fortune. This led him to board a steamship bound for Anchorage, Alaska. He became a partner in a gambling house, and in some miraculous fashion, he acquired the only two taxi-cabs in town.

In 1917, Anchorage was a US government enclave and there were no liquor stores within that community. Allen put his two taxi-cabs to good use. His drivers bought liquor in other communities, where the sale of spirits was legal, and brought the booze to Anchorage where Allen and his associates sold it at what they deemed to be a reasonable mark-up. Business prospered to such an extent that the law-enforcement agencies had the temerity to describe Allen as a "bootlegger" and gave him 48 hours to leave town. His taxi-cabs were seized.

In November 1918, Allen left Alaska on a southbound steamer and chose to disembark at Vancouver. The young would-be promoter took one look at Canada's West Coast port-city and fell in love with it. Before a month had passed, he was staging a fight show in the old Dominion Hall on Pender Street.

Vancouver, in the decade after the Second World War, provided Jack Allen with one of his rare periods of continuing affluence. Clubs, selling liquor to their "members," were operating full-blast and gambling games and bookmaking establishments abounded in the city core. Jack obtained a club license and, in his downtown premises, provided card games which obliged him to keep the club open 24 hours per day. At one stage, he was employing three shifts of bartenders.

But his heart really was in the boxing game. He acquired his own stable of pugilists, including Vic Foley, who became Canadian bantamweight champion. But to fill his boxing cards, it was necessary to import talent from the United States. Later, he was fond of recalling that two fighters from Portland, who fought for him in Vancouver, rejoiced in the names of Broken Blossoms and Papa Too-Sweet.

Allen, who may have inherited some wanderlust from his father, the itinerant telegraph operator, couldn't remain permanently in one city. Watching the successes of his mentors, Ancil Hoffman and Jack Kearns, he couldn't resist the lure of the big time. New York's Madison Square Garden was the mecca for every fight manager.

Passage to New York City was provided eventually by the emergence of an earnest young Vancouver welterweight named Bill Townsend. Allen signed him when Billy still was an amateur fighting at the Dominion Hall. Allen recognized that Townsend was the type of fighter who would appeal to Madison Square Garden crowds — clean-cut in appearance, blond and willing to absorb an opponent's punch in order to land a punch of his own.

Allen had little difficulty convincing matchmaker Johnny Johnston that Billy Townsend had all the equipment to merit regular appearances on boxing cards at Madison Square Garden. In addition to making Allen his assistant in the matchmaking department, Johnston bequeathed one of his own heavyweights to Mr. Allen — just to keep him busy as a manager of pugilists. The heavyweight in question was Yale Okun.

Yale Okun was magnificently built and exceptionally strong, but he displayed a consistent reluctance to be the aggressor in his bouts. Instead of punching his opponents with vigor, he had a distinct fondness for wrapping his arms around his opponent and clutching and tugging him.

After watching Okun in a bout at the Garden, Damon Runyon wrote in his New York newspaper column that, in all probability, Okun had been the inspiration for that famous college football chant: "Hold 'Em, Yale!"

Billy Townsend, for his part, was a smash hit at Madison Square Garden. He became a New York headliner — fighting in three Main Events at North America's shrine of pugilism. In one of those main events — on July 26, 1932 — he lost a very close decision to Benny Leonard, former lightweight champion of the world.

It was a thrilling bout. Many ringside critics felt that Townsend deserved at least a draw, but sentiment impelled the judges to vote for Leonard, the old champion. On the strength of his showing against Leonard, Townsend was assured of three more main events at the Garden in the coming year.

Things were much too good to last. Jimmy Johnston was fired as matchmaker at the Garden and Allen's services no longer were required. Simultaneously, something even worse occurred. Although Townsend had a contract for three bouts in the coming year, he suddenly was overcome by homesickness. To put it succinctly, Billy was pining for his girlfriend back in Vancouver. The lights of the Great White Way were enticing to his rollicking manager while Townsend was essentially a homebody whose greatest desire was to marry and settle down in a little cottage on the Pacific coast.

The Deacon was appalled by the thought that any fighter could turn down the lure of international attention as a Madison Square Garden headliner, but he recognized that Billy Townsend was his current meal ticket — and, if Billy was dead keen on returning to Vancouver, his manager might as well resign himself to that inevitability. So they climbed into the smart new roadster which Allen had bought himself — largely from his share of Townsend's ring earnings — and drove all the way back to Vancouver.

July 1932 was the high point in Jack Allen's career as a manager of pugilists. After that, there were some cheering ups and depressing downs but, on balance, there were more downs than ups.

The nadir of his promotorial career was the year 1936. He was managing Gordon Wallace, another outstanding Vancouver welterweight, and he induced Barney Ross, the world champion, to come to Vancouver for a bout with Wallace on March 11.

Ordinarily, a champion wouldn't be anxious to go to Vancouver, but Ross was managed by Sam Pian and Art Winch, who had been late-night playmates of Allen in his

Madison Square Garden days. Furthermore, on the strength of having a world champion on display, Allen had scared up a bankroll of $20,000 for purses.

It proved to be a great bout — Barney Ross, who was a brilliant champion, had his hands full in earning a ten-round decision. It was an entertaining bout — but there were few spectators. On the day of the fight, Vancouver was hit by one of the worst unexpected snowstorms in the history of the city. More than 12 inches of soggy snow fell, and the city was paralyzed. Public transportation was cancelled, radio stations warned citizens to refrain from driving their automobiles, and people were reluctant to stir from their homes, with the result that the promoter took a financial bath of shocking proportions.

As usual, Allen had friends in the boxing world who were willing to come to the rescue. Max Baer had lost the world heavyweight championship, but he was still the "biggest draw" in pugilism and Allen's former mentor, Ancil Hoffman, offered to bring Baer to Vancouver for a bout if Allen could find a suitable heavyweight opponent.

There wasn't a heavyweight within 500 miles of Vancouver who was willing to risk his head in the ring with Baer. But an importunate young impresario, Dave Cavadas, convinced Allen that he had a fighter who would fill the need. Cavadas's candidate was James J. Walsh, nicknamed the Alberta Assassin. This was no mere coincidence. Cavadas was an admirer of Edmonton reporter Dick Jackson who, a few years earlier, had given the Alberta Assassin nickname to Heartless Harold McMasters. The bout was set for August 19, 1936, at the old Vancouver Arena, a hockey building at the corner of Georgia and Denman streets with a capacity of 10,200 spectators.

Three days before the show, Allen and Cavadas went to the C.N.R. depot to meet James J. Walsh, arriving on the train from Edmonton.

Allen damn nearly dropped dead when he had his first sight of the Alberta Assassin. Walsh weighed more than 200 pounds, but he wasn't more than five feet ten inches. The thought of this tubby little guy in the ring with the tall, magnificently built Max Baer was almost too ridiculous for contemplation. Nevertheless, the bout had been advertised, many tickets had been sold, and it was too late to get a substitute opponent.

The promoter, thinking quickly, told Cavadas: "Take your fighter to his hotel room where he can get a good night's rest. Then bring him to the gymnasium for a workout at 8:00 A.M."

"At 8:00 A.M.," Cavadas blurted. "At that hour in the morning, none of the boxing writers will be out of bed to see the workout."

"That," said Allen smoothly, "is the general idea." James J. Walsh remained almost completely inconspicuous around Vancouver until the night of the fight.

Breaking with tradition, Allen had arranged for Baer to be the first fighter to enter the ring. Baer was greeted by mixed cheers and boos. When Walsh came into the ring, the crowd buzzed with confusion and broke into outright laughter when Walsh took off his bathrobe.

At the opening bell, Walsh rushed across the ring and threw a wild punch which missed. Baer didn't waste any time. He threw a solid right to Walsh's belly and the Alberta Assassin collapsed like a pricked balloon.

Later that night, the Vancouver Arena broke into flames and burned to the ground. Allen and Hoffman, who had been drinking in a bootlegging joint, arrived to see the fire at its height.

Allen said to Hoffman: "I think that someone in Vancouver is trying to tell me something." He made immediate plans to move to Toronto where he became matchmaker for boxing promoter Jack Corcoran at Maple Leaf

Gardens. Allen took a stable of good fighters to Toronto.

Although throughout his entire lifetime his closest associates included gamblers, bookmakers, bootleggers and hustlers of dubious distinction, Allen avoided incarceration in the slammer.

He had a close call in Winnipeg during the early years of the Depression. An American promoter named C.C. (Cash & Carry) Pyle had dreamed up a gimmick known as Walkathons or Dance Marathons. Allen became a partner in an enterprise which staged a Dance-Marathon in the Playhouse Theatre in Winnipeg. The situation was complicated by the fact that a competing Walkathon was being staged in the Amphitheatre, Winnipeg's hockey arena. There weren't enough suckers in Winnipeg to sustain the two operations, and both were going broke rapidly.

On the fourth day of operation, the Winnipeg Constabulary raided the Playhouse; they bundled Allen and his ragged troupe of competitors into the Ruppert Street police station, which was only one block from the theatre. Allen and the competitors were charged with engaging in a public performance without obtaining a license. Allen's partner, who was supposed to have purchased the license, had ducked out of town when he received advance warning of the impending raid.

En route to the police station, Allen remembered that one of the "ringers" among the walkathon competitors was a con-man who was adept at feigning epileptic fits. So, when the desk sergeant was warning them that, as vagrants with no visible means of support they were likely to receive indefinite jail terms, Allen gave a nudge to the fit specialist. Immediately frothing at the mouth and uttering strange cries, the talented gentleman fell to the floor in front of the desk sergeant.

Then Allen went into *his* act. Banging the desk he shouted, "All these contestants have been under competent medical care while they were involved in our show. If you put this man in the police cells — and if he dies there — our lawyers will sue the City of Winnipeg." The threat, although patently phony, was effective. The constabulary shooed the dance-marathon troupe out of the police station after warning them that they must leave town within 24 hours.

There were other occasions when, possibly, he *should* have been incarcerated. In Toronto, when the boxing game was temporarily in the doldrums, he became a partner of the Mad Russian in a bookmaking operation. The Deacon was operating a training gymnasium on the third floor of a building on Queen Street, directly across the road from Toronto's old City Hall. There were two telephones in the office of the gymnasium and Allen used one of those phones for bookmaking.

A bookmaker had to be very careful not to keep on his person any record of the bets which he had covered. If he were arrested, police always seized such records which would assure them of a conviction in court.

A sensible bookmaking operation required a "Back End." The Back End usually was a small apartment in a residential section of the city. An employee of the bookmaker sat behind locked doors in the Back End all afternoon, recording the bets which were telephoned to him by the bookmaker. His record of bets was written in his own private shorthand on little strips of rice paper. If the Back End heard a knock on his apartment door, he could be reasonably sure that he was being raided by the morality squad. In such emergencies, he flushed his strips of rice paper down the toilet or, if he really was pressed for time, he *ate* the evidence of betting.

Allen was the only *unsuccessful* bookmaker I ever knew. He not only scratched out laughably small profits, but he took a pinch!

One afternoon, he was playing gin rummy with a friend and hadn't bothered to telephone all his bets to the Back End. Scribbled notes, in which he had recorded his bets, were lying on his desk when the morality officers walked in.

It was an open-and-shut case, but Allen always managed to have friends in the right places. The Crown Prosecutor, who long had been a grateful recipient of passes to Allen fight shows, told the presiding magistrate that since Allen obviously was a lamentably unsophisticated bookmaker, a small fine would be a salutary penalty. The magistrate, who also enjoyed boxing shows, suspended sentence. Heaving a sigh of relief as he left the court room, Allen retired immediately and permanently from the bookmaking profession.

When he first settled in Toronto, Jack Allen installed himself in the Walsingham Hotel which was nicknamed "The Dancing Pig." The Walsingham, which wasn't one of the great hostelries of the world, was located on Jarvis Street, approximately three blocks from Maple Leaf Gardens, the centre of indoor athletic productions.

For more than 20 years, he continued to occupy that tiny, crowded room at The Dancing Pig. He had numerous visitors — many of whom dropped in about 2:00 A.M. because they knew that their host was quite likely to be sitting there, fully dressed, toying with a drink and gnawing on one of his cheap cigars, which he described as "heaters."

In the late 1950s, he was enjoying a spell of unusual financial security. He was clearing $1,000 per week for producing local boxing shows for CBC television. He had replenished his wardrobe, he was driving a new car, and he was enjoying himself. But after 20 years, he was living in the same crummy little hotel room.

As we were sitting there drinking one night, I said to him: "Why don't you move out of here? For the kind of money you're paying here you could rent a really nice apartment." He gnawed his cigar, took a drink and said: "Once, when things were tough, I went for an entire year without paying my rent. Not once in that year did the owner threaten to give me the heave-ho. So, considering the way they looked after me when I was broke, I figure that I should be loyal to the old joint now that I'm in the chips." Loyalty was one of Jack Allen's commendable qualities.

Shortly after his arrival in Toronto, Allen "inherited" Mike Levinsky. Mike was a gentle and harmless stray from St. Catharines. He couldn't read or write, was only about five feet tall, weighed about 100 pounds, and seldom shaved. He combed his mop of hair with a towel and could take two steps before his baggy hand-me-down clothing moved.

One day, Allen was standing in his first Toronto gymnasium on Bond Street watching two boxers sparring in the ring. On the far side of the ring, he saw this shabby little guy staring at the fighters through wide eyes.

"Scram!" Allen shouted at the little intruder. "Blow! Get lost!"

Mike didn't move. Allen picked up a broom and rushed around the ring. Mike sped down the stairs from the second-floor gymnasium and fled right into the street with Allen shouting at him.

The goofy foot-race was repeated four more times that day. Mike showed enough speed to escape without being clouted by the broom. Later that night, the Deacon locked up the gymnasium and went home to The Dancing Pig. The following afternoon he returned to his gymnasium. There, standing uncertainly in the middle of the boxing ring, was Mike Levinsky. Apparently, he had hidden himself under the ring the previous night before Allen locked up.

Allen accepted the inevitable. Mike lived on handouts of meal money and cigarettes from Allen and the other gambling-and-boxing characters who frequented the gymnasia. Everyone realized that Mike lived in a private dream world and most people were protective of him. He earned a bit of money by sweeping the floors, hanging up the equipment and washing and drying the towels used by the athletes in the gym.

Mike had no home and his sleeping arrangements were largely hit-and-miss. In Allen's lifetime, Mike usually slept in Jack's gym. When Allen died, Mike found another gym proprietor who gave him similar privileges. Laurie Vassalo, who owned an electrical supply business on Ossington Street, permitted Mike to sleep on an old chesterfield in his office.

One of Mike Levinsky's protective friends was Joe Fink, the perpetual night manager of the New Statler Hotel on Queen Street. The New Statler was a beer parlour hotel close to City Hall. The few bedrooms on the second floor were rented out on an evening basis to Queen Street prostitutes. When one of the girls indicated to Mr. Fink that she would be making no further use of the room on that particular night, Joe would give the room key to Levinsky. I am writing about events of 45 or 50 years ago and one wonders if, in the much more violent atmosphere of today, a Mike Levinsky could survive in Canada's most populous city.

John Finlay Allen was an unabashed hedonist, drinking enough to hospitalize most normal men, eating rich and expensive foods without any dietary supervision, and spending his money without any thought of the day of reckoning. Every night he got himself comfortably sloshed, but on New Year's Eve he stubbornly refused to go out on the town to join the traditional revelry. As he settled down in his room at The Dancing Pig, he would say derisively: "New Year's Eve is only for amateurs." There is no doubt that the Deacon was the complete professional in drinking. His cure for hangovers was a couple of Mothersills' Seasick Pills.

He thought nothing of driving 180 miles to Buffalo and back simply to have a pasta dinner in an inexpensive

Italian restaurant where they sold good Chianti. When Eddie Quinn was promoting boxing shows in Montreal, Allen went there frequently and spent most of his time in Slitkin and Slotkin's. I came back with him from one of those trips and I don't know why we bothered to pay for a compartment because we sat up all the way to Toronto, drinking with two professional card-sharks, John the Pipe and Johnny Cairo. The two Johns eagerly were awaiting the post-war restoration of transatlantic passenger liner service. Prior to the war, while "playing the tubs," they had become internationally renowned for their skill in reducing the assets of wealthy first-class passengers.

Allen was seemingly indestructible. I was 20 years younger than he but after keeping up with him for 15 years, I was forced to quit drinking when I was 46. Nevertheless, I continued to spend evenings with him at The Dancing Pig.

Many people had duplicate keys for Allen's hotel room. Tommy McBeigh, who came from Vancouver to train Allen's pugilists, had a key. I had my own key. Sam McKelvie, the night clerk of the hotel, had a key. A cheerfully blowsy blonde, nicknamed "Miss Halifax," had her key. Jack never betrayed a hint of surprise when he came home late at night and found two or three visitors sitting in the room, sampling his generous supply of liquor.

Allen inherited the blonde in much the same way that he inherited Mike Levinsky. She lived somewhere nearby and she developed the habit of dropping in when she was thirsty — which was frequently. In Allen's room, he had his own private telephone so that he could make long distance calls in connection with assembling his fight shows. The blonde apparently had a boyfriend in Halifax. Letting herself into Allen's room, she would put in long distance calls to Nova Scotia. It was after Deacon received his telephone bill one month — and noted that it included $86 in calls to Nova Scotia — that he nicknamed the blonde "Miss Halifax."

Jack never would get upset when people took advantage of him. When an upstart attempted to muscle in on Allen's boxing promotion preserves in Toronto, I gave some vigorous opinions on the interloper's moral dishonesty. "Tut, tut," said the Deacon soothingly, "the poor slob only *aspires* to be a con-man."

For a man who spent most of his adult life managing pugilists, Allen was remarkably pacific by nature. I remember him throwing punches only twice. The first occasion was the day his favourite cocker spaniel died. The Deacon was sitting in his second-floor gymnasium office when a bailiff walked in and handed him a summons to appear in court. The enormity of the bailiff's intrusion on his moment of grief for his canine companion so enraged Allen that he rose and knocked the bailiff all the way down the flight of steps.

The other occasion was one night when he was sitting drinking in his Dancing Pig room with Max Orgel, who managed a fighter named Joey Ferrier. Both men were quite drunk and when Allen opined that Ferrier "couldn't lick his lips," Orgel picked up a thick glass tumbler and broke it over Allen's head.

They stood up, and as they exchanged punches, the blood from Allen's wound spattered the walls of the room. They went out into the corridor, Allen relentlessly driving Orgel towards the front door of the hotel. As they continued to punch, the blood spattered the walls of the corridor.

The next day, Tommy McBeigh used his key to let himself into Allen's bedroom. The old promoter was lying on a pillow which had been soaked by the blood from his head cut.

"What the hell happened to *you*?" McBeigh demanded.

Opening one eye blearily, Allen croaked: "I dazzled the son of a bitch with footwork."

Allen took very poor care of himself when he collected the gate receipts after a successful fight show. He'd stuff the cash into his pocket and go out to celebrate. After he had closed the legitimate bars, he'd wind up at a bootlegging joint owned by two pickpockets who were our acquaintances. Frequently, he managed to be relieved of much of his money before he made an early, dawn return to his hotel.

After this happened a few times, he devised a plan for saving his gate receipts from pillage. After the show, he'd go first to his room at The Walsingham. Stacked against the walls of his room were all the last month's copies of the three local newspapers — the piles usually were about five feet in height. Allen would peel off several hundred dollars for "walking around money." Then he'd take the major portion of the gate receipts and conceal the cash between the layers of stacked newspapers.

About eight o'clock one night, I let myself into his room and found Allen and McBeigh down on their hands and knees as they rummaged among the newspapers scattered all over the floor. Allen explained: "After last night's fight show, I came home and hid the gate receipts in this stack of newspapers. Now I can't find the damn cash." I got down on the floor and helped them unfold the newspapers, page by page.

We were just about ready to give up when Sam McKelvie, the night clerk, opened the door with *his* key. Sam had dropped by on his way to have his evening meal.

"I guess you're looking for your bankroll," McKelvie said to Allen. "Well, last night, you were quite sloshed when you arrived from your show at Massey Hall. So, before you went out on the town, I took $3,500 from you and I locked it in the hotel office safe."

At one time or another, every prominent figure from the world of boxing who visited Toronto spent some time in that room at The Dancing Pig. There we drank with Jack Dempsey, Jack Kearns and rotating platoons of New York sports writers who had come to know Allen in the course of his fistic peregrinations.

We drank indiscriminately. For one long period, our drink was Bols Apricot Brandy, a liqueur. I suggested that a diet of Apricot Brandy, consumed by the tumbler, might undermine our health. "Nonsense," retorted my host. "This is merely the juice of the fruit. And what could be more healthy than fruit juice?"

Time was running out for him, but for several years I believed sincerely that the Deacon finally might hit the jackpot. First, he had Alan McFater, a young Toronto featherweight who grew into a welterweight. McFater headlined many shows in Toronto, but he stopped just short of becoming a genuine world-class contender. Later, John Finlay Allen had a stroke of almost unbelievably good fortune. He found himself managing George Chuvalo, an iron-chinned young heavyweight. Every manager of pugilists has dreamed of having a protégé like George Chuvalo — a white heavyweight with the potential to fight for the world championship.

Chuvalo was a gem beyond price — a white heavyweight and a genuine championship contender in an era when the division was dominated completely by black fighters such as Mohammad Ali, Sonny Liston, Floyd Patterson and Joe Frazier.

There was, of course, no way that his story could have a wildly successful conclusion. With his past performance record of more than 45 years of promotorial pratfalls, it was perhaps inevitable that Jack Allen should flub his final chance to take off a Big Score.

Through sheer carelessness more than anything else, he provided the opportunity for Irving Ungerman, a wealthy Toronto chicken plucker, to deprive him of Chuvalo's services. Allen steered Chuvalo into some profitable pay days, but the fighter became impatient when Allen appeared to be dragging his feet in pushing him into the Big Time. The Deacon was stunned when Chuvalo asked to be relieved of his existing contract and indicated that he wished to be managed by Ungerman.

Although he had lost the last big opportunity of his life, I never heard him say anything bitterly resentful about Ungerman. What was truly remarkable about a man who had survived so long in a cut-throat business was the fact that I never heard Allen say many unkind words about *anyone*.

Jack really was on his uppers after he lost Chuvalo's contract. I had left the racetracks to return to the Southam newspapers and our mutual friend, Trent Frayne, had succeeded me as public relations director for the Ontario Jockey Club. Frayne hired Jack as an all-round assistant in the publicity department.

Allen was a most efficient acquisition. Over the years, he had established a warm rapport with all the sports news media in the Toronto, Hamilton, Buffalo and Niagara Falls areas. After a lifetime of practice, he was no mean hand at typing out printable press releases. And everyone liked the grizzled old geezer.

By the time that the Deacon lost Chuvalo's contract and joined the staff of the Jockey Club, he had been living for several years in a pleasant bed-sitting-room apartment on the shore of Lake Ontario.

On an early October afternoon in 1964, we talked for the last time. Ten days later, when I was on assignment in Naples, my wife called and told me that John Finlay Allen had dropped dead. They were delaying the funeral service until noon Saturday, in the hope that I might be able to get home in time.

Allen would have enjoyed the story of how I managed to catch a plane out of Rome the following morning in order to arrive in Toronto, via Lisbon, on Friday night. Italy's unionized railway workers were staging one of their peculiar strikes and shutting down the operation of all trains — from 7:00 each night until 8:00 the following morning. If I waited for Friday morning's first train, I wouldn't reach Leonardo da Vinci Airport in Rome in time to catch the plane for Canada.

The concierge had the answer to my problem. The concierge had a brother-in-law who, for a negotiated fee, would pick me up at 5:00 in the morning and drive me to the airport in Rome.

Promptly at 5:00 A.M., the brother-in-law was waiting for me in a beaten-up Fiat which looked as if it had survived the shelling from the US offshore battleships before the landing at Salerno. We took the "coast road" instead of going by the much longer but better paved inland highway.

It was a crazy journey — right out of an old Mack Sennett slapstick comedy. With the horn blaring — and without slacking speed — we roared through coastal villages scattering chickens, dogs and small children from our path.

I knew that my mad-eyed driver didn't speak English, but by the time we reached the outskirts of Rome, I began to realize that he was probably the only living Neopolitan who never had paid a visit to the Italian capital. He had no idea of where the airport was.

So we sped through the suburban streets, pleading for guidance. The driver leaned through his window and I leaned through mine, both of us crying "Aeroporto? Aeroporto?" The natives responded by pointing and cheering us on. We made it with a good hour before takeoff, but I could have used a couple of Jack Allen's favourite "stingers" to settle my nerves.

On Saturday morning, Frank Lynett's funeral chapel was jammed. Frank had arbitrarily designated my wife and me as the chief mourners and we sat in the front row. Little Mike Levinsky, looking even more bemused than usual, sat with us.

From my vantage point, I was able to watch Murph Blandford, an old baseball umpire and bar manager, go up and kneel in front of the open coffin to pay his last respects. I noticed that Murph reached up and put something into the casket.

I went up and looked at my old friend lying there in the casket. Murph Blandford had shoved two cigars into the breast pocket of Jack Allen's blue suit. The Deacon would have a couple of his favourite "heaters" for his last, long trip.

Allen was a long-lapsed Catholic, but one of our racing friends, Father Flanagan, had agreed to conduct a brief, non-sectarian service. The good Father hit all the appropriate notes. At the conclusion of his brief benediction, he said: "It's almost 1:00. Post-time for the first race at Woodbine is 2:00 P.M. Jack wouldn't want any of us to miss the Daily Double."

It was one of those funerals where a general sense of loss was dissipated by happy recollections. Seldom have I attended a farewell service where so many mourners wore gentle smiles as they thought of a favourite Jack Allen story. The dearly departed left a legacy of laughter.

That morning, I learned the precise details of Jack Allen's demise. On his way home after the last race of the day at Woodbine, he made a couple of stops to shop for what he used to describe as "the necessities of life."

He arrived at his apartment block in the evening, pressed the button for the elevator, and before the elevator door opened, he dropped dead on the lobby floor.

As he fell, he was still clutching the shopping items which he carried. As he lay there, in his arms was a delicatessen-bag containing a barbecued chicken, a liquor-store bag containing two bottles of imported red wine, and finally, the current edition of the *Daily Racing Form*.

There was a man who died the way he lived!

THE GOOD KID, ET AL

WHEN I THINK OF MY EARLY YEARS IN TORONTO, I AM REminded of the immortal phrase of R. James Speers: "There's a little bit of larceny in every man. But you *notice* it more around a racetrack."

Good Kid Louie was a lifelong carnie, a pitch-man who hustled only during the summer months and spent the winter living off his own fat and the largesse of his chief patron, Morris Fishman.

In his younger days, when carnivals played the southern United States in the winter months, The Good Kid had worked year-round. He abandoned such an exhausting schedule later when he learned that he could earn enough in four or five warm months to pay back the money which he had borrowed from Fishman during the previous winter. He said: "The world is divided into two classes of people — borrowers and lenders. Personally, I'm not much of a lender."

The Good Kid was one of those oddballs who came

into my life after I settled in Toronto. My addiction to the racetrack led me into a lasting friendship with Morris Fishman. If you spent much time with Morris, it was inevitable that you spent a lot of time with The Good Kid, who adhered to Morris like a mustard plaster.

Morris, a well-off owner and trainer of thoroughbreds, was a former jockey, a former amateur pugilist and the former owner of a successful gambling house. He didn't *need* The Good Kid any more than he needed "Hopalong Archie" Wetstein but he "looked after" both of them.

Morris always was the bankroll for those two little men in times of need. Maybe he cherished them because, like himself, they were diminutive in stature. It is much more likely that their attachment had been sealed when they were school kids, selling newspapers on the Toronto streets.

I had known Good Kid Louie vaguely for a year or more before I learned his surname. One night, I asked my street-wise newspaper colleague, Joe Perlove, of the Toronto *Star*: "What's The Good Kid's real name?" Joe pondered for a few seconds before he replied: "Damned if I know, really. But I know that he has a brother named Percy Piffles." Finally, it was Morris Fishman who told me that the surname of The Good Kid and Percy Piffles was Drillick.

I became familiar with Percy Piffles on trips to New York City where he was a permanent resident of a small midtown hotel. He was a racetrack tout.

By the time I knew him, Percy had turned his back on the thoroughbred tracks and confined himself to touting on the harness-races at Roosevelt Raceway and Yonkers Raceway.

He preferred harnessracing because it was a sport which was conducted at night. Like his brother Louie, he was constitutionally opposed to rising from bed early in the day. With the coming of night-racing, the schedule enabled him to sleep, if he desired, until early afternoon.

Although his father and his siblings lived in Toronto, Percy Piffles seldom returned to the city of his birth. Harness-racing in New York was conducted seven days weekly and he felt obliged to be available at all times, to service his betting clients.

"These suckers around the harness tracks have no sense of personal loyalty," he told me once as we sipped coffee in a Manhattan automat. "If I missed even a single day at the track, they'd give all their business to some other creep."

The Good Kid was a roly-poly little man who walked as if his arches were in a state of permanent collapse. He dressed in expensive blue serge suits and wide-brimmed fedoras, which he wore squarely on his head but tilted forward sufficiently to shade his eyes. He always had a cigar in his mouth but gave up smoking for the final ten years of his life.

Good Kid Louie worked with every big-time carnival company at one time or another: Johnny J. Jones Shows, Rubin and Cherry Shows, Royal American Shows and the Conklin Shows.

One thing about The Good Kid which always fascinated me was the manner in which he spent money he really didn't have. After a winter in Toronto — during which he didn't work — Louie probably would owe $15,000 or more to Morris Fishman. Forty years ago, $15,000 probably was close to $100,000 in terms of today's money.

If The Good Kid ever worried about anything, he kept his worries a deep secret. On the surface, he was as carefree as a spoiled child with an inexhaustible supply of goodies.

When the horses were running, he bet on them as if money was going out of fashion. And after racing closed down for the winter, he spent most afternoons in Slow Stein's club, near the corner of Queen Street and Spadina Avenue, engaging in interminable games of gin rummy or "klob."

The Good Kid told me that he was a good gin rummy player but I never gave him the opportunity to victimize me. I remembered his story about playing gin rummy with another carnie throughout the entire train trip from Calgary to Winnipeg.

"I beat this gazooney 37 straight games," he said. "Then this sucker won *one* game. So I said to him, 'Let's quit — this game is getting to be too much of a see-saw.'" I suspect that in addition to being a lifelong hustler, The Good Kid also was a compulsive liar.

Molly and Morris Fishman had two sons, Donald and Stanley. While The Good Kid was enjoying his lengthy wintertime sabbatical, there were occasions when the Fishmans induced him to do a bit of baby-sitting.

When Molly and Morris were going out for an evening, they would leave The Good Kid and their two children parked in front of the television. Morris kept a well-stocked bar in the house and it was tacitly understood that the baby-sitter could help himself to refreshments.

The Good Kid was a formidable imbiber for his size. When in the mood, he could knock off an entire bottle of rye without outside assistance.

Usually by the time Mr. and Mrs. Fishman returned from their evening's outing, their baby-sitter was in a state of semi-paralysis. The two Fishman boys still would be wide awake, playing gin rummy for 50-cents a game. The boys were small but very strong; if there had been an outbreak of fire, they could have been relied upon to carry their baby-sitter to safety.

The Good Kid scorned the plebeian facilities of Toronto's excellent public transportation system. He lived with his father and a younger sister in the old family house on Palmerston Avenue and was within reasonable walking distance of most of his winter daytime haunts. However, on most occasions he insisted upon travelling by taxi-cab. (After all, Fishman financed him generously.)

It didn't bother me particularly that The Good Kid never deigned to address me by my first name — invariably he addressed me only as "Coleman." We spent many an hour in the dining-room of The Paddock Tavern — a busy estaminet which Fishman owned in partnership with Harry Lahman and Lou Chesler. On those occasions when I got my head into the pail, The Good Kid used to say, with a shake of his head: "Coleman, you drink just like us Polacks. As soon as you take your first drink, you buy a through ticket."

Because he spent so much time travelling by train when he was a carnival hustler, his conversation was sprinkled with railroading allusions. I took him to a home owned by a very wealthy friend of mine. It was an exceptionally large house — on a lot with a frontage large enough for a small public park. Afterwards, he referred to that house as "that joint where the upstairs bedrooms were a sleeper-jump from the drawing-room."

He believed devoutly in travelling first class. When he worked the Calgary Stampede, he stayed at the Palliser Hotel, the most opulent hostelry in town. In Edmonton, he'd stay at the Macdonald Hotel. In Saskatoon, his address was the Bessborough Hotel. When the carnival moved into Regina, he lived in comfort at the Hotel Saskatchewan.

He'd never dream of attempting to save a few dollars by going down to the hotel dining-room to have breakfast. Instead, at considerably greater expense, he'd insist upon having breakfast in bed, served by a room-service waiter. When he was presented with his breakfast check, he'd scribble his name and room number and he'd give the waiter a generous tip.

He didn't believe in early rising. His habits were late to bed and late to rise. When he was on the road with the carnival, he would seldom leave his hotel room before 11:00 A.M., and even if the exhibition grounds were within walking distance of his hotel, he would blow himself to a ride in a taxi-cab.

The Good Kid always worked with a partner and they'd operate one of those flat-joints, in which they had a revolving wheel which they could stop at any number they desired. When there were enough ticket purchasers to cover almost every number on the wheel, the two big-hearted operators would give away a prize with every spin of the wheel. They had bought the prizes at such job-lot bargain prices that, even if they gave one away each time they spun the wheel, they still were making a profit. At those big western Canadian exhibitions, a carnie could make a profit of several hundred dollars a day without breaking a sweat.

When The Good Kid had a particularly good week at the Calgary Stampede or the Edmonton Exhibition, he would take a taxi-ride down to the telegraph office and send as much as $5,000 to Fishman, his "banker" back in Toronto.

The Good Kid would come home triumphantly in September. He would pay off his total debt to Morris. He would be equipped with a considerable bankroll and looking for action.

At the racetrack, he prowled tirelessly in search of feed-box information. He never trusted his own intuition about horses — he had to have a tip from some racetracker, even from a groom, whose employer was starting "a good thing" in the next race. It seems strange that carnies, who depend for their livelihood on the gullibility of fairgrounds suckers, become gullible themselves when they venture onto the racetrack.

Nothing could anger The Good Kid more than to be advised, belatedly, that he had missed out on a good thing. There was the afternoon at the Long Branch track in Toronto when Fishman was starting a horse named Indian Giver. This was one of those can't-miss situations — when Morris gave you "the word" about a horse, you could bet with confidence.

In this particular case, Fishman's partners — Harry Lahman and Lou Chesler — contrived a coup. Lahman and

Chesler were known as heavy betters, and two bookmakers, Slow Stein and Palooka, had been attempting to get their betting trade. This afternoon, Chesler and Lahman took the two bookies to the track and all four of them were in Lahman's car, parked close to the six-furlong starting gate, when Indian Giver's field was going to the post.

Lahman and Chesler had been plying the bookies with rye. Palooka was becoming quite expansive and he was boasting that he and his partner were quite capable of handling big bets.

"Could you handle $2,000 on a horse?" Lahman asked silkily.

Palooka and Slow said that they could cover a $2,000 bet without blinking an eye.

"Well," said Lahman, "I'm betting you $2,000 to win on Indian Giver in this race."

The bookies were cooked! There was no way they could get to the pari-mutuel machines to lay off any part of the $2,000 bet.

And as they sat there in the car, trapped, the field broke from the starting gate.

Indian Giver won handily and he paid $13.65 for every $2 wager.

Lahman and Chesler had "beaten" the bookies for $13,650.

After the race, Morris Fishman and I were on our way back to the barn to have a drink; at the paddock gate, we bumped into The Good Kid.

"Hey, where were you?" Morris said genially. "If I'd seen you, I would have told you that Indian Giver would win the last race."

The Good Kid erupted furiously. He was genuinely cheesed-off. He shouted: "Don't give me *results*! In my business, I'm looking for *tips*." He sulked for an entire day and refused to be mollified even when Morris offered to cut him in for $500 of the money which had been won by Lahman and Chesler.

The Good Kid had many very odd friends and expected me to know *all* of them because I was a newspaperman. He once mentioned an acquaintance named Pushcart. In exasperation, I asked: "Who the hell is Pushcart?" He looked at me as if I had lost my senses and he snapped: "You *must* know Pushcart! He's Squinchy's brother-in-law."

One winter, about December 20, The Good Kid telephoned me at my office and asked if I had completed my Christmas shopping.

"I haven't even started," I replied.

"Okay," said The Good Kid, "just give me your shopping list and I'll pass it along to my good friend, Helen the Booster. She likes you and she'll do your shopping for free."

It took me a few minutes to realize that Helen was the lady with whom we had been drinking at The Paddock two nights earlier and who was, by profession, a highly talented shoplifter.

For several summers, Good Kid's partner on the carnival circuit was Middle of the Road Red. Red acquired his nickname after he was walking along the sidewalk in a western town one night and an automobile jumped the curb and knocked him down. After that, he always avoided sidewalks and insisted on walking down the middle of the road.

The Good Kid told me that, when travelling on day coaches, Middle of the Road Red would sit down next to a particularly dumb-looking traveller and indulge in a stratagem known as "Playing the Snooze."

Sighing wearily, Red would say to this prospective sucker: "Pardon me, I'd like to take a snooze, but there are some suspicious-looking passengers on this coach. I'll be grateful if you hold my wallet in your pocket while I take my snooze." Before the train was due at the station where he intended to disembark, Red would pretend to awaken, refreshed, and say to the sucker: "Thank you very much for looking after my wallet. Now, why don't *you* take a little snooze. And I'll hold your wallet for you while you're having your snooze." There were, of course, limits to my tolerance for The Good Kid's more outrageous anecdotes.

The Good Kid's lifelong aversion to physical exercise and a propensity for a high cholesterol-count probably contributed to his downfall. He was playing gin rummy in a Toronto club when, without warning, he fell out of his chair and was unconscious when he hit the floor.

Fortunately, Dr. Sam Shaul, who was medical doctor to most members of the local gambling fraternity, was playing gin rummy at another table in the same room.

After examining the seemingly unconscious Louie, feeling for his pulse and listening for heart beats with his ever-ready stethoscope, the good doctor said gravely to the assembled friends of The Good Kid: "He's still alive — but I'll lay five-to-one that he'll be dead before morning."

The Good Kid, who hadn't twitched a muscle since he was stricken, opened one eye and, with great effort, whispered distinctly: "Bet!"

The Good Kid won that bet. He continued to live for another four or five years. He had more strokes, but eventually became so frail that it was necessary to lodge him permanently in Baycrest Hospital for the Aged. He had access to a pay phone and, almost every day, he called bets to his favourite bookmaker. To the very end his expenses, including his bets, were underwritten by his lifelong friend Morris Fishman.

I have known many carnies in my time, but none as intimately as I knew Good Kid Louie. I was honoured to be one of the active pall-bearers at his funeral. That was the first time I witnessed an old-fashioned Yiddish graveside custom. As the pall-bearers held the casket, the officiating rabbi opened the lid. He placed a penny on each of The Good

Kid's closed eyelids. At the time, I felt that Louie would have been derisive. With his free-spending habits, he would have been willing to settle for nothing less than a $1,000-bill on each eyelid.

Although The Good Kid was opposed to working in wintertime, many of the carnies spent the winter working as "telephone salesmen" for Toronto's mining-stock promoters.

When first I settled in Toronto, many of the carnies were working "on the blower" for my old friend Murray Wallace Caldough, who specialized in promoting moose-pasture mining stocks. Many of those carnival hustlers became so successful as stock salesmen that they retired permanently from the road.

Wally was operating out of a tall Yonge Street office building, just a few doors south of King Street. Each of his salesmen was equipped with a sucker list which had been assembled over the years by other promoters in this shady type of business. When Wally first showed me one of those lists, I was genuinely surprised to see that it included the names of well-established businessmen, as well as professionals such as doctors and lawyers. I was dumbfounded when I found that the list included the name of the publicist for the Kentucky Derby. I knew that he was a sucker for slow horses but I didn't realize that his weaknesses included penny stocks.

This type of operation was known as a Boiler Room. When business was booming, Wally had so many salesmen working on so many telephones that his Boiler Room resembled the main switchboard at AT&T. Usually, when a Boiler Room operator finally was "nailed" by an investigator from the Ontario Securities Commission, it was because the investigator had access to the files of Bell Telephone and noticed that an inordinately large number of long distance calls were being made from a certain brokerage office. Of course, the Securities Commission also was receiving written complaints from widows and pensioners who had been sweet-talked into buying those moose-pasture stocks.

Wally, a very stout man with a perpetually optimistic disposition, had come from a conservative family of dispensing chemists in Winnipeg. He began his business career as a teenager by selling candy, fruit and magazines on the trains between Winnipeg and the summer resort of Winnipeg Beach. Another young candy butcher tipped him off to the fact that if he stuck 10 percent of every sale into his own pocket, the man who employed him wouldn't know the difference.

Thus was launched a bumpy, but generally successful, business career. Somewhere along the line before he arrived in Toronto, Wally had been convicted in a slight case of petty larceny; so that his police record wouldn't disqualify him from obtaining a stock promoter's license in Ontario, he had changed his name legally to Caldough.

He operated "Bucket shops" for some "legitimate" brokers who were members of the Stock Exchange. Of course, those brokers would have denied any connection with Caldough's operation. Wally was the "front man", and if anything went amiss, he "would take the fall." That was a nice way of saying that he would face court charges and possible incarceration.

It was fortunate that he was equipped with an equable disposition because he made and lost modest fortunes frequently. I sold him his first race horse, a two-year-old filly named Isaldwana, for $500. Isaldwana wasn't a world beater, but she whetted Caldough's interest in racing and, within a year, he had a stable of four or five horses. He became a regular attendant on the Ontario tracks, all dolled-out in white Palm Beach suits and Panama hats, resembling a corpulent facsimile of Bet-A-Million John Gates.

He had been something of a desperado in his young days as a con-man. He told me about one of his early adventures in selling moose-pasture stocks to suckers in British Columbia. One of his salesmen was a handsome young fellow who caught the fancy of a wealthy bordello operator in Victoria. Wally tried to persuade the young salesman to go through a form of marriage with the Madam so that they could get her to invest her fortune in the penny stock which they were promoting.

Wally freely acknowledged that he was in a messy game, selling highly speculative stocks to gullible suckers who were contacted by telephone. However, he pointed out that a moose-pasture stock, promoted by one of his colleagues, became one of the most productive mining properties in the history of Ontario. Many of the original investors made fortunes. Speaking of his former colleague's bonanza, he said wryly: "All his lies came true."

Caldough had no illusions about his own role. Once he told me defensively: "When I die, there's one thing about me that all my critics will be forced to admit. I never sold one share of these blankety-blank stocks to a friend or a relative."

Wally was married to Nellie Woodall, who had been a hoofer in the chorus of the old daily stage shows at the Capitol Theatre in Moose Jaw.

They were prodigious drinkers and, among their Toronto acquaintances, they were known as The Battling Caldoughs. Nellie was a lady with a very short fuse and a great left hook. When annoyed, she was known to take off one shoe and whack Wally over the head with the spiked heel. Wally frequently came to work with his scalp displaying more drill-holes than one of his mining properties.

With my own thirst deeply established, it was perhaps inevitable that I spent much time in company with the Caldoughs and their business associates. One night, when they were in their cups, Wally said proudly to his wife: "Darling, show Coleman the new diamond ring I gave you."

Nellie coyly raised her left hand for me to admire the sparkler which was approximately the size of a locomotive headlight. Leaning over to me, Nellie said in a half-whisper: "It's quite a rock — but I would have liked to have seen the finger that came with it."

To their tumultuous union, Nellie brought her son, Georgie, a product of her previous marriage to George Woodall, who had been a dance-band musician in Moose Jaw.

George adopted the surname of his colourful stepfather and by the time he was a teenager, it became apparent that he had absorbed a great deal of his stepfather's guile. He was an exceptionally bright student in school but preferred to tootle his saxophone in Bobby Gimby's Band which was playing gigs at the Brant Inn and other Ontario dance halls. Everyone predicted a bright future for George, but only time would reveal which of his talents he was likely to utilize. One thing was certain: he exuded boyish charm from every pore.

In the early 1950s, the Ontario Securities Commission decided that the time had come to clamp down hard on the boiler-room operators. Wally lost his license when an investigation revealed that the long distance bills from his office totalled almost $100,000 over a very short period.

Realizing that Ontario had become too hot for them, most of the telephone salesmen moved their operations to Montreal. But before long, the Montreal authorities also began to crack down on the penny stock promoters. Many of them — still the survivors of the old gang of carnies — took the hint and, almost en masse, they moved out to Vancouver where the Securities Commission was thought to be more liberal.

Wally Caldough had been all over this same route in his youth and nothing was new to him. After Nellie died in Toronto in 1952, Wally moved to Vancouver. He was no longer willing to be "front man for a stock joint," and confined himself to obtaining a salesman's license. In those days, the British Columbia authorities weren't overly interested in prosecuting salesmen — they wished to "nail" only the actual promoters of dubious stock deals.

By this time, Wally had saved enough money to keep himself in comfort for the rest of his days. Not only had he cleaned up his act, but he had given up drinking permanently.

When my curiosity took me to the Pacific coast to observe the debut of the B.C. Lions football team in the autumn of 1954, I was bemused to find my one-time drinking companion, Murray Wallace Caldough, sipping afternoon tea and nibbling daintily on a crumpet in the old Tea Room of the Hotel Vancouver. Observing him, clear-eyed and merry, I began to have some sharp pangs of doubt about the course which my own disorderly life was taking.

We fell to talking about Wally's errant stepson, Georgie. The previous year, George had been working with a boiler-room crew in Montreal and was lodged in the slammer — a 60-day stretch in Montreal's Bordeaux Jail.

Blithely impenitent, George dined at Café Martin, one of Montreal's finest restaurants, on his first night out of Bordeaux. Then, he went to Toronto, loaded his wife and children into a new Cadillac convertible, and started out for the Pacific coast — a trip which took him almost two months as he stopped off to test business prospects in cities along the way.

When George was reunited with his stepfather in Vancouver, there was a dramatic change in their roles. By then Wally was content to be the salesman, free of the risks which were involved in being the proprietor of a boiler room. George had become The Boss — the genius who floated the stock promotions and took the major risks.

When Wally and I sipped afternoon tea at the Hotel Vancouver, the elder Caldough was painfully aware that

George was heading for a major calamity. "This kid is just too damn much of a desperado," Wally said earnestly. "Everyone keeps warning him that he's heading straight for a long stretch in the jug but it doesn't worry him one bit."

George certainly had been cutting a wide swath in Vancouver. He personified the wealthy and expansive boulevardier. He dressed handsomely in dark double-breasted suits, tailored for him in London's Savile Row. He wore a Christy's black bowler, carried a furled umbrella and, invariably, smoked a big cigar.

When his boiler-room operations extracted a steady flow of money from naive investors, George was a one-man spending wave in Vancouver. He entertained lavishly, drank expansively and became a "media personality" in the city, which is always a dangerous practice for anyone whose business activities are likely to attract the attention of the law enforcement agencies. Shortly after establishing headquarters in Vancouver, George opened a branch office in Edmonton.

George had sexual appetites to match his thirst and he kept a hotel room where, on alternate afternoons, he had a shapely blonde and a shapely brunette as his playmates.

A shakedown artist who knew of George's afternoon frolics rented the adjoining room in the hotel and bored a hole in the wall. Using a telescopic lens, he took a series of interesting photographs with George in flagrante delicto.

One day, George was sitting in his Edmonton office when his secretary stuck her head through the door and told him that a Mr. Ferguson was waiting to see him. The name didn't mean anything to Caldough but he told the secretary to show Mr. Ferguson in.

"Now, Mr. Ferguson," George said genially, "what can I do for you?"

The prospective blackmailer simply handed George a brown envelope which contained two photographs.

But the blackmailer had pulled a blank. George didn't give a damn if "Mr. Ferguson" took his pictures to be published on the front page of the Edmonton *Journal*.

George looked at both pictures intently and said: "I don't care much for *this* one, but you can sell me a dozen prints of the one with the blonde."

Georgie continued to live recklessly. When he and his friends partied at the Panorama Roof of the Hotel Vancouver, Caldough often would go up on the bandstand, borrow a saxophone and sit in with the regular musicians for a set.

When the axe fell, it "finished" George as a stock promoter. The RCMP raided his offices on West Pender Street and charged him with fraudulent stock operations in connection with two companies in the Yukon.

The news of George's arrest was circulated nationally by the Canadian Press wire service. He had become something of a celebrity in the previous two years. The Canadian Press stories linked George with Errol Flynn, who had died in Vancouver just a few weeks previously after partying with Caldough. In fact, George was a visitor in Flynn's suite at the Sylvia Hotel when the film actor, complaining of a sore back, lay down on the floor and died suddenly of a heart attack.

Deacon Jack Allen telephoned to tell me about George's arrest. Like myself, Allen had known George when he was barely out of short pants. The old boxing promoter was chuckling as he told me the Canadian Press story had mentioned that Errol Flynn had visited Vancouver because George was negotiating to buy Flynn's yacht, *Zaca*.

"Now, why in hell would George wish to buy a yacht?" Allen said rhetorically. After a pause for effect, he added slyly: "After all, he knows damn well that he can't take a yacht to jail with him."

Always the genial con-man, Georgie had a grandiose plan for the yacht. He was planning to use the *Zaca* for a Treasure Hunting expedition to the islands of the South Pacific. When the RCMP interrupted his business operations, he was working on the production of a brochure designed to sell share certificates for a company to be known as Treasure Hunters, Limited. It's unfortunate that he didn't pull it off. The thought of Georgie, wearing a sea captain's uniform and leading an expedition of treasure hunters to the Tahitian Archipelago always has appealed to me.

While the RCMP were sifting through his files, George skipped bail and fled the country. But he had to be near the centre of action so he chose London as his sanctuary and lived under an assumed name.

Of course he couldn't keep his identity to himself. He told a young lady who he was and the net closed on him. He had gone on the wagon and was sipping a lemon-squash in his favourite "local" one noon-time when two very nice detectives from Scotland Yard walked up to him and discreetly asked if he was "George F. Caldough."

Brought back to Canada, he was a picture of good-natured bonhommie as photographers greeted him and his Scotland Yard escort at Vancouver Airport.

There was a long trial in Vancouver and the court — which somehow failed to be charmed by Georgie's exploits — sentenced him to six years in the penitentiary after the jury found him guilty of a $385,000 stock swindle. There were other charges, but the Crown, having obtained a satisfactory conviction, didn't press them.

George was so resilient emotionally that, as they say in con-men circles, he served his time "standing on his head." He was a model prisoner, made himself invaluable as a counsellor to other prisoners in Oakalla Penitentiary, and was paroled after three years of his six-year sentence.

While he was in jail, his wife divorced him and grabbed what assets were available. When he got out, the federal government was suing him for unpaid income taxes.

Three years in the can had not quenched George's incredible optimism. He had written his autobiography for *Weekend Magazine* and it was published in three installments of Canada's largest weekly newspaper supplement. He had a tremendous amount of untapped ability and kept himself busy in legitimate enterprises in Toronto until his parole expired.

George always had felt that London was his personal oyster. After his parole expired, he moved to London where quickly he re-established himself. He wrote and published a newsletter for small investors and had a paid circulation of 16,000 devoted subscribers. He was flying high again, but this time, he had become a paragon of respectability.

George re-established contact with me in 1977. Perhaps he had reached the stage of life when one comforts oneself with nostalgia. Nellie and Wally were long-gone, but George wanted to hear from someone who had been their friend.

We began a lively correspondence and he extracted a promise that we would lunch at his club on my next trip to London. The picture of the mischievous and dashing George lounging among sedate British clubmen tickled my imagination.

In December 1977, my wife and I were going to spend Christmas at my daughter's home in Kent. In preparation for my reunion with George, I dug up an old photo of Nellie and Wallie with Isaldwana, the filly which I sold to them for $500. I wanted to show it to George over lunch in his club.

On the morning of the day we were leaving for England, I noticed George's obituary in the *Globe and Mail*. He had died in London three days earlier. George had died at 48, but he had done more than enough living for any man of 96.

RACETRACKERS REMEMBERED

ON THOSE MORNINGS WHEN THE SUN IS SHINING WITH particular benevolence, I wish that I could write the entire story of my lifelong love affair with the racetrack.

There are so many people to whom I wish to pay a final tribute, so many good and brave horses gone to ground without a line of print to rekindle memories of their brief taste of glory.

Flaming Lizzie may not have been the greatest mare in the history of racing, but she was the only race horse to come to the track on a *raft*! Her owner Geordie Brown lived on a little farm about 200 miles northwest of Edmonton. Every spring, he'd load Flaming Lizzie on a raft and float down the river to Edmonton. Geordie would pole the raft to shore at the foot of 82nd Street and walk Flaming Lizzie to Northlands Park where a stall was reserved for her. After the mare had regained her land legs, she'd *win*.

Jack Smith was a barber by trade and one year he wintered his mare Chattahoochee at Jim Alcock's farm in South Edmonton. Alcock also was boarding some circus animals, including a house-broken lion.

One morning, Chattahoochee was grazing in her paddock when the lion got loose and playfully leaped on the mare's back. The mare was so startled that she jumped the fence and ran down the C.P.R. line, heading south.

At the Edmonton racing meeting a few months later, Chattahoochee ran and won — first crack out of the box! The performance prompted Presiding Steward George W. Schilling to observe: "That crazy barber has revolutionized racing. To get his mare ready for a winning race, he used a lion for a jockey and he used the C.P.R. right-of-way for a training track."

Few people have written books about jockeys in recent years. There have been many books about hockey players and baseball players with multi-million-dollar contracts. However, jockeys were, for a long time, the world's highest-paid professional athletes. A dozen or more jockeys in North America were earning more than $100,000 a year, back when no man in baseball had surpassed Babe Ruth's long-standing salary record of $80,000 per year. In that same period, the top players in the National Hockey League were being paid about $10,000 per season.

Jockeys ranked among the most admirable of all professional athletes — half a dozen times every afternoon they perch atop a thunderbolt. Being a jockey is much riskier than piloting a supersonic fighter plane. If the plane blows apart, the pilot is ejected and his parachute is activated. When a jockey rides that thunderbolt, a single mis-step can result in serious injury or even death. When his thunderbolt makes a crash landing, the jockey quite often is at the bottom of the wreckage.

Two of the best jockeys ever to ride in Canada — George Woolf and Avelino Gomez — died as a result of racetrack accidents. Many horsemen of his era regarded George Woolf as the outstanding North American race rider. A member of a Mormon family from Cardston, Alberta, George began his career on western Canada tracks but rocketed to fame soon after moving to the United States.

He was an intelligent but taciturn man and this latter quality, combined with the chilly efficiency with which he rode his races, caused him to be nicknamed "The Iceman." He could be charming, but he had little time for platitudinous pleasantries.

In more than 60 years around racetracks, I had the good fortune to see (or at least know) all the great Canadian jockeys including Woolf, Johnny Longden, Red Pollard, Willie (Smokey) Saunders, Frank Mann, Chris Rogers, Ronnie Turcotte, Sandy Hawley and Avelino Gomez.

I had a particular affection for Longden, who was one of my heroes when I became a racetrack "regular" as a teenager. He was born in Wakefield, England, but was brought to Canada as a baby and raised in Taber, Alberta. He was a physical marvel — his weight remained close to 105 pounds throughout his 40-year career — but he had the strength of a pocket Hercules.

Although he enjoyed a lifetime of international celebrity, Johnny never severed his emotional ties with Canadian horse-racing.

When he was zeroing in on the 6,000th win of his career, Longden decided that it would be appropriate to return to a track in western Canada for that milestone victory. Accordingly, it was at Exhibition Park in Vancouver that he rode Prince Scorpion to register his 6,000th win on August 16, 1965.

Johnny continued to ride until he was 59; very fittingly, it was a Canadian-bred horse which he selected for the final race of his career. He had ridden George Royal to victory in the 1965 renewal of the San Juan Capistrano Handicap. A year later, George Royal was entered for the 1966 renewal of the San Juan Capistrano.

The night before the race, Johnny "called the shot." He was talking with Bill Shoemaker and said to The Shoe: "I'm going to ride George Royal tomorrow afternoon, and, when he wins, I'm going to retire — permanently."

The following afternoon, the 59-year-old jockey gave George Royal a million-dollar-ride. Throughout the long run of one mile and three quarters, Longden gauged his final charge perfectly and George Royal won a thrilling photo-finish. True to his promise, after jumping from George Royal's back in the winner's circle, Johnny never rode in another race.

Longden has one record which is unique in the history of American horse racing. He is the only man who ever rode the winner of a Kentucky Derby and, later in his life, became the *trainer* of a Kentucky Derby winner.

In 1943, Longden rode Count Fleet to win the Kentucky Derby. Count Fleet, with Johnny in the saddle, went on to win the other two US Triple Crown Races — the Preakness Stakes and the Belmont Stakes — in the colours of John D. Hertz, the founder of the car-rental industry.

Then, 26 years later in 1969, Longden was the trainer of Majestic Prince which won the Kentucky Derby for Frank McMahon of Vancouver. Majestic Prince also won the Preakness but he finished only third in the Belmont. After the Preakness, Longden told the owner that the horse should be retired for the year. McMahon over-ruled his trainer and insisted that Majestic Prince should run in the Belmont. Longden was right — the horse never ran again after that losing start at New York.

When I was growing up under Hudson's Bay Rules, jockeys

weren't always trying to win. Some trainers didn't *wish* to win except on those occasions when they were *betting*. Woe betide a jockey who won on a horse after the trainer had instructed him to "give the horse an easy one."

When I first became associated with Morris Fishman, I asked a veteran trainer, Bill Campbell, if Morris had been a good jockey during his professional career in the saddle.

Mr. Campbell removed the cigar from his mouth, pondered judiciously and said: "Morris was a very strong jockey. He could stop an elephant reaching for a bale of hay."

I got the message. I knew that Morris had done most of his contract riding for Jimmy Boden, an old Irishman who "didn't let his horses run" unless he and his associates were betting. Thus, Morris was obliged to "stiff" a great many of the Boden horses which he rode.

Curiosity being the stock-in-trade of all newspapermen, the time came when I was bold enough to ask Fishman: "What was the best day you ever had as a jockey?"

Morris replied without hesitation: "It was one afternoon at Bowie when I rode six horses for Mr. Boden. I won on four of those horses and I pulled the other two. I *could* have won all six races."

It was an era when purses were small and an owner-trainer had to be sure of winning an occasional bet in order to make ends meet. It was common practice for a trainer to give his horse "a couple of easy ones" before "turning him loose" on the afternoon when he was betting his own money.

Always there have been trainers who insisted on giving riding instructions to their jockey before every race. In most cases, this type of instruction, given in the paddock after the horse has been saddled, is superfluous. Any really expert jockey who has previous experience in riding this particular horse doesn't require any last-minute advice from the trainer. But those paddock conversations are intriguing for the watching spectators. And the owner of the horse — particularly if he is new to the game — is flattered to be party to the mysterious communications between trainer and jockey.

When it came to giving pre-race instructions to a jockey, one of my favourite trainers was the late Ted Mann who campaigned successfully on Ontario tracks for many years. Ted's advice to his riders always went like this: "Jock, I've got this horse as fit as human hands can make him. I've trained him to perfection for this race. Now, you get on his back; go out on the track and screw up everything I've done."

There was one era in which four Canadian jockeys, Longden, Woolf, Red Pollard and Smokey Saunders, were considered among the best jockeys in the entire world.

Saunders, who came from Edmonton, rode Omaha to victory in all three US Triple Crown races in 1935. Pollard, who also was an Albertan, was Seabiscuit's regular rider when The Biscuit was at his peak. Ironically, it was a third Albertan — George Woolf — who replaced Pollard as Seabiscuit's rider when The Biscuit defeated War Admiral in a famous match race at Pimlico.

Chris Rogers, a harum-scarum equestrian genius from Hamilton, Ontario, was junior in age but partially contemporaneous with those other outstanding Canadians. Chris was a superb horseman but he wasted many of his best years frolicking under the bright lights. He was my jockey for the first race I won on an eastern Canada track. I had a western-bred two-year-old named Broom Time and Chris rode him when the gelding broke his maiden at Stamford Park in Niagara Falls. To steel myself for watching my horse in action, I had taken several stiff drinks and, when I congratulated Rogers after his winning ride, his keen sense of smell detected a kindred spirit.

We became lifetime friends. While he was still riding at the age of more than 50, he became an active member of

Alcoholics Anonymous and was instrumental in saving the careers of several young jockeys who were about to go off the deep-end. I had the honour of being asked to deliver the eulogy at Chris's funeral. I am certain that honour fell to me because I, too, was a member of A.A.

Often I've wondered what feats Chris Rogers might have performed if some man of genuinely strong character had taken over as his manager-agent when first he came around the racetracks. Rogers was only 19 when he deserted Ontario and went away to ride on the major tracks in New York and Florida.

From the very outset, he was a hell on horseback. He had amazing skills; but his obvious love for liquor and night-life influenced many trainers to avoid selecting him to ride their horses in stakes races because they just couldn't count on Chris turning up sober. In those days there were no breathalyzer tests for jockeys and many riders kept a mickey hidden among their gear in the jockeys' room.

Vic Sovinski was one leading American trainer who had no illusions about Chris Rogers. Sovinski was keenly aware of Chris's nocturnal habits when he engaged Rogers to ride Lincoln Road in the 1958 Kentucky Derby.

Tim Tam, owned by the all-conquering Calumet Farm, was the hot favourite for the Derby. Lincoln Road was, primarily, a sprinter, but Rogers had induced him to carry his speed far enough to finish a good second to Tim Tam in the Florida Derby, at one mile and one eighth. It was debatable whether Lincoln Road could go the entire Kentucky Derby distance — which was 220 yards longer than the Florida Derby.

On the day prior to the big race at Churchill Downs, as hundreds of media reporters attended a press conference to quiz the most prominent trainers, Vic Sovinski gave an immortal pre-Derby quote.

A reporter stood up at the press conference and asked Sovinski if he was "worried about his horse." Sovinski replied with engaging honesty: "I'm not worried about my horse — I'm worrying about my *jockey*!"

The night before the race, Sovinski hired a private detective to sit all night outside Roger's room.

The next afternoon, Rogers rode a magnificent race in the Derby. Lincoln Road led from the first jump out of the starting gate. Rogers kept him on the inner rails and saved every possible inch of ground. Lincoln Road, a sprinter, was being asked to go much farther than he wished, but wanted to lie down and rest 300 yards from the finish post. However, Chris, employing his complete repertoire of tricks, kept the colt running but was beaten only in the very last strides, losing to the favoured Tim Tam by a quivering nose.

Rogers earned big money in his twenties but managed to spend it as quickly as he collected it. He went where the lights glowed brightest and the liquor flowed most freely. He returned to Ontario when someone offered him a suitable inducement and rode the winners of The Queen's Plate three times between 1949 and 1954.

I've witnessed many fine riding performances but one which always stays in my mind was the ride which Rogers gave Collisteo in The Queen's Plate of 1954. At the head of the home stretch, Collisteo hooked up in a nose-and-nose battle with Queen's Own, which was owned by E.P. Taylor and ridden by a very promising youngster, Bert Albert.

Most horsemen agreed that Queen's Own was the better colt but Rogers "stole" that race. As they thundered towards the finish post they ran like a team, stride-for-stride and nostril-for-nostril. Then, on the second last jump, Rogers lifted his head and he yelped at Albert: "You've got me!" Albert, startled by the shout, lost his concentration for one split second. In that wink of an eyelid, he glanced over at Rogers who dropped Collisteo's nose on the finish line and beat Queen's Own by the width of a matchstick.

Chris's *first* Queen's Plate triumph — on Epic in 1949

— caused me some hours of painful soul-searching. That year the Ontario Jockey Club had instituted a rule that an owner could start only *one* horse in The Queen's Plate. Furthermore, the OJC had only a 12-stall starting gate and didn't wish to have an unwieldly field for their major race.

Charlie Hemstead, a Toronto hotel owner, had two horses he wished to run in The Queen's Plate. Two months before the race, he asked me if I'd run one of those horses — a filly named Grandehem — in my name. This would enable him to circumvent the new OJC regulation.

Carelessly, I agreed, never suspecting that there could be any repercussions. However, I insisted upon Hemstead legally transferring Grandehem into my name and that she be turned over to Dr. R.K. Hodgson, who was training some horses for my father. Furthermore, I insisted that, right up until the day of the race, all the filly's training moves be planned and supervised by Dr. Hodgson.

I made a second stupid move after a friend, Gil Darlington, phoned and asked me if I knew a bookmaker who would accept a $1,000 bet on a colt named Epic in The Queen's Plate. The bookmakers had been offering 10 to 1 against Epic which never had started in a race.

Darlington made it clear that the $1,000 was being bet by a man named E.P. Taylor, who owned Epic. At the time, I hadn't met E.P. Taylor and I knew only that he was a wealthy brewer.

I called my bookmaker friend, Curly Litman, and told him that I wanted to bet $1,000 on Epic if he would give me 10 to 1. Curly agreed readily. I called Darlington who brought $1,000 to me at the *Globe and Mail*. Later that night, I met Curly at the Paddock Tavern and gave him the $1,000. It was only two days before the running of The Queen's Plate that the enormity of my situation hit me.

The draw for post positions was conducted and Epic drew Number 13. With only 12 stalls in the starting gate,

Epic would be forced to start from *outside* the gate. This was a colt that had been *trained* to start from the gate and had never raced before. In these circumstances, he might jump in the air at the "break" and lose all his chances for a win.

I fully intended to withdraw Grandehem from the race unless the track was muddy. Her only winning performance as a two-year-old had been a race on a muddy track. Hemstead had agreed that I could scratch the filly if it didn't rain before the race. In the meantime, I was obligated to leave Grandehem among The Queen's Plate entries, at least until scratch time on the morning of the race.

Compounding my dilemma was the fact that the favourite in the race, Speedy Irish, was owned by George McCullagh, who paid my salary at the *Globe and Mail*.

Suddenly, I was feeling pressure from two sides. Everyone was very polite about it. Darlington, who worked for E.P. Taylor, asked casually if Grandehem would be a starter. George McCullagh dropped into a chair beside me in the *Globe and Mail* cafeteria on Thursday afternoon. He, too, casually asked if I was going to scratch the filly. If she ran, Epic would be compelled to start from outside the starting gate, militating against his chances of winning.

The decision was made for me by the whims of the weather. By Saturday morning, not a drop of rain had fallen and Dr. Hodgson informed the stewards that Grandehem wouldn't run.

Later that afternoon, Epic, making the first start of his life, broke alertly from the Number 12 stall and, with Chris Rogers in the irons, ran splendidly to win The Queen's Plate.

You can guess who finished second: It was Speedy Irish, owned by George McCullagh, my employer.

On the following Monday afternoon, I collected the $10,000 and gave it to Gil Darlington, who came to my office. I presume that he turned it over to E.P. Taylor.

In retrospect, every aspect of my involvement in the 1949 Queen's Plate smacked of excessive stupidity. As a favour to Charlie Hemstead, I had permitted a Queen's Plate candidate to be entered in my name (a contravention of the racing rules); I had bet $1,000 on a rival horse on behalf of the owner (also a breach of the rules); I had collected $10,000 from a bookmaker to hand over to E.P. Taylor, who didn't know me from a hole in the ground; I had risked antagonizing my employer, George McCullagh. I had compromised myself seriously in the eyes of any outsider who looked at the deal closely. However, I hadn't profited by as much as a nickel.

Two weeks before the race, jockey Chris Rogers had told me that Epic would win "by as far as a strong-armed farmboy can throw a rosy, red apple." I ignored Chris's advice. I didn't bet even a dollar on Epic. Instead, in a drunken moment, I telephoned Curly Litman and bet $50 on Grandehem at odds of 25 to 1.

The final, ironic twist to the incident came more than three years later when, after spending two years as publicist for Thorncliffe Raceway, I was hired by E.P. Taylor to handle public relations for all the Ontario thoroughbred-racing establishments which he was re-organizing under the banner of the Ontario Jockey Club.

Although I worked for Mr. Taylor for ten years — and although there were many occasions on which I made bets in the thousands of dollars for him on our own tracks — never once did he mention the $10,000 which I had collected for him from a bookmaker after the 1949 Queen's Plate. I'm reasonably sure that he didn't realize that I had been the agent who made his bet.

My employment by the Ontario Jockey Club put me "on the other side of the fence" from the bookmakers, but my duties put me in daily contact with John J. Mooney, who was, in my opinion, the best racetrack operating official in North America.

There was absolutely nothing about a racetrack that John Mooney didn't know. You could say that he had been born and raised in a tackroom. His father was J.D. Mooney, an American jockey.

John had intimate knowledge of every inch of a racetrack. As a kid, he had mucked-out stalls, he had been an exercise boy, and, since he had been growing up in the years of unbridled larceny, he was aware of every trick which had been perfected by oldtime trainers and jockeys.

One year, while his father was campaigning in New Orleans, John earned his pocket money in an unsual way. Many of the jockeys at New Orleans were carrying "joints" or small hand batteries to encourage their mounts when they rode in races. Such electrical stimulation was, of course, highly illegal. A jockey who was caught with a "joint" would be given the heave-ho.

Accordingly, after the finish of a race, a jockey surreptitiously would toss his "joint" into the infield as his horse was easing up around what is known as the Clubhouse Turn.

At New Orleans, young John Mooney would be lying on his belly in the grass of the infield. After the jocks jettisoned their batteries, John would retrieve and return them to the riders later that evening. It was his first experience in the area of profitable free enterprise.

John Mooney and I had a happy and profitable association for ten years until I returned to the newspaper business. After I left, he became president of the Ontario Jockey Club. When we worked together, we also lunched together every racing day and operated well together as a team. John added to my racetrack education and I like to believe that I added to his store of knowledge by introducing him to many of my oddball sporting friends from other sections of the country.

The jockey Avelino Gomez was an exceptionally agile athlete with great equestrian skills and an enduring love of the spotlight. For years he brought colour, excitement and laughter to Canadian horse-racing.

Gomez always put on a show for the spectators. When he returned to the winner's enclosure after capturing a race, Avelino would propel himself out of the stirrups — straight up in the air until both feet were above the level of the saddle — and land on the ground on the balls of his feet like an expert gymnast. In the 1950s, he was a frequent visitor to the Winner's enclosure — three, four or even five winners in a single afternoon weren't unusual for him.

Racing spectators developed a curious love-hate relationship with Gomez. They loved him because he was a frequent winner but hated him because, sometimes, he *didn't* win when they bet on his mounts. That type of fan reaction was deep-dish apple pie for Avelino. When he was coming through the homestretch with a clear lead on a horse which the betters had permitted to get away at juicy odds, he'd wave derisively at the crowd or thumb his nose at them.

The stewards threatened him with a long suspension if he didn't keep his thumb to himself, but generally, the stewards were inclined to side with Gomez in his feuds with the public. They realized that he was one of racing's major crowd attractions.

Gomez always was much in demand for interviews by newspaper reporters and radio-TV commentators. He never completely mastered the nuances of the English language, but he was an intelligent and extremely quick-witted man. He realized that his mildly fractured English was part of his very considerable public charm.

Benny Sorenson, who had been stable-rider for the powerful E.P. Taylor outfit, soon found himself being overshadowed by Avelino and wisely went to Detroit after Gomez had established himself in Ontario. Sorenson, in his first season at Detroit, gave an interview to the *Daily Racing Form*, during which he said that he had been "The King of Canada's jockeys."

Gomez simply couldn't let that pass without rebuttal. He sped to the Woodbine press box and wrote out the following telegram to be sent to Sorenson in Detroit: "Benny. You was not the King. You was only the Queen."

When Gomez first arrived in Toronto, another celebrated occupant of the jockeys' quarters was Ronnie Behrens. Behrens wasn't the world's greatest jockey, but he had an astonishingly large appetite for a little man. The manner in which Ronnie knocked off 12-ounce beefsteaks and other goodies was a constant source of amazement for his fellow-jockeys, most of whom were forced to hit the steam box every day to keep their own weight at a reasonable level. Gomez used to shake his head in amazement as he watched Behrens destroy the groceries.

Avelino was very interested in investigating the cultural resources of Toronto. Shortly after his arrival in the city, his agent, Dick Woolgar, took him on a tour of the Royal Ontario Museum.

It was getting late in the afternoon and they hadn't eaten since morning. Woolgar suggested that they should drop into the museum canteen for a sandwich and coffee. As hungrily they looked around for the canteen, they came upon the skeleton of a huge dinosaur that had been re-assembled in one of the great halls of the museum.

Gomez looked up at the massive display of bare bones. He tugged Dick Woolgar by the arm, saying: "Let's get out of here. We're too late to eat — Ronnie Behrens has been here before us."

Avelino's athletic nimbleness enabled him to survive many racing spills, but finally, his luck ran out in 1980 when he was still actively competitive at the age of 52. The filly he was riding in the Canadian Oaks at Woodbine tripped over another filly which had fallen in front of her. Avelino was flipped to the track and, before he could roll out of the way, another horse crashed on top of him, completely collapsing his chest cavity. Avelino died 12 hours later.

Jockeys can't continue to ride interminably. Increasing weight terminates the careers of most of them. Some become successful trainers, some become officials on racetracks, and some acquire enough money to live in contented retirement. There is an occasional indestructible — such as Bill Shoemaker, who continued to compete daily until the age of 59.

In Vancouver, every time I venture into Exhibition Park, I am reminded of "Alex Haller's Last Ride."

Alex Haller had been a competent rider on the tracks of western Canada for many years, but a slight strain of larceny and a magnificent thirst often resulted in him serving lengthy suspensions imposed by the sympathetic but exasperated stewards. Most of his colleagues in the jockeys' room liked Alex Haller, although they deplored the unfortunate fact that he was a lush.

It was at Vancouver's Exhibition Park that Alex Haller had his last opportunity to "Take Off a Big Score" on August 14, 1958.

He could no longer control his weight, so he decided that he'd ride his final race on a horse named Lord Glenlivet — and win a big bet to celebrate his retirement.

No one is certain how much money his friends managed to bet for Alex Haller on Lord Glenlivet in the first race of the afternoon of Thursday, August 14, 1958. The money was bet with bookmakers so that it wouldn't cut down the price of the horse in the pari-mutuel machines at Exhibition

Park. Consensus of opinion among surviving oldtimers in Vancouver is that enough was bet to provide Alex Haller with a walking-around bankroll of more than $5,000.

Alex Haller wasn't leaving anything to chance — he was going to carry a battery when he rode Lord Glenlivet, a six-year-old gelding which had been known to respond dramatically to electric stimulus.

Haller's coup appeared to have gone off perfectly. Lord Glenlivet was sluggish in the early stages of the six-furlong race but when Alex gave him a taste of the battery, the gelding ran like a startled gazelle and flew through the homestretch to win by a nose.

When Haller came back to the winner's circle and dismounted, he glanced at the infield odds board and noted with approval that the odds against Lord Glenlivet were 20 to 1. The horse would pay $42 for every $2 wager.

One minute later, Haller was in the jockeys' room, chuckling to himself, warmed by the thought that he and his betting confederates "had killed the country." He was just going to sit down when presiding Steward Wilson Dunn strode into the room.

Dunn confronted Haller and said: "Alex, did you use a joint on that horse?" Alex, believing that Judge Dunn already had flashed the "official sign" permitting the payoff prices to be posted on the odds board, replied cheerfully: "Yes, Judge." He reached into his right riding boot and pulled out the tiny battery which he handed to Wilson Dunn.

For Haller, it was stark tragedy. Judge Dunn *hadn't* declared the result of the race to be "official." The payoff prices *hadn't* been posted on the infield odds board. As soon as Haller handed that battery to Judge Dunn, the public in the stands was informed that Lord Glenlivet had been "disqualified and placed last." For Haller's part, he knew that he was going to be ruled off the racetrack but at that point he was beyond caring — because he had blown his last chance to win a nest egg.

Even today, I feel a bit sad when I recall how Alex Haller blew it. But, you don't stay sad for long in my business.

The past is glowing with warm memories, but it is the future which will be full of surprises. When I go to bed each night, I get down on my knees and I offer a prayer of thanks for the love and happiness which have illuminated my long ride on the hobby-horse.

But, even in those contemplative moments, always I can feel a glow of excitement as I look forward to the uncertain future.

Tomorrow may be the day when I'll receive that wake-up telephone call for which I have been waiting a lifetime.

The hoarse voice at the other end of the telephone line won't require any identification. The hoarse voice will say: "The Big Horse runs today. He'll win by as far as a strong-armed farmboy can throw a rosy, red apple."

Until tomorrow, then!